The Politics of Autism

The Politics of Autism

Navigating the Contested Spectrum

John J. Pitney, Jr.

ROWMAN & LITTLEFIELD
Lanham • Boulder • New York • London

Published by Rowman & Littlefield
A wholly owned subsidiary of The Rowman & Littlefield Publishing Group, Inc.
4501 Forbes Boulevard, Suite 200, Lanham, Maryland 20706
www.rowman.com

Unit A, Whitacre Mews, 26-34 Stannary Street, London SE11 4AB

British Library Cataloguing in Publication Information Available

Library of Congress Cataloging-in-Publication Data

Pitney, John J., Jr., 1955– , author.
The politics of autism : navigating the congested spectrum / John J. Pitney.
p. ; cm.
Includes bibliographical references and index.
ISBN 978-1-4422-4960-8 (cloth : alk. paper) — ISBN 978-1-4422-4961-5 (electronic)
I. Title.
[DNLM: 1. Autistic Disorder—United States. 2. Education, Special—United States. 3. Policy Making—United States. 4. Politics—United States. 5. Public Policy—United States. WS 350.8.P4]
RC553.A88
362.19685'882—dc23
                                        2015013910

♾ ™ The paper used in this publication meets the minimum requirements of American
National Standard for Information Sciences Permanence of Paper for Printed Library
Materials, ANSI/NISO Z39.48-1992.

Printed in the United States of America

Contents

Preface

I have seen autism close-up, but this book is not a first-person story. There are already many fine memoirs about autism, which you may find in the endnotes. I did not think that I could add much to this genre, so I decided to analyze autism as an issue of politics and public policy. Apart from valuable studies by Dana Baker and the late Trudy Steuernagel, there is surprisingly little work on this subject in the field of political science. Accordingly, this book draws heavily from other disciplines, such as psychology, sociology, and medicine. Although I have grounded the book in citable sources, my experiences guided the analysis every step of the way.

Personal knowledge has its limits. Because I do not have a diagnosis of autism myself, I cannot claim authority on what it is like to be autistic. There is a burgeoning literature by autistic people, including some who cannot speak but instead communicate by way of technology. I quote this literature frequently, though it cannot capture the diversity of the autism experience.

I have tried to write a clear, straightforward book about a subject whose hallmarks are complexity and uncertainty. It is necessary to use certain specialized terms, but wherever possible, I have kept jargon to a minimum. I have also tried to give a flavor for the mass of often-conflicting information that parents and autistic people have to master, and to do so without confusing readers. If you belong to the world of autism, you will notice many places where I could have gone into greater detail. For readers who are new to the subject, however, less is more.

A major theme of this book is that just about everything concerning autism is subject to argument. There is not even any consensus on what one should call people who have autism and other disabilities. "In the autism community, many self-advocates and their allies prefer terms such as 'Autistic,' 'Autistic person,' or 'Autistic individual' because we understand autism as an inherent part of an individual's identity," writes blogger Lydia Brown.[1] Other writers prefer "people-first" language (e.g., "persons with autism") since it puts the persons ahead of the disability and describes what they have, not who they are.[2] For the sake of stylistic variety, this book uses both kinds of language, even though this approach will satisfy neither side. I can only say that I mean no offense.

Much of the book is about problems in public policy. Let me stress that I do not think that people with autism are themselves a "problem." Autistic Americans are citizens, friends, coworkers, sons, daughters, fathers, and mothers. Whenever they do not have a chance to take part in our country's social and economic life, everybody loses out. Just think of all the inventions and works of art that never happened because autistic people could not get the education and training that they needed. In part because of laws such as the Americans with Disabilities Act, things are changing. People with autism are not just the object of public policy, but they are also participants in policy debates. As I explain in the final chapter, that role will become even more important in the years ahead.

In my research, I have tried to piece together much of what we know about autism, but there is much that we do not know. Fundamental blocks of information are simply missing, such as historical data on the size of the autism population. This book thus cannot be the last word on the subject, and I hope that it encourages other scholars to fill in some of the gaps. For instance, we need much more work on the comparative politics of autism policy. Although the book makes references to other countries, its focus is on the United States. It would be extremely helpful to have thorough analyses of how other nations handle autism, including the provision of education and the protection of civil rights. If you are a graduate student in search of a dissertation topic, consider yourself nudged.

I have many people to thank. Mark Munro and John-Clark Levin provided an abundance of research help. Dana Baker, John McNulty, Brad McKay, Alex Rajczi, and Ernie Bensinger have all shared their thoughts and experiences. For invaluable comments on various portions of the manuscript, I salute Jeremy Shane, David Menefee-Libey, and Shanna Rose. Marjorie Charlop and Sienna Greener-Wooten not only gave me advice on the project, but have been a source of strength and guidance throughout the years. My gratitude to them knows no bounds. Of course, any mistakes in this book are mine alone.

My wife Lisa has been an inspiration. Our precocious daughter Hannah has contributed far more than she knows. And then there is the awesome Joshua: as our hero Stan Lee would say, "'Nuff said."

Chapter One

Introduction

Autism is political. It involves all kinds of government policy—from provision of education and social services, to regulation of insurance companies and medical professionals, to public funding of scientific research into its causes and treatment. The connections between government and autism reach farther than most people know. For example, many police officers and other first responders get training in how to deal with autistic people, who might react in unexpected ways during emergencies and crime investigations. Many organizations lobby policymakers and try to influence what government does about issues involving autism. Thomas Insel, director of the National Institute of Mental Health (NIMH), told journalist Andrew Solomon: "We get more calls from the White House about autism than about everything else combined."[1]

Autism is "political" in a broader sense. Political conflict involves ideas and arguments for which the information is often murky, incomplete, interpretive, and open to manipulation.[2] Just about everything concerning autism is subject to dispute. What is it? What causes it? How many different kinds of it are there? Who has it? What can we do about it? Is it even the right problem to be thinking about? All of these questions, and many others, are the stuff of bitter political battles. The stakes are high: according to one estimate, the national cost of supporting people with autism adds up to $236 billion per year.[3] Of course, such numbers themselves entail controversy. An alternative perspective is that they do not represent the cost of autism, but rather the cost of discrimination against people who have it, and the failure to help them lead independent lives.[4]

And yet with only a few exceptions, political science has barely begun to analyze autism policy and politics. This inattention is unfortunate, because the discipline can tell us much about how the issue has emerged and what

1

government is doing about it. Conversely, the study of autism politics can contribute to a more sophisticated understanding of policymaking.

Autism is more than an abstract topic for academic discussion. It shapes the lives of the people who have it, as well as their families. Well-meaning observers sometimes refer to autism as a "tragedy," a term that connotes destiny, something irretrievably beyond anybody's control. But many people with autism can do much more than make wallets in sheltered workshops. Under the right circumstances, they can pursue careers, contribute to society, and lead happy lives. Those circumstances, however, are often absent. Many autistic people do not get the kind of education that can help them build their capabilities and improve their ability to interact with others. As a result, many of them have a hard time finding good jobs, maintaining loving relationships, and achieving happiness.

Before looking at the broad scope of the relevant policy issues, we should glance at the ground-level realities of life with autism.

THE MAGIC 8-BALL: THE UNANSWERED QUESTIONS OF AUTISM

Autism refers to a group of complex disorders of brain development. It entails difficulties in social interaction, verbal and nonverbal communication, and repetitive behaviors. The difficulties come in various degrees. For instance, impairment of communication can range from a total inability to speak to rapid-fire talk with odd rhythms. That is why we also use the term *autism spectrum disorder*, or ASD. Unless otherwise indicated, this book will use the terms *autism* and *ASD* interchangeably.

Autism often involves a range of other co-occurring conditions: intellectual disabilities (e.g., low IQ); delays in gross motor skills (e.g., walking, throwing) and fine motor skills (e.g., writing); attention problems and hyperactivity; anxiety; self-injurious behavior; unusual sensitivity to certain sounds, smells, or feelings; extreme food selectivity; and sleep disorders.[5] For autistic people and their families, the co-occurring conditions may cause as much anguish as the autism itself.

Even the idea of a "spectrum" does not fully capture the variety of autism. People in this world have a saying, "If you've met one autistic person, you've met one autistic person." Consider two people with high-functioning autism (not an officially recognized diagnosis, but a term in common usage). Both may have the same IQ scores and both may be able to speak coherently, but the similarities may well end there. One may be even-keeled and affectionate, while the other shows little warmth but a lot of rage. One may hate reading, while the other can spend hours engrossed in a book. One may love to gorge on fruit, while the other rejects it entirely, to the point of retching after a sip of apple juice. In light of the daunting array of behaviors and abilities involved in autism—not to mention the possibility of variations in the underlying biology—some scientists believe that it is more accurate to speak of "the autisms." Neurologist Daniel Geschwind says that if you show him 100 different people with autism, he could "show you exactly 100 different types of autism."[6]

As with so much else in the world of autism, its first signs arrive in a cloud. The condition involves an impairment of social communication, and because we all start life with limited social communication skills, there is still no sure way to distinguish infants who will eventually get an autism diagnosis from those who will not.[7] Many babies who end up on the spectrum will laugh, gurgle, crawl, and walk just like other children. Their parents put checkmarks next to their list of "developmental milestones" with no inkling that these children were different from their peers. For parents of a toddler, the indications may start with things that do *not* happen: talking, pointing, making eye contact, or engaging in pretend play. Other signs consist of behavior such as flapping hands and lining up objects. One at a time, these things do not prove autism. Developmental delays are common, and most children sometimes flap their limbs and line up their toys. But the signs indicate autism if a number of them are present and persistent, that is, if they form a pattern. It takes time to spot a pattern.

Parents do not want to think about autism, so even when warnings seem to mount, it is tempting to ignore or rationalize them. But sooner or later, anxiety will drive them to seek answers from the Internet. Hoping to find reassurance, they may Google a phrase such as "lining up objects." If so, the results will rattle them even more, since most of the hits will have something to do with autism.

Pediatricians may not be helpful at this point. A pediatrician typically sees children for only a few minutes, during which time autistic behaviors might not show up.[8] It is possible to flag a potential case of autism with some screening questions, but less than half of pediatricians routinely do so.[9] In one small-sample study, twelve of thirteen parents of autistic children reported negative experiences when they approached their child's pediatrician with their concerns.[10] Nancy D. Wiseman recalls that she repeatedly voiced her suspicions, "but I received the same responses: 'Don't worry—she'll outgrow it.' 'Let's wait and see.'"[11] If they see something out of the ordinary, pediatricians will refer a child to a developmental pediatrician or psychologist. Often the referral comes much later, at school. Although the signs of autism usually appear by the age of twenty-four months, the median age of diagnosis is fifty-three months.[12]

Diagnosis is painful for parents, even when it comes after months of simmering suspicions and inconsistent comments from doctors. David Mitchell writes:

Faintheartedness is doomed by the first niggling doubt that there's Something Not Quite Right about your sixteen-month-old. On Diagnosis Day, a child psychologist hands down the verdict with a worn-smooth truism about your son still being the same little guy that he was before this life-redefining news was confirmed. Then you run the gauntlet of other people's reactions: "It's just so sad;" "What, so he's going to be like Dustin Hoffman in *Rain Man*?"; "I hope you're not going to take this so-called 'diagnosis' lying down!"[13]

An official diagnosis swaps one set of question marks for another. As parents talk to clinicians and other experts, their frustration boils over. They find ambiguity where they expected guidance and may eventually feel as if they are playing with a magic 8-ball that lacks any affirmative responses.

Why did this happen?

Nobody knows for sure.

Is there some kind of medicine?

There are drugs for some co-occurring conditions, but none for autism itself.

What can we do?

There are various therapies that take a long time and cost a lot of money.

Do they work?

Often they lead to progress. Occasionally they make a big difference. Sometimes they do not help much at all. It is impossible to say in advance.

The only sure thing is hardship. "With rare exceptions," wrote journalist Jane Gross in 2004, "no disability claims more parental time and energy than autism because teaching an autistic child even simple tasks is labor intensive, and managing challenging behavior requires vigilance."[14] Catherine Maurice recalls how she got her daughter to stop self-injurious behavior: "Every time she hit her own cheeks, we calmly took her hands, guided them to her lap, and held them there for two or three seconds, saying nothing. Then, after a couple of seconds, we would praise her, in the succinct specific language of behavioral reinforcement: 'Good hands down.'"[15] Tom Fields-Meyer writes that when his son was little, he was terrified of seemingly innocuous things such as a fishing toy but lacked the fears that he should have had: "He balances precariously on high playground structures; he wanders off to explore the outer limits of the supermarket on his own, not noting or caring that he has lost contact with his mother or father; left unattended for even a second, he wanders into crowds and busy streets."[16]

Getting help can be just as tough. "Once you have that diagnosis in hand, the questions start piling up," writes autism parent Mari-Jane Williams. "What services does he need, and what will insurance cover? What really works, and what is just a hopeful shot in the dark? How can she get the most out of the public school system? Who coordinates all of this? Do you need a small army of specialists or just one really good behavioral or occupational therapist?"[17] Very quickly, parents will learn that there is no one-stop shopping in the autism world. Various providers offer various services, with various levels of support from the government, which largely depends on where one lives. Wherever they turn, parents run into red tape. "Trying to obtain services for a special-needs child is a never-ending process," one mother told a Tennessee journalist. "Taking care of the children is much simpler than taking care of the paperwork."[18]

For children under three, the first stop is an individualized family service plan (IFSP), which maps out early intervention (EI). After age three, children get an individualized education program (IEP) from their local education agency (LEA), that is, their school system. The IEP explains how children will receive a free appropriate public education (FAPE) in the least restrictive environment (LRE). The program may include speech therapy (ST), occupational therapy (OT), physical therapy (PT), adapted physical education (APE), and applied behavior analysis (ABA) interventions including discrete trial training (DTT). Depending on which state they live in, official agencies or insurance companies may also subsidize services from NPAs (nonpublic agencies).[19] As attorney Gary S. Mayerson observes drily: "Given the confusion that all these unhelpful acronyms are causing for parents and professionals, it is not without irony that autism is associated with communication dysfunction."[20]

Once they start receiving services, parents have to become case managers, coordinating the work of multiple providers. Some services take place in the home, but others (especially speech and occupational therapy) require a trip to an office far away. "Appointments. Lots of appointments," says one autism parent who drives two hours from a home in Rolla to a care center in Columbia, Missouri.[21]

When they are not shuttling their children or filling out forms, parents are searching the Internet for various do-it-yourself approaches, including "complementary" or "alternative" medicine. The treatments range from the benign (cod liver oil) to the risky (hyperbaric oxygen chambers). Though largely unregulated by the government and unsupported by scientific evidence, the world of alternative treatments never fails to keep parents busy. A new fad is always around the corner.

Some research suggests that a small percentage of children do lose the diagnosis over time.[22] But contrary to some media reports, the process is neither natural nor automatic. "These people did not just grow out of their autism," said Deborah Fein, lead author of a study of autistic people who had great progress. "I have been treating children for 40 years and have never seen improvements like this unless therapists and parents put in years of work."[23] Families often run up huge out-of-pocket expenses, at risk to their financial futures.[24] The time that goes into the care of an autistic person means less time for earning money, and one study put the resulting average loss of annual income at $6,200, or 14 percent of reported income.[25] Raising an autistic child with special service needs is even more stressful than raising a child with another developmental disability.[26] "It's very difficult to hear your own son say, 'I don't want to have autism, I just wish I was dead,'" says one autism parent.[27]

Many analyses of autism speak as if it were only a childhood ailment and assume that parents are the main stakeholders. But most children with autism grow up to be adults with autism, and they suffer uniquely high levels of social isolation. Almost 40 percent of youth with an autism spectrum disorder never get together with friends, and 50 percent never receive phone calls from friends. These figures are higher than for peers with intellectual disability, emotional disturbance, or learning disability.[28] When school ends, many adults with autism have grim prospects. Though evidence is sparse, it seems that most do not find full-time jobs.[29] Compared with other people their age, they have higher rates of depression, anxiety, bipolar disorder, and suicide attempts.[30]

So instead of looking at the issue only from the viewpoint of parents, change perspectives and try to put yourself in the position of an autistic person. Of course, there are many different kinds of autistic experience. "Autism is often a hidden disability," writes one person with Asperger's. "There is no universally visible signifier—no mobility aid that we all use, no assistive technology or service animal or language common to all or even most autistic people. While many of us use assistive technology, many others go through our days—our lives—passing for nondisabled."[31] But "passing" is not the same thing as avoiding pain. "You look at me and I look articulate, but I suffer, in some way, every single day," says autistic author John Elder Robison. "You know, you look at somebody like me and you think, he looks, you know, so successful and so functional [but] anxiety affects forty per cent of us, depression affects forty per cent of us, several per cent of us kill ourselves. Those are absolutely very real risks every single day for me."[32]

Others cannot "pass" because of their impairments. Ido Kedar, who is unable to speak but now communicates via an iPad, recalls his immense frustration with the behavioral therapists who doubted his intelligence when he was a child.

> It isn't a lack of intelligence to be able to think but to not be able to get your body to show it. It is being trapped. If I put your hands into baseball mitts and your tongue was trapped in gooey sludge and couldn't move right and I bombarded you with questions, I think you would agree you would have a hard time showing that you had an intact mind, especially if those baseball mitt hands moved differently to your thoughts and wishes sometimes, and everyone assumed that people with sludge tongues and baseball mitt hands were intellectually low.[33]

Many autistic people engage in self-stimulatory behavior, or "stimming." Sometimes the stimming involves jumping up and down. In the aptly titled *The Reason I Jump*, autistic adolescent Naoki Higashida explains, "When something happens that affects me emotionally, my body seizes up as if struck by lightning. 'Seizing up' doesn't mean that my muscles literally get stiff and immobile—rather it means that I'm not free to move that way I want. So by jumping up and down, it's as if I'm shaking loose the ropes that are tying up my body."[34]

Just as parents have their own magic 8-ball of autism nonanswers, people on the spectrum face different questions at different ages. Autistic children may ask: *Why do other kids laugh at me?* Adolescents wonder: *Why do my parents see me as such a burden?* With age, the questions get darker. *Why do I have trouble holding a job? Will I be alone for the rest of my life? Why do some people think that people like me shouldn't even be born?*

Yet it is a mistake to portray the world of autism only as a harsh realm of unrelieved pain. With supports and accommodations, many autistic people can make their way in the world. After recounting his son's often-troubled development, Tom Fields-Meyer concludes with his uplifting bar mitzvah speech: "In all my favorite parts of the Torah, God makes miracles. And today feels like a miracle too. I am finally thirteen years old. So let me tell you about me. I am an autistic person. That means my brain works differently than other people's brains. Sometimes I repeat things when I don't mean to. Sometimes it's hard to focus in school. Sometimes autism is very helpful. One good thing is that I have a very good memory."[35]

Some autistic people do indeed have great memories. Some do not. Some can deliver eloquent remarks about their relationship to God. Some cannot communicate at all, even with assistive devices. Nobody is sure why this is so, and on diagnosis day, parents can never be sure where their children will end up. Just as uncertainty is a part of autistic life, it is a defining characteristic of autism politics.

DIAGNOSIS AND DEFINITION: A RIDDLE WRAPPED IN A MYSTERY INSIDE AN ENIGMA

A short form of the public policy process would run this way: identify a problem, measure it, devise alternative solutions, then decide what to do. Autism is not that simple. It is a "syndrome," a collection of signs or symptoms not easily traceable to a specific cause. When we say that someone has autism, we mean that certain kinds of behavior are stemming either from something inside that person's brain, or some interaction between the brain and other bodily systems. Unfortunately, we cannot yet see exactly what that "something" is. Scientists believe that the brains of autistic people tend to differ from those of their typically developing peers, but they have not yet mapped the differences, or connected them to the resulting mix of capabilities and disabilities. Says Temple Grandin, a scientist who has autism: "Even when researchers do think they've found a match between an autistic person's behavior and an anomaly in the brain, they can't be sure that someone else manifesting the same behavior would have the same anomaly."[36]

Unlike people with Down syndrome, most people with autism lack distinctive physical characteristics.[37] No brain scan or blood test can yet diagnose autism with any confidence. Instead, clinicians carry out evaluations by watching behavior and asking questions. Standardization of these techniques did not take place until the 1980s, and the criteria for identifying autism have shifted since then. The American Psychiatric Association published its latest definition of autism in 2013. Psychiatrists and psychologists continue to argue about that definition, which may be subject to future revisions. Asperger's disorder, a form of autism featuring relatively high levels of language and cognitive development, was a separate subtype in the 1994 diagnostic manual but not in the 2013 version. Amid such back-and-forth, there is no universal agreement on what autism is and who has it.

Originally clinicians had a narrow definition, which led them to think of autism as rare. A quarter century ago, the best estimate was that it affected only one child in 2,000. In the 1990s, as the term "autism spectrum disorder" came into common usage, a broader definition (including Asperger's) encompassed more cases. In 2007, a study published by the Centers for Disease Control (CDC) found a prevalence of one in 150.[38] Two years later, another CDC study put the figure at one in 110.[39] Three years after that, it was down to one in 88.[40] A 2013 CDC report found that the prevalence of parent-reported autism among children was one in 50.[41] Although such figures have prompted talk of an autism "epidemic," no one knows how much of the difference represents a true increase.[42] As the 2013 CDC report said: "Changes in the ascertainment of ASD could occur because of changes in ASD awareness among parents or health care professionals, increased access to diagnostic services, changes in how screening tests or diagnostic criteria are used, or increased special education placements in the community."[43] At the same time, a big part of the change remains unexplained, and scientists cannot rule out a true increase.[44]

Uncertainty about prevalence contributes to uncertainty about causation. If we knew that the number of people with autism started to rise in one particular year, we could identify potential causes by looking for what else might have changed at the same time. Without such baseline knowledge, it is hard to resolve the question. One thing is clear: autism tends to run in families, so genetics has something to do with it.[45] Beyond that, the possibilities include such disparate items as paternal age, maternal age, pollution, and immune responses to viruses. Until scientists know what causes autism, when and how it starts in the developing body, and how it expresses itself over time, they will have difficulty in devising medical responses. Studies show that certain behavioral and educational programs can help with symptoms of autism, at least in the short term, but they are not a "cure." And there is little research showing how much these interventions can improve quality of life in the long run.[46]

Information on the outcomes of autism policy is just as sparse. Paul T. Shattuck and Anne M. Roux ask us to picture a big company that tried to do business without financial statements, that is, without data on sales, spending, customer experience, or assets. Obviously, the company would fail. "Yet, this state of affairs is commonplace in many autism services. At a population level, we are almost completely unable to clearly describe the resources expended on services or measurable indicators of the population outcomes we hope to influence—including the employment rate."[47]

THE COMPLEXITY OF AUTISM POLICY

With autism politics, complexity accompanies uncertainty. Autism is a "pervasive developmental disorder," which means that it affects most areas of a person's life. It is also a pervasive policy issue, straddling health, education, scientific research, insurance regulation, and civil rights, among other issues. No government agency has exclusive jurisdiction over all of these areas. The federal government takes the lead with some, while states and localities may be the main arenas for others. At each level, different bureaucracies deal with different aspects of autism. Courts and private organizations also play important roles in autism policymaking. Each place on the autism policy map has its own jargon and rules, hence the "alphabet soup" that bedevils parents. This complexity, rooted in our system of federalism, may sometimes work to the advantage of autistic people. Multiple programs may mean multiple opportunities: when one door closes, others may remain unlocked.[48] Different layers and branches may check each other, as when courts order government agencies to provide assistance. But complexity can also result in the delay or denial of services, especially when autistic people and their families lack the money and political resources to work the system.

A number of the laws and decisions that have shaped government responses to autism were originally not about autism at all. Either they did not specifically cite autism (at least at first) or mentioned it far down a long list of other conditions. For instance, when Congress enacted the basic federal statute on special education in 1975, lawmakers considered autistic students only in passing. Their concerns lay more with deafness, blindness, paralysis, and mental retardation.[49] The major Supreme Court decision interpreting that law—a decision that lurks in the room every time autism parents meet school officials—involved a girl with a hearing impairment.[50] Applying such laws and legal rules to people with autism is complicated.

Because many autism therapies consist of behavioral modifications instead of drugs, some define them as educational rather than medical. Is categorization anything more than an academic exercise? Does it really matter whether we call autism a "health" issue as opposed to an "educational" one? The answer is an emphatic yes. Categories help determine which government agencies support which kind of services, and which laws and rules apply to a particular case. Arguing that autism therapy is an educational service instead of a medical treatment, health insurance companies contend that they should not have to cover it. In cases where state law "mandates" coverage, parents often have to fight insurance companies in court in order to ensure compliance.

The United States has never recognized a "right" to free medical care, even under the 2010 comprehensive legislation.[51] (After all, its most controversial provision is the mandate that many individuals buy their own insurance.) By contrast, states and localities do offer free primary and secondary education to the general public.[52] Until the early 1970s, some schools could bar students with serious disabilities.[53] Advocates for these students won legal battles by arguing that this exclusion violated their individual right to equal treatment.[54] Congress codified this reasoning by entitling handicapped children to a "free appropriate public education" and by arming their parents with legal tools to enforce it. In carrying out the federal law, however, states and local education agencies have had to spend large sums to provide equal treatment of students with autism and other disabilities.

But what *is* equal treatment? This question raises the "dilemma of difference," as legal scholar Martha Minow explains. "When does treating people differently emphasize their differences and stigmatize or hinder them on that basis? And when does treating people the same become insensitive to their difference and likely to stigmatize or hinder them on that basis?"[55] Such questions may land in court. As Tocqueville famously said, "There is hardly a political question in the United States which does not sooner turn into a judicial one."[56] Attorneys have become major figures in the world of autism, because people often need legal counsel to get services from school districts and other government agencies. Soon after a diagnosis of autism, parents seek advice from those who have already been on the path. And soon they will hear, "Get a lawyer."

The rights approach puts a great burden on parents to serve as advocates for their children. Highly educated, affluent parents are in a better position to do so than the poor and uneducated: for one thing, their social networks are more likely to include lawyers and expert witnesses.[57] But even the best-equipped parents are at a disadvantage against school district administrators and other bureaucrats. Like their representatives in Washington and state capitals, they are "repeat players." Their experience and expertise give them an edge that the parents' special-education lawyers can only partially overcome.

Although autism is a public policy issue, much of the action takes place in the private sector. Consider, for instance, decisions on how to define and measure autism. The most authoritative definition of autism lies in the *Diagnostic and Statistical Manual* (DSM) of the American Psychiatric Association (APA). The DSM has had an enormous impact on the number of people who have a diagnosis of autism and on the services they receive. Insurers rely on it to determine who qualifies for coverage (when offered), and many government agencies consult it as well. Western Psychological Services, a Los Angeles publisher, owns key autism screening and diagnostic instruments, including the Autism Diagnostic Observation Schedule (ADOS) and the Autism Diagnostic Interview-Revised (ADI-R). The company charges a fee for each administration of the tests and passes part of the royalties on to the developers. "I don't think there's any other condition in medicine in which you have to pay a royalty to a publishing company in order to make the diagnosis," says neuroscientist David Skuse.[58]

Outside of school settings, nonpublic providers carry out the lion's share of autism therapy. A 2009 survey of the Association of Professional Behavior Analysts found that only 29 percent work directly for government agencies.[59] Most of the others either work for private agencies or for themselves. These providers draw much of their income from vendor agreements with schools and social service agencies. Even government does not furnish the money itself; it is often making someone else pay. More than thirty states have enacted laws requiring health insurance companies to cover behavioral therapy.[60] With autism, though, a "mandate" on the insurers is not a "guarantee" for the parents, who often have to fight insurance companies in court to ensure compliance.

State governments regulate some kinds of providers. Physicians and clinical psychologists are subject to licensing requirements, as are speech therapists in most states. Some states license behavior analysts, though the same requirements do not apply to the paraprofessionals who actually spend time with autistic people. There is no "pill for autism," but physicians treat co-occurring conditions (e.g., anxiety) by prescribing medications that are subject to regulation by the Food and Drug Administration. Amid scientific uncertainty about the causes of autism, many parents believe that various nutritional supplements can mitigate or even "cure" autism. Provided that the manufacturers do not directly make medical claims, these supplements can elude the strict FDA rules that apply to drugs.

FACTIONS

Whatever the underlying reality, the increase in the number of people with the autism label means that more Americans see themselves as part of the issue, and so the boundaries of the autism world keep moving outward. When boundaries change, so do political struggles.[61] Some students who would once have had the label of "mentally retarded" or "intellectually disabled" now have the label of "autistic." Their parents seek help appropriate for people with autism, and they join forces with other autism families to seek changes in public policy. As their children grow up and age out of the educational system, many of them join the fray as well. The rising demand for government action translates into increasing numbers of providers, researchers, and others with a professional stake in autism policy.

To the extent that the stakeholders form a "community," it is a quarrelsome one. James Madison identified the causes of faction, including a zeal for different ideas and interests. In autism politics, the factional disagreements are diverse and deep.[62] Emotions run high because the stakes are high. Few things are more frightening to parents than not knowing whether a child will ever be able to live independently, indeed to survive without them. For people with autism, the issue involves their very identity.

The most basic questions trigger angry arguments. For instance, into what category do we put autism in the first place? In 2013, President Obama said that "we're still unable to cure diseases like Alzheimer's or autism or fully reverse the effects of a stroke."[63] The language of "disease" and "cure" offends some in the autism community. "We don't view autism as a disease to be cured and we don't think we need fixing," says Ari Ne'eman of the Autistic Self Advocacy Network. "We do feel comfortable with the word *disability* because we understand what it means."[64] From this perspective, autism is difference that requires accommodation, not an illness that requires eradication. Adherents of this position liken autism to homosexuality, which psychiatrists once deemed to be a disorder. Conversely, some parents take offense at opposition to a cure. "Anyone with the mental and verbal ability to challenge autism research is not autistic on a scale that I care to recognize," writes autism parent James Terminello. "Opposition to finding a cure is particularly hurtful to parents who still mourn the loss of the child that could have been. A line has been crossed."[65]

Those who support the search for a cure are divided among themselves. Uncertainty opens the way to wildly divergent ideas about causes and medical response, and adherents of each theory band together in their own groups. Those who believe that vaccines cause autism are especially zealous. Dr. Paul Offit, a leading expert on vaccines, writes that his criticism of that belief has led to threats against him and his family.

While sitting in my office, I got a phone call from a man who said that he and I shared the same concerns. We both wanted what was best for our children. He wanted what was best for his son, giving his name and age. And he presumed I wanted what was best for my children, giving their names and ages and where they went to school. The implication was clear. He knew where my children went to school.[66]

Nearly every detail of autism policy is contentious. What kinds of behavioral therapy work best? Who should deliver it? Who should pay for what kind of intervention? What kinds of accommodations do autistic adults need? Such questions catch the attention of a wide array of interest groups. Some examples are the American Academy of Pediatrics, the American Psychological Association, the National Education Association, and groups representing occupational therapists and speech therapists. Easter Seals, originally the National Society for Crippled Children, is perhaps best known for its work with paraplegics, but in the past twenty years it has become the nation's largest nonprofit provider of autism services.

Every issue has its own warring camps. Intense arguments over strategy and tactics have pervaded movements for civil rights, environmental protection, and nuclear disarmament, among others. Tea party groups and conservative religious organizations also engage in intramural fights. Despite their factionalism, these unwieldy issue communities have sometimes managed to come together for common purposes, however briefly and inconsistently. In the case of autism, the interested groups cannot agree on what the issue is about. Science has failed to deliver a definition of autism that goes beyond a list of symptoms, and that list continues to evolve. Everyone has a theory; no one has a narrative that embraces the diversity of experience and channels that energy toward a shared purpose.[67] Susan Senator, an autism parent, has written a lament:

This may sound like the old Monty Python's "Life of Brian" bit where two obviously like-minded religious groups—the People's Judean Front and the People's Front of Judea—were fighting to the death against each other. Or like the Mensheviks versus the Bolsheviks. You're all crazy, a curse on all your heads, my great-grandmother would have said. But in the autism community, the rift among advocates is serious. And far from being funny, it is causing me a lot of pain. . . . Why does this happen to causes? Why can't people see when they are all in something together? Why aren't we trying harder to listen and connect?[68]

Another obstacle to action consists of the one thing that many participants in the autism world do have in common. It is exhausting to be either an autism parent or an autistic person. Parents have to devote time and money to the care and treatment of their autistic children; much of the time, they have little left over for political advocacy. Autistic people have to struggle with everyday tasks that the rest of us take for granted, and then they have to struggle for work and education in a world that does not always welcome them. Like their parents, they often lack political resources.

THE REST OF THE BOOK

The second chapter puts the problem into historical perspective, laying out how autism became a national issue. Three subsequent chapters look at different realms of autism politics. Chapter 3 examines science and medicine. Here, the battles take place largely at the national level, involving the federal government and the big advocacy organizations. Chapter 4 looks at education. This theater of conflict is all about intergovernmental relations. States and localities are primarily responsible for education, but federal statutes set the rules of engagement. Chapter 5 considers life for autistic people outside the classrooms. Here, the federal government is less dominant, though still relevant. Chapter 6 ponders the future of the issue in light of legal, demographic, and scientific trends. For all the uncertainties about the true prevalence of autism, we do know for sure that the number of children with an autism label has grown, which means that the number of adults with that label will also grow. Some are finding a voice. Those who lack a voice are finding the shelter of the education system gone and the future very daunting. Our political system is not always good at managing this kind of issue.

Chapter Two

A Short History of Autism

For an issue to enter the public agenda, people must first see it as a problem. That process is less straightforward than it sounds. A situation may fester for years before the general public notices it. Manufacturers had been selling tainted goods long before the outcry that led to the Pure Food and Drug Act of 1906. In other cases, people may know of a condition for a long time without thinking of it as an urgent public concern. The classic case is racial segregation. Before the 1960s, most white adults were vaguely conscious of racial barriers: they just did not care much.[1] Problem recognition thus involves a change in awareness or attitudes.

For public policy, a "problem" is more than just an unwanted state of affairs. The late political scientist Aaron Wildavsky told of a soldier in New Zealand who had orders to build a river bridge without enough workers or material. "He stared along the bank looking glum when a Maori woman came along asking, 'Why so sad, soldier?' He explained that he had been given a problem for which there was no solution. Immediately she brightened, saying 'Cheer up! No solution, no problem.'"[2] For something to become a problem of public policy, people have to believe some remedy is possible: otherwise, why argue about it? Many policy debates involve senior citizens, but aging itself is not the issue, because nobody can stop it.

It is likely that autism has always been with us. The first lines of the first issue of the *Journal of Autism and Developmental Disorders* (then called the *Journal of Autism and Childhood Schizophrenia*) put it this way: "One is entitled to wonder: What happened until recently to unfortunate children who, through no fault of man, were condemned to sufferings now belatedly recognized as psychotic ailments?"[3] In some cases through the early nineteenth century, parents simply left them to die: "feral children" probably were people with autism who survived abandonment. But autism did not become a major policy issue until late in the twentieth century. Its emergence hinged on its identification as a distinct disorder, on public knowledge of its existence, and on changing beliefs about what causes it and what to do about it.

Issues do not grow in isolation: they have family trees. In the nineteenth century, for instance, concern about management of public lands led to the creation of the Department of the Interior. In the early 1900s, the conservationist movement expanded the department's responsibilities with the creation of new national parks and monuments. In the middle of the twentieth century, conservationism helped give birth to the contemporary environmental movement. Similarly, autism can trace its ancestry both to the broad issue of civil rights and the more specific issue of disability rights.

But before delving into the issue's genealogy, we should first consider its birth as a public concern.

AUTISM EMERGES

In 1910, Swiss psychiatrist Eugen Bleuler drew the word *autism* from the Greek *autos*, meaning "self."[4] He was not talking about autism as we define it today, but rather an extreme social withdrawal that he had seen in his schizophrenic patients. (Bleuler had also coined the word *schizophrenia*.) During the next three decades, psychologists used the term loosely to refer to introversion or fantasy. Sometimes it even made its way into literary and artistic criticism. During the 1930s, an Austrian pediatrician named Hans Asperger was talking about children with "autistic psychopathy," and he would write up some of his findings in a 1944 article.[5] But the article appeared in German and behind enemy lines during the Second World War, so few Americans knew about it.

In 1943, Dr. Leo Kanner of Johns Hopkins University became the first to publish an English language article describing autism as a distinct disorder.[6] A pioneer of child psychiatry, Kanner reported on eleven children who seemed to have more interest in certain inanimate objects than in other people.[7] In listing symptoms, Kanner employed terms that are still in use, including *echolalia* (repetition of words or phrases spoken in the autistic person's presence) and *stereotypy* (repetitive movement such as hand flapping).

Though Kanner got some important things right, he also made misjudgments with lasting effects. In a 1949 article, he suggested that autism is a form of schizophrenia: "The basic nature of its manifestations is so intimately related to the basic nature of childhood schizophrenia as to be indistinguishable from it. . . . Early infantile autism may therefore be looked upon as the earliest possible manifestation of childhood schizophrenia."[8] Though subsequent research would sharply distinguish autism from schizophrenia, one can see how early research could confuse the two. Those on the autism spectrum often talk to themselves and move their bodies in odd ways, making it look as if they are hallucinating. Nonverbal people with autism may react to harsh internal pain by thrashing about. Because they cannot tell others what is happening, others might see the behavior as a sign of a psychological disturbance.

The confusion persisted and spread to the popular press. A "sympathetic" description in the *New York Times* put it this way: "They can see, but with the glazed stare of a doll. They can hear but show no sign. They can make sounds but do not speak. Their wild movements are purposeless. Their illness is called autism; it is a form of childhood schizophrenia."[9] Three years later, an article in *Time* magazine began: "The most tragic, and in some ways most mysterious, form of mental illness in children is infantile autism. Autistic children live in a lonely and unbreakable trance."[10] These passages reveal two aspects of the public understanding of autism at midcentury. The first is the assumption that autism is an affliction of the young. Although it should have been obvious that autistic young people would become adults, there was little effort to identify older people with the condition. The second is the label of "mental illness." The public's psychological vocabulary was cruder than it is today, and for many laypeople, "autistic" was just one way to say "crazy."

Clinicians and researchers treated autism as they treated mental illnesses. Techniques included electric shock, stimulants, tranquilizers—and even LSD.[11] The use of LSD seems bizarre, but well-credentialed scientists thought that it held promise. A 2007 retrospective study concluded that "judged by the standards expected in today's randomized controlled trial or the properly controlled and systematically replicated single-case study, the vast majority of these initial Autism/LSD studies were so flawed that the resulting data are little better than anecdote."[12]

While many people with autism received the tag of "mentally ill," even more fell into the category of "mentally retarded."[13] Again, the reasons for the label are easy to grasp. Some people on the spectrum do have low IQs, though not as many as researchers once thought. More important, poor attention to task may cause intelligent people with autism to stumble on standardized tests. "Mental retardation" was a convenient catchall category for people with low scores and unusual behavior.

The classification of autistic people under other labels sometimes meant institutionalization. One common belief is that autistic people usually ended up in some kind of big institution, either for the mentally ill or mentally retarded. Surely, some met this fate, but as with so many aspects of the issue, there is a thicket of question marks. If we suppose that the true prevalence of autism has always been more or less constant at 1 in 150 Americans, we can make a rough guess about total number of autistic people in each census year.[14] Table 2.1 compares these figures with the total number of residents of institutions for the mentally ill and mentally retarded.

In each year, the estimated number of autistic people *exceeded* the total number of people in these institutions—and it is nearly certain that most of the latter were dealing with something other than autism. So if our assumption about prevalence is right, then most people with autism were *not* in institutions. So what happened to them? Did they manage to make independent lives? Did they stay with family members? Or were they homeless? We do not know. It is plausible, though unprovable, that some scratched out a living in jobs requiring physical labor instead of social skill. In 1940, 20 percent of people with occupations were laborers or domestic servants. By 1990, this share was down to 5 percent, so there were fewer places where they could toil in the shadows.[15]

Of course, it is also possible that the assumption is wrong and that the true prevalence of autism was lower in the past. In that case, we have to ask what caused it to increase during the past few decades—a question to which we shall return.

BLAME AND BEHAVIOR

In his 1943 article, Kanner emphasized that all of the autistic children that he had studied were from "intelligent families," implying a causal link. What he actually saw was a referral bias, meaning those most likely to seek out a university psychiatrist in the 1940s were the most highly educated.[16] Although he referred to autism as "innate" and "inborn," he also observed that the children's families tended to lack warmth and that several of the parents had divorced. In another article six years later, he came closer to pronouncing parental guilt: "Most of the patients were exposed from the beginning to parental coldness, obsessiveness and a mechanical type of attention to mate-

Table 2.1. Estimated Number of People with Autism and Total Population of Institutions for the Retarded and Mentally Ill

	Total Population	Population/150	Total in Institutions
1940	132,164,569	881,097	578,222
1950	151,325,798	1,008,839	705,375
1960	179,323,175	1,195,488	769,682
1970	203,302,031	1,355,347	580,956

Source: U.S. Department of Commerce, Bureau of the Census, *Historical Statistics of the United States: Colonial Times to 1970* (Washington, DC: Government Printing Office, 1975), 84–85. Online: www2.census.gov/prod2/statcomp/documents/CT1970p1-03.pdf.

rial needs only. . . . They were kept neatly in refrigerators which did not defrost. Their withdrawal seems to be an act of turning away from such a situation to seek comfort in solitude."[17] In seeming to blame the parents, he mixed up cause and effect, overlooking the emotional burnout that autism can inflict on family members.[18]

By the late 1940s, popular literature had begun to repeat Kanner's hint that autism stemmed from cold or indifferent parenting. In a 1948 article titled "Frosted Children," *Time* reported on his young patients: "How did they get that way? Dr. Kanner took a hard look at their parents. . . . Were the cold parents freezing their children into schizophrenia? Dr. Kanner did not say yes or no; but he has found no case of infantile autism among children of 'unsophisticated' parents."[19] As late as 1960, Kanner told *Time* that autism was often the product of parents who were "just happening to defrost enough to produce a child."[20]

Years later, Kanner would absolve parents of blame, but in the meantime, the "refrigerator mother" theory gained a powerful advocate in Bruno Bettelheim. The director of the Orthogenic School, a Chicago institution for disturbed children, Bettelheim was a shrewd self-promoter who built a reputation as an expert on psychology even though he lacked a degree in the subject. (His Ph.D. was in aesthetics.) In 1959, *Scientific American* published "Joey: A Mechanical Boy," Bettelheim's article about an autistic boy who acted like a machine.[21] Working under the assumption that autism was a form of schizophrenia, Bettelheim pointed at the mother: "Schizophrenia often results from parental rejection, sometimes combined ambivalently with love. Joey, on the other hand, had been completely ignored." He noted the mother's "total indifference as she talked about Joey. This seemed much more remarkable than the actual mistakes she made in handling him."[22] *Reader's Digest* excerpted the article for its much larger readership, amplifying its impact. The next year, the CBS television program *Armstrong Circle Theater* presented "The Hidden World," a favorable dramatization of the Orthogenic School, with actor Peter von Zerneck portraying Bettelheim.

Bettelheim claimed that he had had close personal ties to Sigmund Freud, an impressive credential at a time when psychodynamic theories were at the peak of their popularity. His status as a survivor of Dachau and Buchenwald gave him additional moral authority with a public that was learning about the Holocaust. Although researchers were starting to find clues that origins of autism were genetic, many people associated genetic theories of behavior with Nazi eugenics.[23]

Parental blame reached its high point with Bettelheim's 1967 book, *The Empty Fortress* (1967). His assessment was blunt: "Throughout this book I state my belief that the precipitating factor in infantile autism is the parent's wish that the child should not exist."[24] Despite skepticism in the scientific community, the book got a warm reception in the mass media.[25] Editors and producers liked Bettelheim because he seemed to convey a sense of authority.[26] The book's questionable research and dubious conclusions spread popular misunderstandings that would take years to correct.

Books such as *Silent Spring* or *Unsafe at Any Speed* put issues on the agenda by defining problems and identifying culprits (chemical companies, automakers) that can plausibly be subject to legislation. *The Empty Fortress*, by contrast, helped keep autism *off* the agenda. If maternal coldness caused autism, there was little that government could do (at least by the standards of the time). Moreover, the "refrigerator mother" stigma discouraged the networking and organizing that are necessary for political advocacy. To anyone who believed in Bettelheim's notions, coming forward as an autism parent was the same as making a public confession of guilt.[27] (By contrast, no such stigma attached to the parents of children with mental retardation, and they organized as early as the 1950s.[28]) In 1970, psychologist Bernard Rimland said:

> [These] theories have been widely subscribed to by most professionals who deal with the children and the result has been DISASTER for tens of thousands of children, and for their families. The psychogenic theory has cast blame on the parents, and thus immobilized the child's strongest ally in what should be his struggle to recover. It has caused stagnation in research—which biochemist wants to analyze a "fractured Oedipus complex?" It has caused educators to shrug their shoulders and leave the problem in the hands of the psychiatrists, psychologists and social workers. It has cost families untold fortunes in money, time, convenience and human dignity. And, worst of all, it has cost far too many children their lives. Such children are not medically dead—just psychologically dead, existing like human vegetables in institution after institution.[29]

A resistance was already under way, however. In the late 1950s, Rimland had learned that his son was autistic, and then began to review the literature. "After four years I had read everything I could find on the subject of autism . . ." he later recalled. "I learned that, despite the supreme confidence (arrogance) with which the authorities proclaimed the mothers were to blame, I could find no shred of scientific evidence for such a belief."[30] In 1964, he published *Infantile Autism: The Syndrome and Its Implications for a Neural Theory of Behavior*. Drawing on studies that had escaped the attention of the general public, the book identified autism as a neurological problem. Kanner, who had revised his thinking, wrote the foreword. Rimland had fewer readers than Bettelheim, though he did gradually make an impression on psychiatrists and psychologists.

In 1962, British parents formed the National Society for Autistic Children (later the National Autistic Society), the world's first national autism group. Americans followed suit in 1965, when Rimland and Ruth Sullivan founded an organization with the same name. (In 1987, the U.S. group changed its name to the Autism Society of America [ASA] to acknowledge the problems of autistic teens and adults.) The group opposed the Bettelheim approach and instead praised the work of UCLA psychologist Ole Ivar Lovaas, who was getting results through behavior modification: praise and other positive reinforcement for desired behavior and punishment for undesired behavior.

Life magazine—still a major force in American journalism—had featured the Lovaas method in a 1965 article titled "Screams, Slaps, and Love: A Surprising, Shocking Treatment Helps Far-Gone Mental Cripples."[31] The article featured dramatic photographs of therapists shouting at writhing autistic children. According to Rimland, the piece did not advance the cause of behavioral therapy. On the contrary, it "horrified many people who had been conditioned by Bettelheim and other mother-haters to believe that autistic children were physically normal youngsters who had withdrawn totally in response to a purported lack of maternal affection." He added: "Lovaas and his co-workers were appalled at the *Life* article. Like all behavior modification programs, his was 98 percent *positive reinforcement*, with only a trace of aversive. Yet, true to the journalistic tradition, the *Life* article used only those few photographs showing aversive events, out of the hundreds they had taken."[32] As he refined the approach, known today as applied behavior analysis, Lovaas dropped the aversive techniques, but they would provide ammunition to his critics for decades to come.

Rimland and other fledgling autism activists did not yet focus most of their attention on politics. But broader social movements were already clearing the political pathway.

CIVIL RIGHTS AND DISABILITY RIGHTS

"Civil rights" usually referred to the fight against racial segregation. In several ways, this struggle set the template for other civil rights issues, including disability rights. First, cases such as *Brown v. Board of Education* demonstrated that disadvantaged groups could gain protections in the courts. Second, movement leaders found that nonviolent protests could gain public sympathy and put pressure on elected officials. Third, civil rights statutes that helped African Americans would also point to means by which the government could protect other excluded groups.

Throughout this period, disability activism was on the rise. The ranks of the disabled had spiked with the return of wounded veterans of the Second World War, who joined groups such as the Paralyzed Veterans of America. In 1950, parents from around the country formed the Association for Retarded Children of the United States (later the Association for Retarded Citizens, and then "the Arc"). During the next decade, the disabled got some modest legislative help from Congress, and in 1960, they gained an important ally with the election of John F. Kennedy, whose sister Rosemary lived in an institution for people with severe intellectual handicaps. (Important facilities for developmentally disabled people now bear the family name, including the Kennedy Krieger Institute in Baltimore and the Eunice Kennedy Shriver Institute in Boston.)

Shortly after his inauguration, Kennedy created the President's Panel on Mental Retardation. In a 1963 message to Congress, he called for a reduction "over a number of years and by hundreds of thousands, (in the number) of persons confined" to institutions for the mentally ill and mentally retarded. He said that these persons should be able to return to the community "and there to restore and revitalize their lives through better health programs and strengthened educational and rehabilitation services."[33] Though he did not use the term at the time, JFK was calling for deinstitutionalization. Over the next several decades, more and more people with disabilities such as autism would stay with their families or remain in their communities instead of entering institutions.

In 1973, Congress passed the Rehabilitation Act. Section 504 of the statute provided that no qualified person with a disability "shall, solely by reason of her or his disability, be excluded from the participation in, be denied the benefits of, or be subjected to discrimination under any program or activity receiving Federal financial assistance or under any program or activity conducted by any Executive agency or by the United States Postal Service."[34] Senate committee staffers added this provision with little public debate or fanfare, and they drew its wording straight from Title VI of the Civil Rights Act of 1964.[35] As we shall see in a later chapter, Section 504 would have its greatest direct impact in the field of higher education. It would also help change the disability rights from a scattered, largely local movement to a focused, national one. Several years later, disability activists protested the slow implementation of the law with demonstrations in several cities, including Washington, DC, and San Francisco.[36]

In the same year that Congress passed the Rehabilitation Act, Marian Wright Edelman founded the Children's Defense Fund. She had studied census figures showing that 750,000 children between ages seven and thirteen were not in school. At first, she assumed that they were African American victims of segregation. But closer study led to a startling discovery. "Handicapped kids were those seven hundred fifty thousand kids," she said. "We'd never thought of handicapped kids. But they're out there everywhere."[37]

In those days, public schools could close their doors to disabilities. In fact, a Pennsylvania law explicitly let them bar students who had not reached a mental age of at least five years. In a federal class action suit, parents and advocates argued that this law violated the Equal Protection Clause of the Fourteenth Amendment. The U.S. District Court agreed and ordered the state not to deny a free public education to any child with mental retardation.[38]

Another court ruled that the District of Columbia had to provide all of its school-age children "a free and suitable publicly-supported education regardless of the degree of the child's mental, physical or emotional disability or impairment." The district could not exclude any disabled child "on the basis of a claim of insufficient resources."[39] Significantly, both courts cited *Brown v. Board of Education*, with the latter quoting this passage: "In these days, it is doubtful that any child may reasonably be expected to succeed in life if he is denied the opportunity of an education. *Such an opportunity, where the state has undertaken to provide it, is a right which must be made available to all on equal terms*"[40] (emphasis added by district court).

These decisions focused congressional attention on special education. In 1975, Congress passed the Education for All Handicapped Children Act, which required that states receiving federal special-education funds provide a "free appropriate public education" to handicapped children. Supporters invoked the civil rights struggle, and the Senate report on the bill used the same quotation from the *Brown* decision.[41]

Although this law would play a central role in the lives of young people with autism, lawmakers gave scant notice to autism at the time of its passage. The legislation did not specify autism as a covered condition, and the Senate report did not include the word even once. Another 1975 law did mention autism by name. As a result of lobbying by the National Society for Autistic Children, the Developmental Disabilities Act required states to set up protection and advocacy services in order to receive federal grants for developmental disability programs, and listed autism as one of the disabilities that these programs had to serve.[42]

A 1988 protest marked a turning point in the broad movement for disability rights. The president of Gallaudet College, a venerable institution for the deaf, announced his retirement. Many alumni and students hoped that Gallaudet would use the opportunity to choose its first deaf president. When it opted for a hearing person, the campus erupted. Students boycotted classes and attracted television coverage by gathering together and collectively saying "Deaf President Now" in sign language. Because the uprising took place in Washington, DC, it made the national news. Students used early-model telecommunications devices to reach journalists and supporters across the country. Gallaudet's trustees quickly yielded, appointing a deaf president and board chairman.[43]

Up to this point, Americans had tended to see disabled people as unfortunates in need of charity. Now they got a glimpse from another perspective: the disabled as citizens demanding their due. After Gallaudet, the news media slowly started to frame disability as a rights issue.[44] These changing viewpoints were one reason for the 1990 passage of the Americans with Disabilities Act, a far-reaching measure that built on previous civil rights legislation to ban many forms of discrimination based on disability.

The policymakers who pushed for enactment of ADA were thinking of "visible" or "physical" handicaps. Senator Tom Harkin (D-IA) had a deaf brother, and Senator Bob Dole (R-KS) had lost the use of his right arm in the Second World War. Evan Kemp, chair of the Equal Employment Opportunity Commission, used a wheelchair, which has become the iconic symbol of disability. During congressional deliberations, autism came up only in passing, and the word appeared nowhere in the text of the bill. Yet ADA did set key precedents by expanding federal antidiscrimination law and bringing official recognition to the disability community. [45]

In the same year, Congress also reauthorized the Education for All Handicapped Children Act, renaming it the Individuals with Disabilities Education Act. The new law changed "handicapped children" to "children with disabilities" and named autism as one of these disabilities. The House report on the bill concluded that "autism has suffered from an historically inaccurate identification with mental illness. This inclusion of autism is meant to establish autism definitively as a developmental disability and not as a form of mental illness." [46] Nevertheless, the lawmakers did not spend much time discussing autism, nor did they define it. Indeed, they left room for administrators to use a fairly expansive definition of the disorder. In his remarks on the conference report, Representative George Miller (D-CA) said: "The bill makes clear that children with an autistic condition or traumatic brain injury, *regardless of its severity* [emphasis added], are entitled to a free, appropriate public education and related services." [47] The inclusion of autism was uncontroversial—the bill passed by voice vote in both chambers—and got virtually no press. Yet it would have major consequences.

AUTISM: PROFESSIONAL AND PUBLIC UNDERSTANDING

While this legislative and political action was under way, there were changes in the professional and public understanding of autism. These changes stemmed from broader shifts in psychology and psychiatry, which had begun to recognize that Freudian theories were more impressionistic than scientific. In a 1971 study, British and American psychiatrists viewed videotapes of patient interviews and came to starkly different diagnostic conclusions. [48] In 1973, psychologist David Rosenhan reported on a team of "pseudopatients" who had fooled psychiatrists into admitting them into mental facilities. [49] (They said that they had heard voices, but then otherwise acted normally.) During the same year, the emerging gay rights movement persuaded the American Psychiatric Association to declassify homosexuality as a "mental illness." These developments raised doubts about the reliability and validity of the categories that clinicians and researchers had been using. Such doubts sped the movement of psychiatrists and psychologists toward more rigorous practices and away from psychoanalytic theories (though they would continue to reign in places such as France).

One result of this movement was an expansion and revision of the American Psychiatric Association's *Diagnostic and Statistical Manual of Mental Disorders*, which went much farther than previous editions in standardizing diagnostic criteria and categories. Whereas the first (1952) and second (1968) editions did not even include autism as a separate diagnostic category, the third edition (DSM-III) did so in 1980, listing six symptoms necessary for a diagnosis of "infantile autism." DSM-III originally had a related category called "childhood onset pervasive developmental disorder," but a 1987 revision merged the two into "autism disorder." Although DSM-III was a step toward standardizing a definition of autism, diagnosis was still an impressionistic affair. It became more systematic at the end of the decade with a new diagnostic instrument, the Autism Diagnostic Observation Schedule (ADOS) and a related research instrument, the Autism Diagnostic Interview-Revised (ADIR-R). These tools offered a way to spot autism as early as age two. The introduction of these instruments, along with the training of many test examiners, revealed that many more people met the criteria for autism. Previously, most of them would have had a different label or none at all.[50]

Researchers were getting past Bettelheim and "refrigerator mothers." Some were mining old studies for new insights. In 1981, British psychiatrist Lorna Wing, one of the founders of the National Autistic Society, drew upon Hans Asperger's work from the 1940s and coined the term "Asperger's syndrome" for a form of high-functioning autism.[51] Others were confirming Rimland's argument that autism is a neurological condition. In 1985, Margaret Bauman and Thomas Kemper linked specific brain abnormalities with autism.[52] This work pointed more and more autism research in the direction of biology.[53]

As noted at the start of this chapter, a difficulty becomes a public policy problem only if there is a plausible remedy. Identifying autism as a neurological condition was a key step that opened the way for more scientific research. In the 1980s, this research did not yet point to any effective *medical* treatment (which still remains out of reach). There were, however, glimmers of hope for developmental and behavioral approaches.

In the 1970s, psychiatrist Robert Reichler and psychologist Eric Schopler founded TEACHH (Treatment and Education of Autistic and Related Communication Handicapped Children). Whereas Bettelheim recommended cutting autistic children off from their parents, TEACHH tried to engage parents as co-therapists.[54] The trend was toward helping children in natural settings, not institutions. Whereas the old model consisted of psychiatrists and institutions, the new model involved a wider array of professions:

psychologists, occupational therapists, speech therapists, and special education experts.[55]

Even more prominent was the rise of applied behavior analysis (ABA). As noted earlier, Ivar Lovaas had become prominent in the field during the 1960s. In 1973, he published an article showing the efficacy of discrete trial training, a structured ABA technique that breaks down skills into small, "discrete" components.[56] Fourteen years later, he wrote another article that caused a much bigger stir. After administering more than forty hours a week of discrete trial training to very young children, he reported that nearly *half* had recovered normal intellectual and educational functioning.[57] The notion of *recovery* would reverberate throughout the autism world. His work got widespread notice in clinical circles, and parents eventually learned of it from *Let Me Hear Your Voice*, a 1993 book in which Catherine Maurice credited ABA techniques with the recovery of her two autistic children.[58] Despite criticisms that Lovaas had exaggerated his findings, discrete trial training and other elements of ABA would eventually gain a reputation as the "gold standard" of autism therapy.

There would be an increasing demand for therapy, since public policy toward people with mental disabilities was evolving away from warehousing. The deinstitutionalization of the mentally ill consisted mainly of large-scale discharges ("dumping"), while the deinstitutionalization of the mentally retarded was much more likely to involve the reduction of new admissions to state institutions.[59] The latter would be more significant to the rise of autism numbers. What we today consider "severe autism" shows up during the toddler years. When parents institutionalized children, they usually put them in facilities for the retarded: the population of mental hospitals consisted mostly of adults.[60]

Outside the realm of medicine and government, ordinary Americans were hearing more about autism. The entertainment media can sometimes stir concern about social afflictions. In the 1960s, for instance, millions of Americans became more aware of child abuse when the problem inspired plotlines in television soap operas and prime-time dramas.[61] In the case of autism, a key event was the 1988 movie *Rain Man*, which won several Academy Awards and did well at the box office. Its depiction of an autistic savant (Dustin Hoffman) likely had mixed effects. It spread autism awareness and exposed millions of audience members to the term "high-functioning." Yet it also reinforced an old stereotype when one of its characters said—incorrectly—that most autistic people "can't speak or communicate." It also fed the false impression that high-functioning autistics have superpowers of memory and math.[62] In fact, true savant syndrome is rare.[63]

During the 1990s, legislative, scientific, and social trends converged to make autism an increasingly prominent political issue.

SHIFTING GOALPOSTS AND RISING NUMBERS

In 1980, as noted above, the DSM-III established autism as a separate diagnostic category. In 1994, the fourth edition of the manual (DSM-IV) led to even more diagnoses. It listed five "pervasive developmental disorders" (which would soon become known as "autism spectrum disorders" or ASD): autistic disorder, Rett's disorder, child disintegrative disorder, Asperger's disorder, and pervasive developmental disorder-not otherwise specified (PDD-NOS). Although Lorna Wing had written of Asperger's some years earlier, it had not been an official diagnosis until this point. According to Yale psychiatrist Fred Volkmar, who persuaded a reluctant American Psychiatric Association to accept it, Asperger's disorder was "a total add-on."[64]

DSM-IV had more inclusive criteria than the previous volume. Furthermore, according to Roy Grinker, the manual's authors missed an error in the manuscript. They had wanted a person to qualify for a diagnosis only if she or he had impairment *in more than one area*, but by mistakenly writing *or* instead of *and* in a key passage, they required impairment in only *one* area for a diagnosis of PDD-NOS.[65] A 2000 revision of the DSM-IV fixed the mistake, but by that time, the criteria had become part of clinical practice.

Whatever difference that error may have made, the new definition redrew the map of the autism world. People who once would have had a different diagnosis—or no diagnosis at all—could now fall under the banner of autism spectrum disorders. (In 2000, at the age of forty-six, Pulitzer Prize–winning music critic Tim Page got a diagnosis of Asperger's disorder, which was not even in the DSM when he was growing up.[66]) Were their ranks growing? It was impossible to say for sure, because in the early 1990s there was no firm baseline from which to measure a change. Although researchers had made scattered studies of autism prevalence in various locations, there had never been a systematic national effort to gather data under the DSM-III definition.[67] Even if there had been, the numbers would not have been comparable to data under the DSM-IV definition.

Around the same time, schools started to provide different kinds of statistics relating to autism. Until this point, children with autism could only qualify for special education services under one of the older classifications, such as mental retardation.[68] With no separate category for autism, such children instead showed up in the statistics under these other headings. Under the 1990 Individuals with Disabilities Education Act (IDEA), they would have their own line in the data tables.[69] And a continuing provision of the 1975 law required states to find out which children with disabilities were getting services and which were not. Now that this requirement specifically applied to autism, schools had to get into the business of identifying autistic children.

In any policy area, the act of gathering data brings out cases. Counting may legitimize discussion of uncomfortable topics. It enables people with a condition to come forward as a group instead of solitary individuals. Official record keeping opens a channel for reporting: once an organization announces that it is keeping count, people send it information. Such reactive effects are especially strong when benefits attach to membership in a category.[70]

With a greater public awareness of general disability issues, and with the new language of IDEA, parents of autistic children began pressing local school districts to get their children into the system. Psychiatrist Allen Frances writes of a "positive feedback loop" between advocacy and the provision of services.[71] As changes in diagnosis increased the population of identified autistic people and their families, they were better able to push for services, thereby increasing the number of people receiving such services. In just a few years, the number of students receiving services for autism more than quadrupled. During the same time, autistic students went from less than 1 percent of all students getting IDEA services to more than 7 percent. So had autism prevalence really risen fourfold or sevenfold? Certainly not. Much of this change stemmed from the "feedback loop" that Frances describes. In any event, a count of students receiving services for autism is not a direct measure of prevalence in the first place. The latter is the share of people who have a *medical diagnosis* of autism, usually by a physician using the DSM. Under IDEA, by contrast, an *educational determination* of autism comes from a team consisting of various school professionals who may or may not consult the DSM. Dr. James Laidler found that the criteria used by school districts to label children as autistic "are neither rigorous nor consistent." Accordingly, he concluded, the Education Department's data "are not reliable for tracking the prevalence of autism, and they in fact never were meant to fill this need."[72]

It is not even certain that true prevalence had increased at all, but by the year 2000, more stories about autism were breaking into the nightly news.[73] Press reports were describing an autism "epidemic."[74] A piece in the *New York Post* was typical:

> Locally, the Department of Mental Health estimates there are 11,000 people in the city with autism, but adds that number could be higher. The Board of Education reports a 60 percent increase in the number of students in its autism programs, from 1,544 in 1996 to 2,450 this year. Statewide figures have doubled, from 2,550 preschool and school-age kids in 1994, to 5,142 by the end of 1998.
>
> Movies like "Rain Man" and celebrities who have autistic children, including actor Sylvester Stallone and football stars Doug Flutie and Dan Marino, have helped raise awareness of autism. But for decades, autism was a hidden, gross-

ly misunderstood condition, labeled as a psychological disorder caused by bad parenting by "refrigerator mothers." Fortunately, the medical community now realizes it's a neuro-biological condition that is probably influenced by more than a dozen genes. Still, scientists don't know exactly what causes it—genetics alone, a virus or a toxin—or why the numbers are skyrocketing.[75]

A *Wired* magazine article titled "The Geek Syndrome" suggested that Silicon Valley had an unusually high prevalence of autism and speculated about the reason. It said that the tech industry attracts people with Asperger's, and when they marry, they pass autistic traits to their children. Though the evidence for this linkage was shaky at best, the article fostered the broader idea that prevalence was increasing, especially in certain "hot spots."[76] It quoted Rick Rollens, cofounder of the MIND Institute, a major autism research center: "Anyone who says this epidemic is due to better diagnostics has his head in the sand."[77]

Politicians were taking notice of autism. In 1998, Bobbie and Billy Gallagher of Brick, New Jersey, told Representative Chris Smith (R-NJ) about their concern that their community might have an unusually high prevalence of autism. Smith asked the Centers for Disease Control and Prevention (CDC) to look into a possible autism cluster in Brick. CDC concluded that the prevalence of ASD in the community was within the range of studies using thorough case-finding methods among small populations.[78] Smith maintained his interest in the issue, and in 2001, he and Representative Mike Doyle (D-PA) founded a congressional member organization devoted to autism, the Coalition on Autism Research and Education.[79]

Representative Dan Burton (R-IN) developed a zeal for one specific aspect of the issue. Believing that vaccines had caused his grandson's autism, he used his chairmanship of the House Committee on Government Reform to provide a forum for advocates of the vaccine theory. In 2000, he took testimony from Andrew Wakefield, a British physician who had published a *Lancet* article suggesting a link between autism and the measles, mumps, rubella (MMR) vaccine.[80] The hearing raised Wakefield's profile in the United States and drew more press coverage to the theory. (Years later, *The Lancet* retracted the article, and Britain's General Medical Council stripped Wakefield of his medical license for ethical violations, including his failure to disclose funding from lawyers who were working on a case against vaccine makers.[81]) The following chapter will discuss the vaccine controversy in greater detail.

Alongside the rising attention from the general public and the political community came greater activism among interest groups focusing on autism. This activism, in turn, would help make the issue bigger than ever.

GROUPS

For many years, the lead national organization was the Autism Society of America (formerly the National Society for Autistic Children). It was primarily a chapter-based self-help group for parents, who thought of it as a fraternal organization.[82] Despite playing a part in the 1975 developmental disabilities law and some other measures, it did not have a strong voice in national politics. In the late 1990s, it was spending about $20,000 a year on lobbying, barely a widow's mite by Washington standards.[83]

Organizing stakeholders was a challenge. At least until DSM-IV broadened the definition of autism in 1994, most of the people with the diagnosis had severe impairments in social communication. They would have found it hard to lobby on their own behalf. Their parents often served as their advocates in dealings with schools and social service agencies. After haggling with bureaucracies, providing care at home, and trying to earn a living, many parents did not have the time or resources for efforts to change the laws. And if they did try to organize, they hit another barrier: finding one another. For privacy reasons, there has never been a publicly available national directory of people with autism. And in the 1980s and 1990s, diagnosed cases of autism were scarcer than they are today.

The Internet helped create networks of stakeholders. In 1992, psychology professor and autism parent Roy Kopp founded Autism List (Autism-L). One parent later recalled her discovery of the Listserv: "It was an eye opener. Not only were we able to connect with other parents who had been there and done that, we were also able to connect with autistic adults who were finding each other for the first time, and building a strong, vibrant autistic community."[84]

During the 1990s, new organizations came onto the scene. In 1994, autism parents launched the National Alliance for Autism Research (NAAR) to support research in hopes of leveraging funding from the National Institutes of Health.[85] In 1995, autism parents Portia Iversen and Jon Shestack founded Cure Autism Now (CAN), which raised money for autism research and lobbied for federal support. CAN's efforts contributed to the passage of the Children's Health Act of 2000 (P.L. 106-310).[86] The new law mandated the establishment of the Interagency Autism Coordinating Committee (IACC), which was to coordinate federal autism research and programs. Shestack lobbied for three years for the law's autism provisions and testified before a congressional subcommittee.[87] As a movie producer (*Air Force One*), he was in an unusual position to raise money and get attention. He arranged for actress Rene Russo to testify with him. Although her only link to the issue was her friendship with Shestack and his wife, her fame drew publicity and her emotional delivery gained the panel's sympathy.[88]

Despite modest legislative success and rising media interest, the autism groups were not particularly effective at mobilizing the general public. A content analysis of newspaper reporting between 1996 and 2007 found that while many articles discussed solutions broadly, few furnished readers with mobilizing information that would enable them to act or to join autism advocacy efforts.[89]

Money was one constraint. Even with famous supporters, interest groups must work to gain and keep financial resources. One solution to the problem is to find patrons in the form of government agencies, nonprofit foundations, or wealthy individuals.[90] For autism, that solution arrived in 2005. After learning that their grandson had autism, Bob and Suzanne Wright founded Autism Speaks. As chairman and CEO of NBC Universal, Bob Wright had the wealth and connections to help the new organization grow fast. It had an early victory with the 2006 passage of the Combating Autism Act (P.L. 109-416), which authorized an expanded federal role in autism research, prevention, and treatment. (Congress renewed the law in 2011 and 2014.) Autism Speaks was soon raising millions of dollars, and by 2007, it had merged with both NAAR and CAN. It rapidly became the most prominent group in the field, funding scientific research and increasing public awareness. Its federal lobbying expenditures grew from $112,000 in 2005 to $525,000 in 2013.[91] Within a few years, it had persuaded dozens of states to mandate health insurance coverage of applied behavior analysis.

With prominence came criticism. Leaders of groups focusing on other conditions (e.g., Down syndrome) worried that it was competing with them for research funds.[92] Autism Speaks also fell into the crossfire between proponents and skeptics of the vaccine theory. Katie Wright, the daughter of Bob and Suzanne Wright and mother of their autistic grandson, made a public break with the group because it did not fully embrace the vaccine theory.[93] She joined the boards of groups propounding the theory and blogged for *Age of Autism: Daily Web Newspaper of the Autism Epidemic*.[94] On the other side, senior executive Alison Singer quit Autism Speaks because she considered it *too* accommodating toward the vaccine theory. She then founded her own group, the Autism Science Foundation.[95] (In 2015, Autism Speaks revised its policy statement, coming down squarely against the vaccine theory: "Over the last two decades, extensive research has asked whether there is any link between childhood vaccinations and autism. The results of this research are clear: Vaccines do not cause autism. We urge that all children be fully vaccinated."[96])

Further criticism came from groups of autistic people themselves. Before the 1990s, it would have been hard to picture such a thing. To the extent that Americans thought of autism at all, they saw it as a children's disorder. The adults with a diagnosis of autism tended to have serious deficits that kept them out of politics. With changing diagnostic standards, however, the autism spectrum grew to encompass people whose impairments were less severe and who could engage in political activity. At the same time, the emergence of social media helped them find one another and build communities that transcended geography. Online communication is particularly valuable to people who have challenges with face-to-face communication, which is of course a characteristic of autism.[97]

In 2006, nineteen-year-old Ari Ne'eman, who had a diagnosis of Asperger's, cofounded the Autistic Self Advocacy Network (ASAN) in response to what members saw as the absence of autistic voices in policy debates on autism. As a motto, the group adopted a saying from the broader disability rights movement, "Nothing About Us Without Us." ASAN gained national publicity in 2007, with a successful campaign against billboards by the NYU Child Study Center depicting autism as a kidnapper. The ads, said the group, stigmatized people with autism by suggesting that their condition was hopeless. Although billboards appeared only in New York City, the response was nationwide. ASAN used the Internet to join forces with other disability rights organizations and gather thousands of petition signatures.[98]

ASAN faulted Autism Speaks for its emphasis on cure over accommodation. In 2009, it protested a video by the group titled "I Am Autism." Directed by Alfonso Cuarón (who would later win an Academy Award for *Gravity*), the video showed images of autistic children, with a voice-over: "I am Autism. . . . I know where you live. . . . I live there too. . . . I work faster than pediatric AIDS, cancer and diabetes combined. . . . And if you are happily married, I will make sure that your marriage fails."[99] Under fire for the ad's fear appeal and inaccuracy (parents of autistic children do not have unusually high divorce rates), Autism Speaks soon removed the video from its website.

ON THE AGENDA

In October 2008, the School of Psychology at the Florida Institute of Technology released the first-ever national survey of the public's understanding of autism. Thirty-nine percent of survey respondents reported that they knew a person with autism, and 83 percent said that finding a cure for autism should be a national priority.[100]

In the same year, the presidential candidates talked about autism. Hillary Clinton reminded audiences that she had the most extensive experience in the issue. As a law student, she had studied autism issues at the Yale Child Study Center. As a young canvasser for the Children's Defense Fund, she had helped Marian Wright Edelman discover that public schools were shutting out children with disabilities. And as a U.S. senator, she had supported the Combating Autism Act and other related proposals.[101]

John McCain often mentioned that his wife had been a special education teacher and that his running mate Sarah Palin had an autistic nephew. Accepting the GOP nomination, he said that he was fighting for people like Jake and Toni Wimmer of Franklin County, Pennsylvania. "They have two sons, the youngest, Luke, has been diagnosed with autism. Their lives should matter to the people they elect to office. They matter to me."[102] Barack Obama said: "Some conditions like autism don't appear until age two, so infant screening is not enough. And to meet the needs of the growing numbers of Americans with autism, we need a comprehensive approach that includes not just screening, but early intervention, research, and education services."[103]

Autism showed up as an issue in other campaigns as well. In the 2010 Nevada Senate race, Republican candidate Sharron Angle denounced legislation to require insurance companies to cover autism therapy. "They just passed the latest one," she told a Tea Party rally. "Everything they want to throw at us is covered under 'autism' so that's a mandate that you have to pay for." Video showed her using air quotes around the word *autism* to drive home her point.[104] Angle's comments drew intense criticism from autism advocates across the country and contributed to her defeat in a race that Republicans had hoped to win. Other politicians drew a lesson from Angle's fate. Four years later, another conservative Senate candidate took a completely different approach. Thom Tillis sported a lapel pin bearing the logo of Autism Speaks and emphasized that he had tried to pass an autism mandate as speaker of the North Carolina House.[105] In support of Tillis, an outside spending group made a television ad featuring autism parents expressing their gratitude for his work.[106] Although it is hard to tell how much the issue helped him, Tillis narrowly defeated incumbent Democrat Kay Hagan.

There was general agreement to "do something" about autism. But what? In 2010, President Obama nominated Ari Ne'eman to be the first autistic person on the National Council on Disability. The nomination was controversial because of his contention that society should accept people with autism instead of curing them. Jon Shestack, the founder of Cure Autism Now (which had merged with Autism Speaks), said: "Why people have gotten upset is, he doesn't seem to represent, understand or have great sympathy for all the people who are truly, deeply affected in a way that he isn't."[107]

There were also divisions among those who preferred cure to acceptance. Some believed that vaccines caused autism, and that the answer lay in radical changes in the vaccine schedule and in chemical treatments to strip mercury from the body. Others pointed to a wider array of potential causes and advocated diverse medical and behavioral interventions.

It is time to turn to the politics of science.

Chapter Three

Medicine, Science, and Math

If we can land a man on the moon, why can't we cure autism? Frustrated parents may ask that question, remembering that when John F. Kennedy committed the United States to go to the moon, NASA scientists and engineers figured out how to get there. Ever since Neil Armstrong stepped off the lunar module in 1969, politicians have held up the Apollo project as a model for solving all kinds of problems.[1] But autism is not rocket science. Contrary to the usual meaning of that expression, I hardly suggest that autism science is simple; rather, it is more puzzling than rocket science.

When the moon program was getting under way, there was consensus about the fundamental terms and facts. Although the engineering details were challenging, the basic math and physics behind the mission dated back to Isaac Newton. Autism is different. As we have already seen, it is a contested concept with many uncertainties. Just picture an Apollo program in which experts saw different kinds of moons in different parts of the sky and were not quite sure about the laws of motion.

In the 1960s, laypeople did not think that they knew better than NASA when it came to operational decisions such as the use of multistage liquid-fuel rockets. Apart from a handful of cranks, they did not buy into the theory that the moon landings were a hoax.[2] People accepted scientific authority in this case because the science seemed settled and did not clash with folk wisdom. With autism, not only is the science in flux but it has to compete with alternative sources of belief. Parents consider themselves experts on their own children, as Jenny McCarthy suggested to Oprah Winfrey: "I do have a theory [based on] mommy instinct. . . . What does it take for people to start listening to what the mothers of children with autism have been saying for years—which is that we vaccinated our babies and something happened." When Winfrey read a Centers for Disease Control (CDC) statement denying the vaccine theory, McCarthy answered to loud applause: "My science is Evan, and he's at home. That's my science."[3]

After the Soviet Union quit the space race and the wave of patriotic fervor subsided, political debates about lunar exploration were largely about costs and benefits. Support waned because Americans thought that there were better uses for the money, not because they saw anything inherently wrong about shooting rockets at the moon. With autism, the politics cuts deeper because some take offense at the very notion of "cure." From their perspective, the problem is not just that research into cures will divert resources from projects that can help autistic people today, but rather that eradicating autism means eradicating an identity.

In short, the Apollo program used well-known scientific principles to reach a lifeless object. Autism science is groping for a basic understanding of an ill-defined issue with debatable goals. The subjects of the inquiry are human beings: they and their loved ones have their own opinions about what happened to them and what should become of them. Not rocket science, indeed.

DIAGNOSIS AND PREVALENCE

Lord Kelvin famously said that "when you can measure what you are speaking about, and express it in numbers, you know something about it, when you cannot express it in numbers, your knowledge is of a meager and unsatisfactory kind."[4] Any discussion of autism science should begin with the numbers—which are meager and unsatisfactory.

Starting in the 1940s and for decades after, clinicians referred to the condition as "infantile autism," a term sounding like "infantile paralysis," long a synonym for polio. A comparison between autism and polio is instructive. A British physician provided the first clinical description of polio in 1789, and it took 120 years to find the virus that caused it. Several more decades passed before polio vaccines were available. Those vaccines have been effective in preventing polio, but they do not help people who already have it. Even today, there is no cure.

For all of our twenty-first-century technology, autism is roughly where polio was a century ago. Before reliable lab tests were available, physicians could diagnose polio only by looking at symptoms. Because paralysis has many other causes (infections, injuries, tumors, toxins), doctors often mislabeled polio as something else, or vice versa.[5] Autism presents a similar muddle. "To diagnose autism reliably, we need to better understand what goes awry in people with the disorder," writes Harvard biostatistician Nicholas Lange. "Until its solid biological basis is found, any attempt to use brain imaging to diagnose autism will be futile."[6] As the previous chapter noted, psychologists have to rely on questionnaires and observations of behavior. Therein lies a problem. Says Thomas Insel, director of the National Institute of Mental Health (NIMH):

> Unlike our definitions of ischemic heart disease, lymphoma, or AIDS, the DSM diagnoses are based on a consensus about clusters of clinical symptoms, not any objective laboratory measure. In the rest of medicine, this would be equivalent to creating diagnostic systems based on the nature of chest pain or the quality of fever. Indeed, symptom-based diagnosis, once common in other areas of medicine, has been largely replaced in the past half century as we have understood that symptoms alone rarely indicate the best choice of treatment. [7]

Moreover, the definition of behavioral symptoms rests on Western—and specifically American—expectations about the behavior of children and adults. But what is "autistic" in this context may be "normal" in another. In rural South Africa, for instance, young children avoid direct eye contact with adults because their culture considers it disrespectful. [8]

Nevertheless, the standardized schedules for observations and interviews are quite reliable—provided that all concerned parties are unbiased. Unlike blood tests and brain scans, these methods involve judgments that might reflect opinions and incentives. Once parents get over their initial denial, they have strong reason to seek a diagnosis of autism spectrum disorder (ASD) for troubled children, since it can trigger thousands of dollars in assistance. Allen Frances says: "Having the label can make the difference between being closely attended to in a class of four versus being lost in a class of 40. Kids who need special attention can often get it only if they are labeled autistic." [9] Roy Grinker quotes a leading scientist who also has a clinical practice: "I am incredibly disciplined in the diagnostic classifications in my research, but in my private practice, I'll call a kid a zebra if it will get him the educational services I think he needs." [10] Bias can run in the other direction, too. If a school district does not really want to provide services, its psychologists might feel pressure to code behavior in a way that spells "normal."

As noted in the last chapter (and as the next chapter will discuss in greater detail), a further layer of confusion arises because an educational determination of autism is different from a medical diagnosis. A person can be "autistic" by one standard and not the other. State education agencies vary considerably in their definitions and evaluation procedures, [11] so school data give a blurry picture.

Over the years, estimates of prevalence have varied by 134-fold, with rates ranging from 0.7 to 94 per 10,000. [12] So why not get a "hard count" by establishing a registry of everybody with a diagnosis? West Virginia launched such an effort in 2004. Physicians, psychologists, and other professionals have to fill out a form and send it to the registry upon diagnosing anyone with an autism spectrum disorder.[13] Implementation has been hard. Some families do not seek a diagnosis in the first place, while others go out of state for an assessment. "Compliance has been an issue," says the coordinator of the state registry. "The big centers—the ones that diagnose on a daily basis—are reporting. But we're missing tons of tiny reporting centers all over the state. They just aren't reporting."[14] Rhode Island established a confidential registry in 2013, but a senior scientist with the project reckoned that it would take ten years to enroll all eligible state residents.[15]

The most prominent analysis of autism prevalence among a "total population" is a study of thirty-seven thousand children (ages seven to twelve) in a South Korean community.[16] Researchers found a prevalence of one in thirty-eight, or 2.64 percent—much higher than previous estimates. It is not clear whether this figure suggests something about overall prevalence, or whether it reflects certain characteristics of that one community. It is also possible that the researchers overdiagnosed borderline cases.[17] The point here is that, even within a single community, a comprehensive prevalence survey of a total population is time-consuming. It took a year to administer the initial screening questionnaire to parents and teachers and another three years to carry out diagnostic assessments of those whose screening results were positive.

Another way to measure prevalence would be to sample the national population and assess individuals in person. This method would be impractical. To capture something that perhaps affects one or two people out of a hundred, the sample would have to be huge, and each individual assessment would cost hundreds of dollars at least. Even with ample resources, it would be hard to get a representative sample, since many respondents would opt out of the lengthy and intrusive assessment process.

The CDC tries to get around this problem by taking a different approach. Every few years, CDC gathers data on eight-year-olds from a dozen or so communities around the country. Researchers scour school and medical records for diagnoses or notations of possible autism symptoms. In 2014, CDC estimated that 14.7 out of every 1,000 eight-year-olds had an autism spectrum disorder, a 30 percent jump from its 2012 estimate of 11.3 per 1,000.[18] In both studies, however, the numbers varied from place to place. Writing in *Autism*, David Mandell and Luc Lecavalier ask why ASD should respect state lines. "Could it be that there are characteristics of the physical environment in New Jersey that result in a greater prevalence of autism than in Alabama? Why would the proportion of children with ASD and intellectual disability vary so greatly across sites?"[19] They suggest that local policies, resources, and awareness may be driving the estimates. In that case, the figures are not actually measuring prevalence itself so much as the extent to which clinicians and educators record the symptoms, such as lack of eye contact.[20]

Both of these CDC estimates relied on the DSM-IV criteria, so if Mandell and Lacavalier are correct in their suspicions, then this apparent rise in national prevalence stems mostly from increasing awareness. That is, professionals are just noticing things that they used to ignore. If we use older estimates as a baseline, the changing diagnostic criteria might also account for much of the change. One study found that one in four autistic children in California would have received the label of "mentally retarded" under older criteria.[21] So is the apparent increase in prevalence just a matter of shifting definition and perception? The mushy data do not supply an answer, so the possibility of a true increase deserves ongoing study.[22]

The data also seem to show differences among demographic groups. Multiple studies find higher rates of autism among non-Hispanic whites than among Hispanics or African Americans.[23] Why the disparity? White people tend to have higher income and educational levels, thus greater access to medical professionals and social networks that provide information about autism. Problems of cultural communication and clinician attitudes may delay diagnosis among nonwhites. In particular, primary care pediatricians find it more difficult to assess Spanish-speaking patients, and many do not offer screenings in Spanish.[24]

Further muddying the diagnostic water is the fifth edition of the *Diagnostic and Statistical Manual* (DSM-5), which came out in 2013. The new classification system eliminated several subcategories, including Asperger's syndrome and PDD-NOS, and folded them into "autism spectrum disorder." It collapsed the three domains of autism symptoms (social impairment, language/communication impairment, and repetitive/restricted behavior) into two: social communication impairment and restricted interests/repetitive behaviors. It added a new category called social communication disorder (SCD), allowing for diagnosis of disabilities in social communication without the presence of repetitive behavior.

Dr. Allen Frances, the lead editor of a previous version of the manual, says that the diagnostic instructions are confusing, so the diagnosis will vary from rater to rater and place to place. "It will be even more impossible than it is now to determine rates of autism and why they shift so much over time."[25] A more recent study says that prevalence estimates are likely to decline under DSM-5—but it cautions that policies for service eligibility and diagnostic tools will change in response to the revised criteria. Clinicians may react by looking for more symptoms to back up ASD diagnoses.[26]

And DSM-5 is not the last word. Whereas the titles of previous editions included Roman numerals (DSM-III, DSM-IV), the new one instead has an Arabic numeral to make it easier to designate revisions. The future will bring DSM-5.1, DSM-5.2, and so on, which may include further changes in the way we describe and diagnose autism.

Autistic people have their own opinions about what labels should apply to them. (This issue represents yet another difference between autism science and space science: Pluto did not object when the International Astronomical Union demoted it from planet status.) The inclusion of Asperger's disorder in DSM-IV may have been a "total add-on," but it had the unanticipated consequence of creating a community of interest. John Elder Robison recalls his reaction to his diagnosis at age forty: "The realization was staggering. There are other people like me. So many, in fact, that they have a name for us."[27] Author Gary Greenberg interviewed one young man who had had a diagnosis of Asperger's. "When you hear the word autism, you think of institutionalization, speech delay, diapers. It's a scary word," said the young man. "It's going to make me want to be even more concealed. Would *you* rather say you have Asperger's or autism?"[28] In 2010, American Psychiatric Association president Carol Bernstein wrote that comments to the working group often emphasized self-identity:

> Many criticisms indicated that some individuals diagnosed with Asperger's disorder (self-designated as "Aspies") have developed a strong sense of uniqueness and belonging built around the diagnosis, an identity that is often supported by their families. Categorizing them in these other diagnoses, they argued, would deprive them of their identity and associate them with diagnoses that are more stigmatizing.[29]

Groups representing people with an Asperger's diagnosis lobbied the American Psychological Association to keep it in the manual. Though they fell short that time, they might someday get it back. After an extensive review of the literature, one psychiatrist has argued there is indeed a scientific case for restoring it as a distinct diagnosis.[30] Regardless of what the DSM says, the term is still in common use, and Asperger groups remain active.

Because of the fog surrounding diagnosis and prevalence, one might assume that the solution lies in more scientific research. But decisions about research priorities are seldom about "purely" scientific considerations. Other interests weigh in, and scientists are not the only ones at the table.

RESEARCH PRIORITIES

From the 1960s through the 1990s, parents took the lead in promoting autism research. Some were key researchers themselves, including Lorna Wing in Britain and Bernard Rimland in the United States.[31] In other cases, parents helped organize and fund the research. Soon after founding Cure Autism Now (CAN), Jerome Shestack and Portia Iversen founded the Autism Genetics Resource Exchange (AGRE), an autism gene bank devoted to fostering collaborative work by providing open access to the entire scientific community.[32] (AGRE is now part of Autism Speaks and receives funding from the National Institute of Mental Health.).

Thanks to lobbying by CAN and other organizations, the Children's Health Act of 2000 included a title dealing exclusively with autism. The legislation charged the National Institutes of Health (NIH) with expanding and coordinating research activities, including grants for regional "centers of excellence." The new law required CDC to set up a surveillance program to gather and analyze information about the epidemiology of autism. The law also required the establishment of an interagency autism task force to coordinate research efforts. NIH and CDC funded most of these activities through their lump-sum appropriations. Congress generally did not earmark funds for autism research in appropriations bills.[33]

When the Children's Health Act passed in 2000, NIH was spending $51 million a year on autism activities. Within a few years, that figure nearly doubled. In 2006, Congress passed the first autism-specific federal statute, the Combating Autism Act. It provided for expanded autism activities, authorizing $945 million over five years. It also reconstituted the task force as an official advisory body, the Interagency Autism Coordinating Committee (IACC), which was to draft strategic plans for federal autism activities. Although actual outlays were below the authorized level, funding would continue to increase.[34] Bureaucracies other than NIH came into play—even the Department of Defense. Starting with the 2007 defense appropriations bill, the Pentagon's Office of the Congressionally Directed Medical Research Programs has included the Autism Research Program. Between fiscal years 2008 and 2012, NIH and ten other federal agencies awarded $1.2 billion to fund autism research projects.[35] In the meantime, private organizations such as the Simons Foundation and Autism Speaks also spent millions on autism science.[36]

The surge in funding fostered a surge in published research.[37] At first, these dual trends may seem to be a success story—and who can argue with success? Indeed, the Combating Autism Act and its 2011 and 2014 reauthorizations passed without any recorded opposition on the floor of either the House or Senate.[38] But the authorized sums amount to a tiny fraction of the federal government's multi-trillion-dollar outlays. For lawmakers, autism research is simply not a big-ticket item. Furthermore, Americans approve of federal support for science: in surveys between 2002 and 2012, no more than 15 percent said that the government was spending too much on it.[39] At a broad level, then, passing autism research legislation involves giving pittance to a popular cause. It is a political no-brainer—or to use social science terminology, a valence issue.

In fiscal 2013, NIH spent $186 million on autism research. That figure exceeded funding for cerebral palsy ($18 million), cystic fibrosis ($78 million), and Down syndrome ($18 million).[40] The disparity has caused some resentment. "Why is Down's syndrome funding low? Autism I think is a big contributor," Jon Colman, the chief operating officer of the National Down Syndrome Society told *Nature* in 2007. "It's dominating priorities."[41] Nevertheless, one should not make too much of the notion that autism is crowding out other categories. Autism research accounts for only about .06 percent of NIH's annual outlays of $30 billion.

Despite autism's microscopic share of NIH funding, there has been concern about wasteful spending. Senators Tom Coburn (R-OK), Mike Lee (R-UT), and Jim DeMint (R-SC) briefly held up the 2011 reauthorization until Senator Robert Menendez (D-NJ) agreed to ask the Government Accountability Office (GAO) to see whether there was too much overlap in federally funded studies. In 2013, GAO released its report, which found that 84 percent of such studies "had the potential to be duplicative."[42] At a congressional hearing, however, the author of the report acknowledged that GAO did not actually look at the studies' hypotheses, populations, and methods. By "potentially duplicative," it merely referred to studies that focused on the same goals. Thomas Insel of the NIMH replied that it was good to have multiple studies concerning that same objective, because replication of results is necessary to confirm scientific findings.[43] But recognizing that some of the research might be ill-coordinated, lawmakers added language directing the Department of Health and Human Services and IACC to ensure that autism activities "are not unnecessarily duplicative."[44]

Another issue concerns the basic definition of the problem. From the beginning of parent activism in the 1960s, the prevailing assumption has been that autism is a "disease" or "disorder" in need of a cure. After all, an early autism group was "Cure Autism Now." On signing the Children's Health Act, President Clinton spoke of "diseases such as diabetes, asthma, lead poisoning, cancer, and autism."[45] A few years later, Senator Hillary Clinton (D-NY) said: "I'm certain that through the convergence of scientific, academic, public and political programs we can successfully develop treatments and hopefully a cure for autism."[46] After Congress passed the Combating Autism Act of 2006—a revealing title in itself—President George W. Bush said that new law would "serve as an important foundation for our Nation's efforts to find a cure for autism."[47] On Capitol Hill, the Coalition for Autism Research and Education (CARE), a congressional member organization, declared that its goals include "legislative initiatives that will help facilitate advanced treatments—and ultimately a cure—for autism spectrum disorders."[48] In 2013, Representative Tom Cole (R-OK) backed legislation to shut down the Presidential Election Campaign Fund and switch the money to autism research. "Transforming welfare for politicians into efforts to eradicate this terrible disease is a much better reflection of our national prerogatives," he said, citing "the need to combat autism."[49]

The "disease frame" may seem natural to parents and public officials, but some in the autism community disagree. In 2013, Seattle Children's Hospital ran bus ads showing a smiling boy next to the words "Let's wipe out cancer, diabetes and autism in his lifetime." The hospital pulled the ads after the Autistic Self Advocacy Network's Washington chapter (ASAN-WA) organized an online campaign against it. "Autism is a disability, but it is not a disease. It is not a life-threatening illness," said Matt Young, coleader of ASAN-WA. "The idea it's a state to be wiped out has much negative impact on our lives."[50]

A fuller expression of this point of view came at a 2012 congressional hearing. Michael John Carley, who founded the Global and Regional Asperger Syndrome Partnership, testified about his experiences as a person with ASD. He said:

> Tone, and language may seem like pc-nonsense semantics to many, but not to someone on the spectrum who grows up having to hear words like "cure," "disease," "defeat," and "combat"—words that have no medical basis given the genetic component of autism (for though we may improve dramatically, we're born with this and will die with this) and given the harm these words cause there is also no ethical basis for their usage. Especially when the words come from not just misguided ad campaigns, but coming from people who might genuinely love us, people who use these words because they learned them from experts on TV.[51]

People in this camp have specific concerns about the organization and implementation of autism research. The Combating Autism Act of 2006 required the inclusion of at least one ASD person on IACC (as well as a parent and a representative of an autism advocacy organization). Arguing that autistic people themselves are the main stakeholders, groups such as ASAN have called for increasing this representation. They also argue that too much autism research spending goes to the "disease frame" and that not enough goes into improvement of services and the quality of life. (See figure 3.1.) In 2010, for instance, only 16 percent went to services and only 2 percent went to "lifespan issues" (e.g., the needs of adults on the spectrum).[52]

Some parents, however, argue that the case against cure overlooks differences among people with autism. It is one thing to say that autism is just a "difference" when it involves a high-functioning person with a college degree. It is another when the person is nonverbal or lacks bowel control. One mother told the *Pittsburgh Post-Gazette*: "I say to this one young man who always brings it up to me, 'Look: if my son could be you, that would be a cure.' As a parent who has a child on the more severe end of the spectrum, I think that's a very different thing than someone with high-functioning Asperger's."[53]

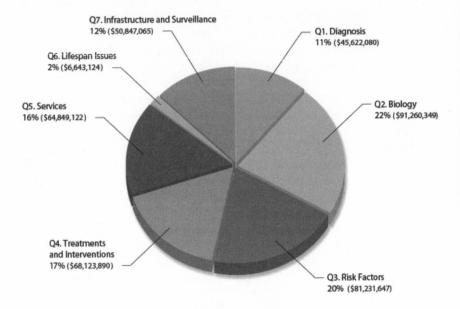

Q7. Infrastructure and Surveillance
12% ($50,847,065)

Q1. Diagnosis
11% ($45,622,080)

Q6. Lifespan Issues
2% ($6,643,124)

Q5. Services
16% ($64,849,122)

Q2. Biology
22% ($91,260,349)

Q4. Treatments
and Interventions
17% ($68,123,890)

Q3. Risk Factors
20% ($81,231,647)

Figure 3.1.   2010 ASD Research Funding. The figures include funding from all sources, 82 percent of which was from the federal government. Source: U.S. Department of Health and Human Services, Interagency Autism Coordinating Committee, "2010 IACC Autism Spectrum Disorder Research Portfolio Analysis Report," July 2013. Online: iacc.hhs.gov/portfolio-analysis/2010/2010_portfolio_analysis.pdf.

When Congress took up the reauthorization of the Combating Autism Act in 2014, self-advocates were disappointed that it neither increased the representation of autistic people on IACC nor mandated greater funding for services research. They did win one small but symbolically important victory. After ASAN ran a hashtag campaign, #StopCombatingMe, the sponsors renamed it the Autism Collaboration, Accountability, Research, Education and Support Act, or "Autism CARES."

The sponsors said that the existing legislation had fostered advances in a variety of areas, such as screening tools. But for autistic people and their families, such advances are merely means to an end. As IACC puts it, one key "aspirational goal" is to develop interventions that are effective for "reducing both core and associated symptoms, for building adaptive skills, and for maximizing quality of life and health for people with ASD."[54] Despite the outpouring of research, progress toward this goal has been limited. There is still no drug for autism per se, and research on behavioral therapy has focused more on appraising existing methods than on inventing new ones. There are several reasons for the frustrating pace of progress.

As suggested at the start of this chapter, the Apollo program involved skillful execution of *applied* science, whereas autism research requires breakthroughs in *basic* science. According to the IACC report: "While in the past, serendipitous findings based on clinical observation have led to treatments for neuropsychiatric disorders without a deep understanding of the underlying biology, it is anticipated that investment in understanding the mechanisms underlying ASD will facilitate the development of the next generation of treatments."[55] That is a bureaucratic-academic way of saying that autism science hinges on other fields of science. There is a long way to go. Despite progress in imaging technology, scientists have only a fragmentary knowledge of the brain and its relation to thinking and behavior.[56] Psychologist Gary Marcus writes: "We know that there must be some lawful relation between assemblies of neurons and the elements of thought, but we are currently at a loss to describe those laws."[57]

At this stage, scientists have identified a couple of important relationships, though with asterisks. First, autism has a strong genetic component. As early as 1977, a study of twins showed important hereditary influences.[58] More recent studies suggest that 50 to 60 percent of the risk for autism may be genetic.[59] But there is still a great deal that scientists do not understand about the underlying genetic mechanisms, the ties between genes and the environment, and the large share of risk that genetics does not account for.

Second, prevalence is greater among males than females. Researchers agree that there is a real gender difference, but it might not be as great as the four-to-one ratio that many studies have found. There could be subtle differences in the way that autism shows up in males and females, so some of the latter might "fly under the radar" on tests geared to male autistic behavior.[60] Beyond such biases in reporting or diagnosis, there also remain major questions about why and how sex differences affect autism risk.[61]

Because scientists lack a grand theory of autism causation—not to mention accurate knowledge of how autism prevalence has changed over the years—research has moved in a bewildering array of directions. Here is just a partial list of correlates, risk factors, and possible causes that have been the subject of serious peer-reviewed studies:

- Pesticides;[62]
- Air pollution and proximity to freeways;[63]
- Maternal thyroid issues;[64]
- Autoimmune disorders;[65]
- Induced labor;[66]
- Preterm birth;[67]
- Birth by cesarean section;[68]
- Maternal and paternal obesity;[69]
- Maternal and paternal age;[70]

- Maternal posttraumatic stress disorder;[71]
- Smoking during pregnancy;[72]
- Antidepressant use during pregnancy.[73]

This diversity of research agendas is partially a result of uncertainty. Amid the darkness, it might make sense to shine searchlights in all directions. Some of it may also stem from the availability of autism research money at a time of tight science budgets. To put it bluntly, publication-hungry scientists may have an incentive to rebrand marginally relevant work as autism-related. Describing her study of how experts on sex differences have landed on the "biomedical platform" of autism, science historian Sarah Richardson says they "have begun to link their very basic research—even if it's on nematodes [roundworms]—to frame it as a contribution to autism."[74]

If the science were not confusing enough, its coverage in the mass media has added another layer of murk. News reports hype tentative findings and weak correlations as "breakthroughs" in the quest for autism answers. When the research yields mixed results, the media headlines can be comically inconsistent. Consider how various publications covered a 2013 study on the impact of in vitro fertilization:

- RARE IN VITRO TECHNIQUE RAISES AUTISM RISK, STUDY SAYS
- IVF PROCEDURES DO NOT BOOST AUTISM RISK
- SOME FORMS OF IVF LINKED TO AUTISM, MENTAL DISABILITY
- IVF, AUTISM NOT LINKED, BUT STUDY FINDS RISK OF INTELLECTUAL DISABILITY[75]

An average reader of the news might well conclude that scientists are clueless about what does and does not lead to autism. In fact, they are sure that they have ruled out at least one purported culprit: vaccination. And yet, according to a 2013 Harris survey, 29 percent of adults and 33 percent of parents agree with the statement that "vaccinations can cause autism."[76] This notion has the support of a passionate grassroots movement that has influenced public policy debates and media portrayals of autism. The causes and consequences of this movement deserve special attention.

SHOTS IN THE DARK

During the 1970s, lawsuits claimed that children had suffered brain damage from the diphtheria, tetanus, and pertussis (DTP) vaccine. Though later research would undercut such claims, some courts awarded damages. Fearful of liability, some manufacturers stopped making vaccines, resulting in a shortage. To reduce the companies' concerns while providing a way to respond to actual harm, Congress passed the National Childhood Vaccine Injury Act in 1986. The law set up the National Vaccine Injury Compensation Program as a no-fault alternative to product liability and medical malpractice lawsuits. With funding from an excise tax on childhood vaccines, the program aimed to encourage childhood vaccination through a less costly and time-consuming system of recovery. The U.S. Court of Federal Claims would decide who gets payment.

The new law did little to allay public fears, as other vaccine scares cropped up. A 1997 law required a government review of food and drugs containing mercury, which can damage the brain and nervous system. In 1999, the Food and Drug Administration reviewed thimerosal, a mercury-based preservative that vaccine makers had used since the 1930s. Although the review turned up no evidence that thimerosal was harmful in the amounts present in vaccines, there was concern that some infants might be getting too much of it after receiving a series of shots. In 1999, the American Academy of Pediatrics (AAP) and the Public Health Service asked makers of childhood vaccines to remove thimerosal as a purely precautionary measure. The statement did not point to any specific risk and did not even mention the word *autism*.[77] Officials thought the move would head off any panic; instead, it fueled the belief that thimerosal was dangerous.

Lyn Redwood, a nurse practitioner in Atlanta, thought that thimerosal had caused her son's autism even though the statement stressed that "there are no data or evidence of any harm caused by the level of exposure that some children may have encountered in following the existing immunization schedule." Writing to the former AAP official who had pushed for the statement, Redwood and her physician husband said: "No evidence of harm does not equate with no harm having occurred!"[78] Redwood started an e-mail list about mercury and autism. As she told author Seth Mnookin: "By word of mouth, people heard about it, so I had ten, then one hundred, and then a thousand, and then four thousand people as part of this list, comparing notes about their children's development [and] mercury. It in essence created a community and a movement."[79]

One recruit to the movement was Danielle Sarkine, a Florida woman with an autistic son and an influential father: Representative Dan Burton (R-IN), chair of the House Committee on Government Reform. On April 6, 2000, Burton opened a high-profile hearing by saying of his grandson: "[A]fter receiving nine shots in 1 day, the MMR and the DTaP shot and the hepatitis B, within a very short period of time, he quit speaking, ran around banging his head against the wall, screaming, hollering, waving his hands, and became a totally different child. We found out that he was autistic."[80] The mother of an autistic child alluded to thimerosal: "I need someone to explain to me why it is acceptable to have products on the market that exposed my son to 37.5 micrograms of mercury in 1 day at a time when he should not have been exposed to more than .59 micrograms of mercury given his body weight."[81] Psychologist Bernard Rimland testified that there was a worldwide epidemic of autism and that vaccines were likely to blame. Though he had no background in medicine, his role in debunking the "refrigerator mother" theory gave him credibility among many autism parents.

The most prominent testimony came from Andrew Wakefield. In 1998, the British physician and a dozen colleagues published an article in *The Lancet* linking the MMR (measles, mumps, rubella) vaccine to autism.[82] He suggested that the culprit was not thimerosal but the administration of three vaccines in one shot. At first, Wakefield drew far more attention in Britain than in the United States. The Burton hearing introduced him to a wider American public.

At the insistence of ranking Democrat Henry Waxman, the committee did take testimony from skeptics of the vaccine theory, but Burton questioned them harshly. Waxman said that Burton had stacked the witness list with advocates of the theory. "What also bothered me was when we asked that we have the American Medical Association or the American Public Health Association or the National Network for Immunization Information or the former Secretary of HHS, Dr. Louis Sullivan—real experts in addition to those we have before us—we were told no, they cannot fit in."[83]

The hearing aired on C-SPAN and got extensive media coverage, including a story in the *New York Times*.[84] Several months later, *60 Minutes* interviewed Wakefield for a segment titled "The MMR Vaccine," thus bringing his ideas to 10.6 million American households.[85] In 2005, both *Rolling Stone* and *Salon* published "Deadly Immunity," an article by Robert F. Kennedy Jr. accusing the federal government of a massive conspiracy to cover up a connection between vaccines and autism.[86] In the same year, in a book titled *Evidence of Harm*, journalist David Kirby did not make definitive claims about thimerosal but treated it as a likely suspect: "If thimerosal is one day proven to be a contributing factor to autism, and if US-made vaccines containing the preservative are now being supplied to infants the world over, the scope of this potential tragedy becomes unthinkable."[87] In 2005, United Press International started publishing Dan Olmsted's "The Age of Autism," a series of articles propounding the vaccine theory.[88] After two years, Olmsted moved to a stand-alone website of the same name, which would become a central hub for adherents.

New organizations were springing up. In 2000, Lyn Redwood and other members of her network founded a group called SafeMinds, short for "Sensible Action for Ending Mercury-Induced Disorders." In 2003, a group of autism parents organized the National Autism Association to encourage self-help and promote "vaccine safety." Two years later, Lisa and J. B. Handley founded Generation Rescue to recover children whose autism purportedly started with vaccines. The group gained a key supporter in actress Jenny McCarthy, who believed that vaccines had caused her own son's autism. McCarthy, who had already gained a great deal of publicity for the vaccine theory by discussing it on *The Oprah Winfrey Show*, became the group's president. (It briefly called itself "Jenny McCarthy and Jim Carrey's autism organization," but the celebrity couple split in 2010.[89])

As press attention went up and stars spoke out, the entertainment media weighed in. In a 2005 episode of *The Shield*, a police detective and his ex-wife contemplated joining a vaccine lawsuit after two of their children got a diagnosis. They talked to a pediatrician, who refused to help them with the suit because the science does not support the vaccine theory.[90] The detective smelled an ulterior motive: "How many shots with thimerosal have you prescribed to kids? Saying that they've been poisoning our kids is just like admitting you've been doing it all along, right?" The 2008 premiere of the short-lived ABC series *Eli Stone* was about a child who had become autistic because of "mercuritol"—a fictional name for thimerosal.[91]

Back on Capitol Hill, Representative Carolyn Maloney (D-NY) and other members supported legislation to require a federal study of vaccines and autism. At a March 2006 news conference at the National Press Club, she singled out Olmsted's reporting as an inspiration for the legislation.[92] Burton, who had continued to hold hearings on the subject, wanted the 2006 Combating Autism Act to include such a requirement. The final version instead just said that research topics should include environmental causes. Senator Mike Enzi (R-WY), chair of the Health, Education, Labor, and Pensions Committee, used a floor colloquy to placate adherents of the vaccine theory. Research into environmental causes, he said, should indeed examine vaccines: "I want to be clear that, for the purposes of biomedical research, no research avenue should be eliminated, including biomedical research examining potential links between vaccines, vaccine components, and autism spectrum disorder."[93]

The vaccine theory made its way into the 2008 presidential race. "It's indisputable that autism is on the rise among children," said John McCain in Texas. "The question is, What's causing it? And we go back and forth, and there's strong evidence that indicates that it's got to do with a preservative in vaccines."[94] At a Pennsylvania rally, Barack Obama said: "We've seen just a skyrocketing autism rate. Some people are suspicious that it's connected to the vaccines. This person included [*pointing to an audience member*]. The science right now is inconclusive, but we have to research it."[95] By now, many Americans were "suspicious." Nearly one in four (24 percent) respondents in a survey believed that it was safer not to vaccinate children at all because vaccines could cause autism, and another 19 percent were not sure.[96]

Secretaries of Health of Human Services, who make the appointments to IACC, have made room for advocates of the vaccine theory. In its public statements, accordingly, IACC has treaded lightly around the subject. In its 2010 strategic plan, it acknowledged that "the link between autism and vaccines is unsupported by the epidemiological research literature." But it also suggested that "the existing population-based studies were limited in their ability to detect small susceptible subpopulations that could be more genetically vulnerable to environmental exposures." Accordingly, it proposed to support studies "to determine if there are subpopulations that are more susceptible to environmental exposures (e.g., immune challenges related to infections, vaccinations, or underlying autoimmune problems)."[97]

Predictably, the committee's position caught fire from both sides. When the committee voted to strike more extensive recommendations on vaccine research, SafeMinds director Mark Blaxill said that both the committee and the Combating Autism Act (CAA) had failed. "CAA was meant to hold the NIH [National Institutes of Health] accountable. It's very clear that they have hunkered down behind the old school orthodoxy. The committee is overtaken by conflicts."[98] Conversely, Yale neurologist Steven Novella, a skeptic of the vaccine theory, slammed the committee for allowing "anti-vaccinationists" to infiltrate the process. At his *NeuroLogica Blog*, he wrote: "This decision by the IACC represents the fruits of that infiltration—a distortion of funding for autism research to suit their anti-vaccine agenda. In fact, two members of the IACC—Lyn Redwood and Lee Grossman, were added specifically to represent the anti-vaccine movement in the (probably misguided) hope of placating that group."[99] The advocates have indeed continued to criticize IACC for not wholeheartedly adopting their positions and for failing to promote research into vaccines and autism.

The anti-vaccine movement rests on the disease frame, which is one reason why many autistic adults oppose it so strenuously. When fear of autism leads to vaccine refusal, they say, parents are not only assuming that autism is a disease but that it is a *worse* disease than measles or pertussis, which can be fatal. In other words, autism is a fate worse than death. Sarah Kurchak, an autistic writer, puts it this way: "Someone who refuses to vaccinate their children because they're afraid of autism has made the decision that people like me are the worst possible thing that can happen to their family, and they're putting everyone at risk because of it." To anti-vaccine activists who claim that they are not referring to high-functioning autism, she responds: "That just means that I will cease to be of any value to these people if I am no longer able to pass as one of them, and that they see no value and no humanity in anyone who communicates or behaves differently from them. Tell me again who has the empathy problem?"[100]

Nevertheless, research into the vaccine theory has been ongoing, with funding both from private sources and the federal government.[101] All the while, the scientific case for the connection has grown weaker and weaker—not that it was ever strong. The "too many shots too soon" version of the theory holds that multiple vaccinations can overload a child's immune system. The immunological challenge depends on the number of proteins in the vaccine. If you were born before 1970 or so, you probably have a small half-moon scar on your right arm, meaning that you got the old smallpox vaccine with its 200 proteins. But the MMR has merely 24, and in fact the entire schedule of 14 childhood vaccines adds up to just 153 proteins. Says Dr. Paul Offit, a leading expert on vaccines: "If immunological overload were the cause of autism, with fewer immunological challenges in modern vaccines, rates of autism should be decreasing, not increasing."[102]

After Wakefield hurled his accusation against the MMR shot in 1998, researchers started looking at the question but could not find any relationship between immunization and autism.[103] In 2004, ten of Wakefield's twelve coauthors signed a statement that "no causal link was established between MMR vaccine and autism as the data were insufficient."[104] Eleven years later, *The Times* of London published a report charging that Wakefield had "changed and misreported results in his research."[105] Early in 2010, a British medical disciplinary panel concluded that Wakefield had been dishonest and was misleading in describing his work. It said he had failed to disclose that he had received payment to advise lawyers acting for parents who thought that vaccination had harmed their children.[106] Britain's General Medical Council barred Wakefield from practicing medicine, and *The Lancet* took the extraordinary step of retracting the article, acknowledging that it had made false claims.[107] In 2014, an exhaustive literature review pounded another nail into the coffin of Wakefield's reputation: "Strength of evidence is high that MMR vaccine is not associated with the onset of autism in children; this conclusion supports findings of all previous reviews on the topic."[108]

The other version of the vaccine theory—that mercury was the culprit—fared no better. After the removal of thimerosal from all vaccines for infants, reported autism prevalence continued to rise, and multiple studies disconfirmed any link to thimerosal.[109] In 2009 and 2010, special masters appointed by the U.S. Court of Federal Claims decided a set of cases involving vaccine-autism theories. They rejected these notions with a thump. One wrote: "I conclude that the evidence is overwhelmingly contrary to the petitioners' contentions. The expert witnesses presented by the respondent were far better qualified, far more experienced, and far more persuasive than the petitioners' experts, concerning the key points."[110]

In 2011, *Salon* retracted Robert F. Kennedy Jr.'s "Deadly Immunity" article. Editor Kerry Lauerman noted that *Salon* had run five corrections in the days after publication. "At the time," he wrote, "we felt that correcting the piece—and keeping it on the site, in the spirit of transparency—was the best way to operate. But subsequent critics . . . further eroded any faith we had in the story's value. We've grown to believe the best reader service is to delete the piece entirely."[111]

Despite these developments, activists have continued to argue for a vaccine-autism link, with some effect. When they packed the room at a 2012 House hearing on autism, several lawmakers voiced agreement with them. More important, they have raised doubts about the safety of vaccines, leading some parents to delay or forgo immunizations for their children. Laws in every state require certain vaccines for students, but all of these laws grant exemptions for medical reasons. Except for Mississippi and West Virginia, all the states grant religious exemptions. Twenty provide for philosophical exemptions for those who object because of personal, moral, or other beliefs.[112] Even in states that do not allow philosophical exemptions, parents can go online to find "vaccine friendly" physicians who will readily agree to medical exemptions.[113] The median rate of exemption is 1.8 percent, with eleven states having rates of 4 percent or more.[114] Oregon has a rate of 7.1 percent, which is about the point at which public health officials worry about outbreaks of vaccine-preventable diseases. Twenty-one Michigan counties, accounting for 44 percent of the state's population, have rates that equal or exceed Oregon's rate.[115]

From January 1 to October 31, 2014, the CDC reported 603 confirmed measles cases, the highest number since 2000, when the United States supposedly eliminated the disease.[116] "The current increase in measles cases is being driven by unvaccinated people, primarily U.S. residents, who got measles in other countries, brought the virus back to the United States, and spread it to others in communities where many people are not vaccinated," said Dr. Anne Schuchat, director of CDC's National Center for Immunizations and Respiratory Diseases.[117] Early in 2015, a measles outbreak that started at Disneyland shone a spotlight on "underimmunization hotspots," places with an unusually high rate of parental refusal and delay of childhood vaccines.[118] Many of the hotspots are affluent, highly educated locales such as Orange County, California.[119]

Concern about autism is not the only reason why people forgo vaccinations for their children, but it does have an effect. The concern is especially potent among the parents of children who already have ASD: they are more likely than others to change the vaccine schedule for their younger children, or do without vaccination altogether.[120]

WHY DO PEOPLE BELIEVE IN THE VACCINE THEORY?

Personal experiences and vivid stories are more likely to stick in people's memories than dry statistics.[121] In the case of autism, the fallacy of *post hoc, ergo propter hoc* ("after this, therefore because of this") often shapes interpretations of these experiences and stories. Children usually receive the MMR and other immunizations around their second birthday, which is also when autism symptoms often show up. If a child gets an autism diagnosis soon after some shots, it is natural for parents to blame the vaccine. Said J. B. Handley, the cofounder of Generation Rescue: "My kid got six vaccines in one day and he regressed."[122] As we have seen, there is no evidence to support a causal link, but the mother and father of a newly diagnosed child are not thinking about the vaccinated children who did not get autism or the unvaccinated children who did: they are thinking about their own child. Parents who believe that vaccines have harmed their children then share their stories, some of which find their way into the mass media—especially if the parent is a celebrity such as Jenny McCarthy.

Autism is just one of a number of issues where anecdotes drive public discussion about risk. Psychologist Daniel Kahneman lays out the pattern: "On some occasions, a media story about a risk catches the attention of a segment of the public, which becomes aroused and worried. The emotional reaction becomes a story in itself, prompting additional coverage in the media, which in turn produces greater concern and involvement."[123] Individuals or groups with an interest in driving the issue then work to keep up the flow of worrying news, and to discredit anyone who questions the hype.

Proponents of the vaccine-autism link circulate stories about children who got a diagnosis of autism shortly after an immunization. They also try to link critics of the vaccine theory to drug companies, which they accuse of trying to hide the connection between autism and vaccines.[124] The pharmaceutical industry is an inviting target: in Gallup surveys of public attitudes toward various business sectors, it ranks near the bottom.[125] This ranking is easy to understand, because the industry has had a number of high-profile failures and scandals, including a 1955 incident in which a bad batch of polio vaccine actually caused forty thousand cases of polio. In 1976, the federal government rushed through a $137 million program to fight what many feared was a looming epidemic of swine flu. But the vaccine seemed to increase risk of a rare condition that causes temporary paralysis and, more rarely, death. More than five thousand people reportedly fell ill after receiving the vaccine, and twenty-five died. The purported flu epidemic never happened.

In public discussions of the issue, pro-vaccine scientists have some disadvantages. Since the pharmaceutical industry finances a great deal of medical research, the anti-vaccine groups can often find some tie (however tenuous) between the scientists and drug makers. More generally, the pro-vaccine side faces the challenge of proving a negative. Notwithstanding the scientific consensus, believers in the vaccine-autism link can always find some limitation in existing studies, or insist on some additional study that is practically impossible (e.g., double-blind study of vaccinated versus unvaccinated). They can also exploit the cautious language that scientists use. At the 2012 hearing, Representative Burton zeroed in on assertions that there is "no conclusive evidence" for a vaccine-autism link: "But that word 'conclusive,' 'there is no conclusive evidence,' creates a doubt. And my question to the presidents and CEOs of pharmaceutical companies has always been, if there's any doubt, if there's any doubt that the mercury in vaccinations can cause a neurological problem, then get it out."[126]

While asserting that vaccines do not cause autism, scientists must also acknowledge how much we do not know about the problem. In public forums, passion trumps doubt. At the same hearing, Representative Carolyn Maloney (D-NY) browbeat a CDC official: "Now, the numbers that he pointed out earlier, that it used to be 1 in 10,000 kids got autism, it's now 1 in 88, and I'd like to ask Dr. Boyle, why? And I don't want to hear that we have better detection. We have better detection, but detection would not account for a [jump] from 1 in 10,000 to 1 in 88."[127]

Burton, Maloney, and their allies have made their mark on the media. In discussing the causes of autism, many stories have cited those who believe in the vaccine-autism link as well as those who dispute it.[128] Graham N. Dixon and Christopher Clarke say that such stories exhibit "false balance," treating sketchy, ill-supported ideas as equivalent to those with overwhelming scientific evidence. They set up an experiment in which respondents read news articles with balanced claims both for and against an autism-vaccine link, articles presenting only one side or the other, or items with unrelated information. Readers who got the balanced material were less sure that vaccines do not cause autism and more likely to think that experts are divided on the subject.[129] Although there are signs that journalists are increasingly likely to refer to the vaccine-autism link as "discredited"—especially in light of the Wakefield scandal—past coverage enabled it to gain many adherents.[130]

In the twenty-first century, however, the mainstream press is only one of many sources of information. One study found that autism was the primary subject of one-quarter of disease-specific blogs.[131] Jenny McCarthy's famous 2007 appearance on Oprah Winfrey's show illustrates the impact of the Internet:

McCarthy: First thing I did—Google. I put in autism. And I started my research.

Winfrey: Thank God for Google.

McCarthy: I'm telling you . . .

Winfrey: Thank God for Google.

McCarthy: The University of Google is where I got my degree from.[132]

One can find good information at "the University of Google," but the Internet is also full of misinformation and conspiracy theory.[133] According to a content analysis of Google search results, those who enter terms involving vaccination risks will come across more websites that propound "vaccine myths" (including the autism link) than those who search for the benefits of immunization. Worried parents will probably find that Google feeds their fears rather than reassuring them about vaccine safety.[134]

One problem is that a good deal of the solid research about autism lies in academic journals behind an Internet paywall, open only to people who have a university library card or can afford the journals' exorbitant prices ($35 or more *per article*). Says neuroscientist Sophia Colamarino: "In today's information age, where essentially anything said by anyone can be made accessible within a matter of moments, it is unfortunate that families have easy access to all BUT the most scientifically valid information, that which can be found in scientifically reviewed research literature."[135] NIH and Autism Speaks have tried to remedy this situation by requiring its research grant recipients to put any resulting peer-reviewed research papers on the PubMed Central online archive, but this policy affects only a fraction of the literature on autism.

Another problem is that average Internet users may have a hard time telling junk from high-quality research.[136] Many articles and blog posts arguing for the vaccine-autism link have the trappings of genuine academic research: tables, graphs, citations, and scientific jargon. Some of the authors have credentials such as M.D. or Ph.D. degrees. None of these things is a guarantee of scientific value, as the history of science is full of crackpot theories (e.g., AIDS denialism) that are the heavily footnoted products of people with letters after their names. But most people will not be able to spot the scientific weaknesses of such work. Outside of academia, few understand concepts such as peer review. Jordynn Jack describes one dubious article that appeared in a non-peer-reviewed publication: "Regardless of the scientific validity of the article, though, the writers perform the writing style quite effectively. It would be difficult for the layperson to distinguish this article from any other scientific research paper, especially if one did not investigate the nature of the journal . . . or of the scientific response to the article."[137]

More fundamentally, many of the advocates of the vaccine theory reject the authority of "the establishment."[138] They believe that scientists and government agencies that support vaccines are blind, indifferent, or corrupt. "No one mentions that these people have everything at stake in this debate," writes one. "If countless parents are right and vaccines have damaged a generation of children, people will be held responsible—the same people who tell us vaccines are safe."[139]

Such sentiments find fertile ground in public opinion, since trust in government has plunged over the past half century.[140] And it is understandable why many parents of autistic children would be especially skeptical of the authorities. Often their first encounter is a bad one. At least until recently, many pediatricians failed to screen for autism or overlooked early signs of the disorder.[141] Jenny McCarthy writes: "I had no idea flapping was a common characteristic of autism. Tiptoe walking and spinning in circles all day are two more that are high up on the list. You would have thought his pediatrician might have noticed something along the way, mind you, but he did not."[142] After pediatricians are clueless about the early signs of autism, parents might question their assurances about vaccines. And once parents start reading up on autism, they will probably learn that clinicians once believed in Bettelheim's "refrigerator mother" theory.[143] If he proved to be a fraud, they reason, will not the same fate meet today's scientists?

Pro-vaccine advocates may find it hard to make converts. An experimental study found that pro-vaccine messages might not always work because their impact depends on existing parental attitudes. One group of respondents saw a CDC summary of scientific evidence against the MMR-autism link. In this group, the information did reduce the belief that vaccines cause autism— but among those leeriest of vaccines, it *decreased* intent to immunize future children. This odd finding reflects "motivated reasoning," the tendency to discount or rationalize evidence that clashes with one's beliefs and intentions. When anti-vaccine respondents got information refuting the autism link, they probably thought, "Yes, but vaccines have many other bad side effects, too." Vaccination advocates often try to persuade people by presenting them with images of sick children or stories about what diseases can do to them. The study also found that these tactics may backfire by increasing belief in serious vaccine side effects.[144]

Some in the anti-vaccine movement play rough. As mentioned in the first chapter, Dr. Paul Offit has received death threats for his advocacy of vaccines. Amy Wallace profiled Offit in *Wired* magazine and later described the response:

> In online comments and over email, I was called a prostitute and the C-word. J. B. Handley, a critic of childhood vaccination and the founder of the autism group Generation Rescue, affiliated with the actress Jenny McCarthy, sent me an essay titled, "Paul Offit Rapes (intellectually) Amy Wallace and Wired Magazine." In it, he implied that my subject had slipped me a date-rape drug. Later, an anti-vaccine website Photoshopped my head onto the body of a woman in a strapless dress who sat next to Dr. Offit at a festive dinner table. The main course? A human baby.[145]

Under these circumstances, the wonder is not that so many people believe in the vaccine-autism link, but that so many do not. In any event, beliefs about autism causation have had an impact on policies concerning autism therapy.

THERAPIES

The proverbial "gold standard" of autism therapy is applied behavior analysis (ABA), which uses the principles of behavioral psychology to teach skills and modify behavior. There are many forms of ABA, but they generally involve breaking tasks into smaller parts and changing behaviors by adjusting the conditions that are present before and after they occur. ABA involves rigorous data gathering, as the most commonly cited report on ABA explains:

> Reliable measurement requires that behaviors are defined objectively. Vague terms such as anger, depression, aggression or tantrums are redefined in observable and quantifiable terms, so their frequency, duration or other measurable properties can be directly recorded. For example, a goal to reduce a child's aggressive behavior might define "aggression" as: "attempts, episodes or occurrences (each separated by 10 seconds) of biting, scratching, pinching or pulling hair." "Initiating social interaction with peers" might be defined as: "looking at classmate and verbalizing an appropriate greeting."[146]

Between the behavioral intervention itself and the meticulous record keeping, ABA is time-consuming and costly. An intensive program may take twenty-five to forty hours of one-on-one attention for one to three years, with rates starting at $50 per hour. The next two chapters will consider the policy implications of time and cost for schools and social service agencies. For now, we ponder a more basic question: what effect does ABA have?

Clearly, it has the strongest empirical basis of any therapy for autism.[147] A large body of literature has documented successful use of ABA-based procedures to reduce problem behaviors and improve skills for people on the autism spectrum. But officials who want to limit spending on ABA can also point to studies contending that ABA looks strong only because the other therapies are so weak. One panel of technical experts found that while ABA and a few other interventions have shown efficacy, the quality of evidence was moderate.[148] An analysis of the literature found that very young children who received early intensive ABA did show improvement, but the size of the effect varied across studies, possibly due to differences among the treatments and the children themselves.[149] One study did find that it is possible that a small number of children with ASD can lose the diagnosis over time, but it did not conclude whether ABA—or any other intervention—was responsible for the change.[150]

According to ABA advocates, however, the key is not whether autistic people lose the diagnosis but whether they can lead better, more productive lives. From this perspective, ABA works to the extent that it enables a person to function well in society even with a diagnosis of autism spectrum disorder. Although analyses of its cost-effectiveness are surprisingly scarce, the research to date does suggest that it is a worthwhile investment.[151] One study compared the costs of eighteen years of special education with the costs of three years of discrete trial training as an early intervention. Results indicated that the state of Texas would save $208,500 per child across eighteen years of education with the early intervention. When the authors applied this figure to the estimated ten thousand children with autism in Texas, they reckoned that the state would save about $2 billion.[152]

ABA has more measurable effect than anything else, but as with so much else about autism, questions and controversies remain. Some self-advocates take issue with the goal of "normalizing" behavior. "We're big supporters of speech therapy or occupational therapy, where the focus is on supporting someone to gain skills or find accommodations," says Julia Bascom, director of programs at the Autistic Self Advocacy Network. "ABA therapy is another story; the stated end goal of ABA is for the autistic child to become 'indistinguishable from their peers,' and we just don't think that's an ethical goal. Would we be able to justify that for any other child?"[153] When autistic people recall their ABA therapy, the memories are not always pleasant. "In ABA years, I lost hope," writes Ido Kedar. "I longed so badly to make my ideas known. I got flashcards instead. Though I liked the teachers as people, I feel I wasted many years in this lonely endeavor. 'Touch your nose.' 'Touch tree.' 'Touch your head.' 'Look at me.' 'Do this.' 'Sit quiet.'"[154]

We do not know why ABA seems to have a big impact on some but not others. A major reason for this quandary is that behavioral therapies are harder to appraise than medical ones. When researchers want to test a medication, they can set up double-blind experiments that others can repeat with great precision. These experiments work because scientists can make the drug look just like the placebo. It is impossible to do the same thing with behavioral treatments. Psychiatrist David M. Allen says: "This is true because, in a sense, the therapist—or more correctly the relationship between the patient and the therapist—*is* the treatment. If the study were to meet the criteria for being double blind, that would mean that the therapists who administer the treatment would have to not know what they were doing."[155] Even though ABA involves detailed protocols and quantifiable results, its success still depends on the therapist's skill, training, experience, and relationship to the autistic person. Even when they follow exactly the same guidelines, two therapists might get different results. One might be more adept than the other, or the autistic person might react differently to different people.

Research on behavioral therapy is not only difficult, but it also gets less attention than other areas. Less than a fifth of autism research money goes into the study of treatments and interventions (see figure 3.1, above), and only a third of that share goes into research on behavioral therapy.[156]

The conventional wisdom is that any kind of treatment is likely to be less effective as the child gets older, so parents of autistic children usually believe that they are working against the clock. They will not be satisfied with the ambiguities surrounding ABA, nor will they want to wait for some future research finding that might slightly increase its effectiveness. They want results *now*. Because there are no scientifically validated drugs for the core symptoms of autism, they look outside the boundaries of mainstream medicine and FDA approval. Studies have found that anywhere from 28 to 54 percent of autistic children receive "complementary and alternative medicine" (CAM), and these numbers probably understate CAM usage.[157]

Many Americans turn to such approaches for a variety of specific conditions or general well-being. "Complementary" generally refers to using non-mainstream approaches *together with* conventional ones, while "alternative" refers to using them *instead of* conventional ones. For the most part, parents of autistic children use complementary methods. Parents with graduate degrees are more likely to use these approaches than those with less education, perhaps because of differences in Internet use and ability to seek out alternative sources of information.[158]

For children with autism, the most common CAM treatment is the use of dietary supplements. After Bernard Rimland founded the Autism Research Institute, he got letters from mothers who had treated their autistic children with high doses of vitamins. Eager to experiment, he contacted vitamin manufacturers and found one that would make flavored vitamins that autistic children would more easily accept.[159] He continued to advocate vitamin therapy until his death in 2006. Although there is no evidence that such supplements work, the Dietary Supplement Health and Education Act exempts them from the regulations that would apply to drugs. When Congress passed this law in 1994, the debate focused on other uses of supplements, not on autism treatment.[160] But because of it, a flourishing industry sells supplements to the parents of autistic children. Manufacturers generally do not make the kind of explicit health claims that would put them outside the protection of the Supplement Act. They do not have to: parents and advocacy groups do it for them, by word of mouth and on the Internet.

Besides supplements, some forms of complementary and alternative medicine are fairly benign. Many parents put their children on gluten-free, casein-free diets. There is only weak evidence suggesting these diets have any impact on autism, but they may have other health benefits and are useful for people who cannot tolerate gluten or casein.[161] And thanks to the broader gluten-free fad, these foods are much more widely available at lower prices than in the past. Other treatments, such as music, massage, or aromatherapy, can be pleasant if not necessarily effective.[162]

Some treatments involve combinations of substances that doctors can order from "compounding pharmacies," which specialize in creating personalized mixtures. The Food and Drug Administration Modernization Act of 1997 exempted "compounded drugs" from the Food and Drug Administration's (FDA) standard drug approval as long as compounders did not solicit the prescription or advertise the compound. The idea was to keep compounding pharmacies from becoming backdoor, unregulated manufacturers. In a 5-4 decision, the Supreme Court held that this provision amounted to an unconstitutional restriction on commercial speech.[163] In 2007, Democratic Senator Edward Kennedy introduced a bill to authorize new limits on compounders. Their trade association ramped up lobbying efforts. At their encouragement, parents of autistic children flooded Kennedy's office, arguing that compounding pharmacies were the sole source of treatments such as chelation. The bill never came up for a vote.[164] But in 2012, drugs from a compounder led to a fungal meningitis outbreak that killed dozens of people. Congress then gave the FDA greater authority to regulate the pharmacies.

Chelation is a particularly risky treatment. Developed to treat industrial workers who had suffered lead poisoning on the job, chelation uses potent chemicals to strip heavy metals from the body. Some advocates of the vaccine theory say that it can treat autism by removing mercury. Of parents with ASD children, 7 to 8 percent have reportedly tried chelation, even though there is no evidence that it works.[165] Even with the 1994 law, the FDA can stop the sale of supplements that are dangerous, and it has cracked down on chelation therapies, pointing out that stripping minerals needed by the body "can lead to serious and life-threatening outcomes."[166]

Although the FDA has primary responsibility for regulating drugs, state governments have also clamped down on certain alternative treatments through their authority to license medical professionals.[167] In 2005, a Pennsylvania doctor faced criminal charges after his chelation therapy caused a five-year-old boy to die from cardiac arrest. Authorities eventually dropped the charges, but the state medical board suspended his license for six months, with two and a half years of probation. Several states disciplined another physician for promoting the "Lupron protocol," which gives autistic children high doses of a drug for chemically castrating sex offenders. In 2014, an Illinois doctor faced fines and agreed to have her Illinois license on probation after state regulators accused her of subjecting children to dangerous therapies that represented an "extreme departure from rational medical judgment."[168]

Until we know more about what causes autism and how to treat it effectively, dubious cures will linger. Dr. James Laidler, a retired physician and father of an autistic son, told *Bloomberg Business Week*: "You always hear the testimonials from the people who got better, not the people who stayed the same or got worse. They don't want to hear somebody saying this is snake oil."[169]

SCIENCE AND STAKEHOLDERS

There was politics in the Apollo program. The clout of Texas lawmakers helped ensure that mission control would be located in Houston.[170] NASA shrewdly built congressional support by parceling out work to contractors in districts all over the country. Still, as noted at the beginning of this chapter, there were many things that the politicians left to the scientists, because the scientists knew what they were supposed to do and how they would do it.

John F. Kennedy said that the goal was "landing a man on the moon and returning him safely to the earth."[171] Little about autism approaches that degree of clarity. Policymakers are trying to accommodate different views on how to define the issue and how to order the scientific priorities. That is why the 2006 Combating Autism Act required that the Interagency Autism Coordinating Committee draw one-third of its members from outside the federal government, including a person with autism, an autism parent, and a representative of an autism organization.

Stakeholders can be allies of science. As we have seen, autistic people and their parents have contributed to our understanding of the condition and engaged in advocacy and fund-raising for autism research.[172] Ideally, the making of public policy should involve both broad-based public participation and thoughtful deliberation based on the best available evidence. But there is a tension between these two goals: public engagement does not equal public enlightenment. As Dana Baker writes, "From the perspective of the relationship between science and democracy, Congressional hearings become an audience of last resort for scientific theories (or discoveries) discerned to be less than credible by the majority of the members of the relevant scientific communities."[173]

When a twelve-year-old autistic Iowan asked about autism policy, Senator Rand Paul (R-KY) said: "Here's the real answer. Government's never going to find—and I'm not saying government can't help, I support some government help for autism—but the answer's going to come from scientists. And politicians get in the way of most answers."[174] Senator Paul failed to reflect that most autism research money comes from the government in the first place. Early in 2015, he further muddied the waters when he said that he had heard of children who "wound up with profound mental disorders after vaccines." Under criticism, he issued an unclear clarification: "I did not say vaccines caused disorders, just that they were temporally related. I did not allege causation."[175]

As long as government funds so much research, politics will shape the questions that scientists ask and determine the kinds of research that receive funding. Politics will even influence which scientists the policymakers will believe and which findings will guide public policy. In the end, science cannot tell us what kinds of outcomes we should want. ABA "works" in the sense that it helps some autistic people become more like their typically developing peers. Most parents regard such an outcome as desirable, but not all people on the spectrum agree. In a 2010 interview, Ari Ne'eman said:

> As a society, our approach to autism is still primarily "How do we make autistic people behave more normally? How do we get them to increase eye contact and make small talk while suppressing hand-flapping and other stims?" The inventor of a well-known form of behavioral intervention for autism, Dr. Ivar Lovaas, who passed away recently, said that his goal was to make autistic kids indistinguishable from their peers. That goal has more to do with increasing the comfort of non-autistic people than with what autistic people really need.
>
> Lovaas also experimented with trying to make what he called effeminate boys normal. It was a silly idea around homosexuality, and it's a silly idea around autism. What if we asked instead, "How can we increase the quality of life for autistic people?" We wouldn't lose anything by that paradigm shift. We'd still be searching for ways to help autistic people communicate, stop dangerous and self-injurious behaviors, and make it easier for autistic people to have friends.[176]

Autism parent Jeffrey Howe has a different perspective. "To the quirky Intel programmer who recently was given a diagnosis of Asperger's, treating autism as a disease to be cured must seem like a personal affront, but for people struggling to raise a child incapable of communication, using the toilet or controlling a physically violent temper, seeing autism as pathology isn't much of a reach."[177] Rather than insisting on the parent perspective, however, he simply calls for tolerance instead of having an "increasingly angry war of words erupt within a community in such desperate need of unity."

Chapter Four

Education

The 1975 Education for All Handicapped Children Act, later renamed the Individuals with Disabilities Education Act (IDEA), asserted that the federal government should support "programs to meet the educational needs of handicapped children in order to assure equal protection of the law."[1] Harrison Williams (D-NJ), the bill's Senate sponsor, said: "This measure fulfills the promise of the Constitution that there shall be equality of education for all people, and that handicapped children will no longer be left out."[2]

In the second chapter, we saw that the disability rights movement grew out of the broader civil rights movement. A major inspiration was *Brown v. Board of Education*, in which Chief Justice Warren wrote: "We conclude that, in the field of public education, the doctrine of 'separate but equal' has no place. Separate educational facilities are inherently unequal."[3] On a high level of abstraction, just about everybody today would agree with the idea of equality. As Deborah Stone points out in *Policy Paradox*, however, *defining* equality in specific cases is the hard part. Debates over such issues as affirmative action remind us that there are many different concepts of equality, leading to different outcomes.[4]

Consider the education of children with disabilities. Although the law encourages inclusion, some disabled children have problems that may require separate educational facilities. And even when they can go to the same schools as nondisabled children, they usually need services (e.g., pullouts for speech therapy) that set them apart. As noted in the first chapter, Martha Minow calls this problem "the dilemma of difference." Policy can reinforce the stigma of difference both by disregarding it and by stressing it, by treating members of a minority the same as members of a majority and by treating them differently.[5] Picture a deaf child in the same classroom as other kids, subject to the same rules without any special accommodations. In one sense, that child is receiving equal treatment. In another sense, the treatment is obviously unequal, since it ensures that she or he will miss most of the oral instruction that the other children are getting. Now picture the school providing the same child with a sign-language interpreter. The child can follow most of the classroom instruction, but only because the school is spending money that it is not spending on other children, and doing so in a way that makes the child stand out. Again, the situation is more or less equal in one respect, unequal in another.[6]

In the case of hearing impairment, Minow suggests that one way out of the dilemma is to have everyone in the classroom learn sign language. Even if one could devise an equivalent approach to autism, it would not work if more than one autistic child were in the room. Because autism has so many different forms, gradations, and co-occurring conditions, each child has a unique mix of challenges requiring a customized approach. Some may be unable to communicate without assistive devices or iPads. Others may be overly talkative and need classroom aides to coach them about when they should and should not speak. Still others may need help with managing tantrums. Finding the right recipe of supports is tricky, especially when parents also want their children to "fit in" with their peers and get the same education as everyone else.

There are further barriers to equality. In our federal system, what you get from the government depends on where you live. Some states, local educational agencies, and individual schools are much more likely than others to identify autism and provide high levels of service. Wherever autistic students reside, IDEA places an unusually heavy burden on their parents to serve as their advocates and to enforce their rights.[7] Parents with college degrees and healthy bank accounts have an easier time fulfilling that role than people without high levels of education and income.

Some of the problems of autistic children may be different from those of other students with disabilities. Their behavioral quirks may cause conflicts with other students and land them in the school disciplinary process. Prejudices about autistic people often color teachers' expectations. Some may confuse autism with intellectual disability and subject their autistic students to what President Bush called the soft bigotry of low expectations. Others may believe in the *Rain Man* myth of savant abilities and conclude that poor performance on a math test can only mean laziness or defiance.

What they all have in common is that they are subject to a federal law that originally did not take these differences into account.

THE BIG IDEA

For most of American history, the states dominated education policy, with the federal government playing a minor role. Whereas the U.S. Constitution does not even mention the word *education*, every state constitution contains education provisions.[8] The balance of power started to change in the 1950s, when the civil rights movement brought the federal government into the struggle for desegregation, and the Cold War prompted the enactment of the National Defense Education Act, which supported instruction in science, mathematics, and foreign languages. The 1965 Elementary and Secondary Education Act added to Washington's role, with grants to state educational agencies to improve K–12 schooling. Meanwhile, the federal government stepped up its efforts to fight discrimination in schools. The 1975 law represented a confluence of these trends: it increased federal funding and regulation of schools and aimed at the inclusion of a minority group in the educational mainstream. (Though disability groups often refer to it as a "civil rights" law, it technically falls under a different category as a funding statute.)

When members of Congress passed the 1975 measure, they assumed that it cost about twice as much to educate a disabled child as a nondisabled one. The bill authorized the federal government to pay 40 percent of each state's "excess cost" of educating children with disabilities. That amount, which advocates for the disabled call "IDEA full funding," equals 40 percent of the national average per-pupil spending times the number of children with disabilities receiving IDEA services. While signing the bill, President Ford warned that Congress would probably never pass appropriations bills that included full funding. "Even the strongest supporters of this measure know as well as I that they are falsely raising the expectations of the groups affected by claiming authorization levels which are excessive and unrealistic."[9] Ford was right. Apart from a short-lived spike during President Obama's economic stimulus program, the federal share has not come close to 40 percent of excess cost. In fiscal 2014, the federal share was just 16 percent.[10]

IDEA requires participating states to provide all disabled children with a free appropriate public education (FAPE). Although the Unfunded Mandates Reform Act of 1995 was meant to keep the federal government from burdening states and localities with duties that it did not pay for, IDEA does not legally count as an "unfunded mandate." IDEA requirements apply only when states accept federal funds for special education.[11] Any state that objected to IDEA could theoretically turn down the funds, though none actually have.

When school officials see an autistic student walk in the door, they see money flying out the window. One recent study pegs the average additional cost of educating such a student at $8,610 a year.[12] That figure, based on a small sample of autistic students, probably understates the cost by a wide margin. An analysis of data from the 1999–2000 school year reckoned the added cost at $11,543, which would be well over $15,000 today.[13] Of special concern to officials are the many students whose services cost much more than the average. In the 1989 case of *Timothy W. v. Rochester, New Hampshire, School District*, the U.S. First Circuit Court of Appeals ruled that IDEA requires school districts to provide special education services to all disabled students regardless of the severity of their disabilities.[14] The decision technically only applies to the First Circuit (four New England states and Puerto Rico), but no other school district has since tried to overturn the "zero reject" principle in court. "This particular case was very important," said Antonis Katsiyannis, the president of the Council for Exceptional Children. "Once you qualify for services under the IDEA, there is no reason whatsoever to be denied services."[15] This story from the *Minneapolis Star-Tribune* suggests how high the price tag can get:

> One of the most expensive students in Minnesota landed in the special education wing of John Glenn Middle School when he was 8 years old. The boy, who was diagnosed with autism and attention deficit hyperactivity disorder, could not speak or communicate with even the most rudimentary symbols, according to District 916 principal Mollie Wise, who helped design the boy's instructional program. At his previous school, he had been disrobing every day and urinating or defecating in class. When staff members tried to remove him, he would become violent, hitting or biting anyone who got too close. "Everyone said this might be the hardest student you'll ever work with," Wise said. District 916 decided to build him his own classroom, one in which his aggression could be contained. It cost $88,000, and is the most expensive of the eight rooms the district has built for individual students in the past five years.[16]

Whatever the exact amount per pupil, we do know that the total cost is rising because the number of students with identified autism is rising. (See figure 4.1.) As we have already seen, it is not clear whether there has been a true increase in autism prevalence. In the past, many of these students might have received services under a different category or received no services at all. For school officials, what matters is that autism can be an expensive label at a time when state and local budgets remain under pressure.

GETTING THE LABEL

The federal IDEA regulation defines autism as "a developmental disability significantly affecting verbal and nonverbal communication and social interaction, generally evident before age three, that adversely affects a child's educational performance." The rule also mentions some other characteristics of autism (e.g., repetitive behavior) and adds that the designation does not

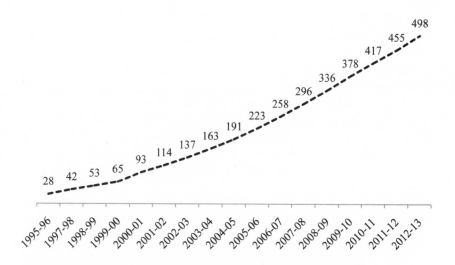

Figure 4.1. Autistic children aged three to twenty-one receiving services under the Individuals with Disabilities Education Act (in thousands). Sources: U.S. Department of Education, Institute of Education Sciences, *Digest of Education Statistics*, 2009 and 2014. Online: nces.ed.gov/programs/digest/d09/tables/dt09_050.asp and nces.ed.gov/programs/digest/d14/tables/dt14_204.30.asp.

apply if the child's academic problems stem from an emotional disturbance. [17]

The process for getting a determination of autism depends on the child's age. If the child is under the age of three, parents get in touch with an "early intervention" agency, often the state health department. (The next chapter will discuss these services at greater length.) If the child is three or older, parents instead contact the special education office of their local school district. At that point, the district arranges for an evaluation by a multidisciplinary team, which must include at least one teacher or other specialist with specific knowledge of autism. IDEA mandates that no single procedure can be the only criterion for setting up the child's education program. Federal rules also require an assessment in all related areas, including health, vision, hearing, communication abilities, motor skills, and emotional status. [18]

Assessment is the first step on an autistic person's long journey through government services. Even at this early stage, inequalities come into play. Although African American and Hispanic students are more likely to be in special education than white students (often with a label of intellectual disability), they are less likely to have an educational determination of autism. [19] One possible reason for this difference is simple racial and ethnic bias on the part of evaluators. Parents' cultural beliefs about child development and education may also be at work: some studies suggest that white families may be more likely than Hispanic families to worry that certain behaviors are signs of autism. [20]

Still another potential source of disparity is economic inequality: nonwhite families tend to be poorer than white families and thus have less access to medical and psychological professionals. [21] Instead of getting an early clinical diagnosis outside of the school setting, these children might not get an autism identification until they start having problems in kindergarten or a later grade—if then. Most measurements of autism and its co-occurring conditions depend on observations of behavior, which may differ from person to person. Because autism is so expensive, school personnel may feel subtle pressure to code these observations so as to point to another label or minimize the severity of the condition.

Although the *Diagnostic and Statistical Manual* (DSM) and IDEA do not define autism in exactly the same way, there is a good deal of interaction between DSM and an educational determination. With a DSM-based diagnosis in hand, parents can then use it as key evidence to seek services under IDEA. In this case, the educational determination would depend in part on the parents' ability to identify a qualified professional, their skill at persuading the school district that their child is eligible, and the district's propensity to agree with them. [22] If the school district does not agree, parents can still get a professional who is not working for the school district to do an independent educational evaluation. The district usually pays for the evaluation, and when it does not, it has to justify its decision at a hearing.

Educated, upper-middle-class parents—who are disproportionately white—are more likely to succeed than poor, uneducated ones. Even when the district is willing to pay for an evaluation, the former are more likely to take advantage of the opportunity and find qualified professionals through their own social networks. Reporter Nirvi Shah writes at *Education Week*: "I have been told by some special educators that while some white students are diagnosed with having autism based on their characteristics, sometimes, black children with identical behavior will wind up with a diagnosis of emotional or behavioral disturbance based on parents' persistence, or lack thereof." [23]

A child's chances of getting an autism label vary by geography as well as social class. On a broad level, state definitions of autism are consistent with the federal definition. At the practical level, there are differences, especially when it comes to assessing social and emotional development, health, vision, hearing, and motor skills. [24] In 2011, 7 percent of students receiving IDEA services nationwide had an autism determination. But the figures varied by state. The states with the highest share of IDEA students with identified autism were Minnesota (12.8 percent), Oregon (10.6 percent), and Connecticut (10.1 percent). The lowest were Iowa (1.1 percent), Puerto Rico (2.1

percent), Montana (2.8 percent), Oklahoma, and West Virginia (3.7 percent each).[25]

FAPE AND IEP

After the assessment comes the meeting to draft an initial individualized education program (IEP), which lays out the child's unique needs and the services that the school district will provide. About 80 to 90 percent of autistic children get an IEP. Not surprisingly, one study found that many of the remainder are Hispanic or have mothers with low levels of education.[26]

The IEP process, which repeats at least once every year for which the child is eligible for services, culminates with a written offer of FAPE in the LRE, that is, a free appropriate public education in "the least restrictive environment." The latter phrase comes straight from IDEA, which requires that disabled children go to school with nondisabled children as much as possible, and that that they attend special classes or special schools only when their condition keeps them from taking part in regular classes.[27] About 90 percent of autistic students under IDEA attend regular public schools, and about two-thirds of these students spend at least 40 percent of their day inside general class.[28] Of those who do not attend regular public school, most go to separate schools for children with disabilities, and a small number get funding to attend private schools. Public charter schools enroll a lower percentage of students with disabilities than traditional public schools, even though the law forbids them to discriminate on the basis of disability.[29] Of more than six thousand charter schools nationwide, about one hundred focus on special education for the disabled.[30] A small fraction of the special-ed charters specialize in serving autistic children.

Schools provide a range of services. One study found that more than four-fifths of preschool and elementary students and two-thirds of secondary students receive speech therapy.[31] The second most common service is occupational therapy, which works on attention span, balance, coordination, sensory processing, fine motor skills such as handwriting, and life skills such as brushing teeth. A related service is adapted physical education, special help for children who have a hard time with running, throwing, catching, and other activities that most kids take for granted. Many students have "one-on-one" aides, paraprofessionals who shadow them through the school day to help them keep up with their schoolwork and manage their interactions with other children. Some districts offer applied behavior analysis, either at school or at home through contracts with private providers.

Lawmakers originally assumed that writing an IEP would be a straightforward matter of matching the services with the student's needs.[32] If you have read this far in the book, you are probably guessing that this assumption proved wrong. IEP meetings often represent a clash of conflicting outlooks. On one side of the table are parents who want the best possible outcome for their children. On the other side are school officials who are usually dutiful but who naturally see the child as one among many. When they say that they care as much about the child as much as the parents do, the parents are thinking, "Oh no you don't!"[33] Even though they deny that that they would ever shortchange autistic kids for the sake of saving money, it is unrealistic to think that they ignore economics. When a Michigan television reporter used a state Freedom of Information Act to request documents from a local school district, they revealed that discussions of cost-cutting repeatedly included the option of cutting enrollment in special education programs. The district even hired a consultant, who suggested that having fewer students in special education would save money.[34]

IEPs can be contentious for any kind of disability, and especially so for autism. At the time of the law's passage in 1975, people thought of autism as an exotic disorder, if they thought of it at all. (As noted in the second chapter, Congress did not add a specific mention of autism to the law until 1990.) The famous 1987 Lovaas study of ABA's efficacy, the identification of Asperger's disorder, and the third, fourth, and fifth editions of the DSM—these things were still in the future. Members of Congress could not have anticipated how many different kinds of children would have a label of autism, what kinds of needs they would have, or what kind of services would be available. They could not have known how complicated autism IEP meetings could get.

At these meetings, the district has several advantages, starting with *Board of Education of the Hendrick Hudson Central School District v. Rowley* (1982), the first IDEA case to reach the Supreme Court. Amy Rowley was a hearing-impaired girl whose parents wanted her to have a qualified sign-language interpreter in all of her academic classes. The court said that the district was already supplying her with sufficient supports and that the law did not require this additional step. Even though the legislation's sponsors said that its goal was educational equality, the majority found that there was no substantive language in the statute itself regarding the level of education that children with disabilities must get:

> While Congress sought to provide assistance to the States in carrying out their constitutional responsibilities to provide equal protection of the laws, it did not intend to achieve strict equality of opportunity or services for handicapped and nonhandicapped children, but rather sought primarily to identify and evaluate handicapped children, and to provide them with access to a free public education. The Act does not require a State to maximize the potential of each handicapped child commensurate with the opportunity provided nonhandicapped children.[35]

The court set a low bar: not the best possible services to ensure equal education, but just a "basic floor of opportunity." In 1997 and 2004, Congress amended IDEA with broad goals suggesting something more: ensuring access to general education, setting high expectations, and preparing students for productive and independent lives, all "to the maximum extent possible."[36] This language, however, appeared in the "findings" section of the statute and did not set specific requirements for IEPs. Moreover, the law did not even mention *Rowley*. Accordingly, the Ninth Circuit said: "Had Congress sought to change the free appropriate public education 'educational benefit' standard—a standard that courts have followed vis-à-vis *Rowley* since 1982—it would have expressed a clear intent to do so."[37] Unless and until Congress or the courts say otherwise, *Rowley* still rules.

The 2004 IDEA amendments specified that IEP services should be "based on peer-reviewed research to the extent practicable."[38] For hearing loss and many other disabilities, the research is fairly clear, at least on the basics. For autism, as we saw in the previous chapter, the literature is scantier. ABA has scientific support, but it also has critics who propound alternatives. Judges and hearing officers have tended to see ABA as only one of many paths to an appropriate education. Even when there is a strong case that ABA is the best therapy for a student, the school district can often get away with other, cheaper approaches, provided that it can offer some scientific evidence that they offer an educational benefit.[39]

The *Rowley* court assumed that the procedures for parent participation would help ensure fair treatment: "As this very case demonstrates, parents and guardians will not lack ardor in seeking to ensure that handicapped children receive all of the benefits to which they are entitled by the Act."[40] In reality, ardor is not enough. School officials not only have the advantage of the burden of proof, they also have the edge that comes with being "repeat players." They have generally handled many cases in the bureaucracy and the legal system, and they have the professional expertise to make their arguments sound convincing. They know the science, the letter of the law, and the informal rules of the game.[41] Most parents have only the experience of their own children's cases, and many are stumbling through the system for the first time. Attorney and autism parent Areva Martin writes about her first IEP for her son Marty:

> New to the whole world of autism, I didn't do much research, because I assumed that the IEP team from the school district was more knowledgeable and would explain the various options to me. I was fully prepared to accept their recommendations. They were the experts. I naively presumed they knew what was best for my child. What a mistake! . . . Because I was inexperienced, I didn't notice that they had already made their choice of a classroom without even asking about Marty's needs and my family's priorities for him.[42]

These meetings can turn nasty, and many autism parents have "IEP horror stories." One parent told me that she tried to ease tensions by bringing cookies to the meeting. The principal then shouted to his staff, "Nobody touch those cookies!" Another parent writes of asking for a sensory diet, a personalized activity plan that helps the student stay focused (e.g., low noise levels for those with a sensitivity to sound). "After just proclaiming she is extremely knowledgeable about Asperger's Syndrome, from the mouth of a school psychologist after we suggested our son needed a sensory diet. 'Our cafeteria does not have the ability to provide this.'"[43]

All parents are at an IEP disadvantage, but some are more disadvantaged than others. Although the law says meetings must take place at mutually convenient times, some parents do not show up. The data show that low-income parents participate at a lower rate than affluent ones.[44] Some may have to take care of their children because they do not have spouses or access to child care. Others may have long, rigid work hours or multiple jobs. Whatever the reason, parents who do not come to the IEP will probably fare worse than those who do. Among those who attend, the more affluent parents can afford to bring special education lawyers (at $200 to $400 per hour) or nonlawyer advocates (at $75 to $150 per hour). "If you have never been to an IEP meeting, you have no idea how intimidating that they can be, even for a very confident person," one parent told the *Orlando Sentinel.* "Everyone should have an advocate to go with them."[45] (Although nonlawyer advocates are less costly, there is some risk in retaining them. There are no educational requirements for serving as an advocate, nor do federal or state rules define "special education advocacy."[46])

Well-heeled parents can also bring their own professionals such as speech therapists. IEPs have to include statements of the student's present level of performance as well as measurable goals and objectives for the coming year. Outside experts can help parents evaluate both. That perspective can be important because schools have an incentive to set low goals and to exaggerate the student's progress. Special needs parent Sharon Lutz recalls her annual experience: "The [school's] speech/language therapist would produce documentation showing nicely graphed charts and wording about how well our son did. We did not really understand what she was showing us." Then she and her husband retained an independent speech therapist, who "explained what was really happening—our son was not really progressing as well as the school led us to believe. She showed us areas that needed improvement. Our therapist put together a new list of items in our son's best interest."[47]

Parents who cannot afford professional advice must become their own experts and advocates. The Internet is their major source of scientific and legal information, but the online world has its own inequalities. As noted, many important journals are not freely available, and people without university affiliations often have to pay to access the articles they need. And it can take a good deal of education to understand the literature and grasp what kinds of evidence would be useful at an IEP meeting. Autism Speaks, Easter Seals, and other organizations help parents with these problems through training workshops and online support sites.

AFTER THE IEP

If parents are unhappy with the IEP, their first step is mediation. In this process, the state education agency pays for a neutral mediator to try to resolve the dispute and reach a mutually satisfactory agreement. In most states, mediation agreements usually include payment toward the parents' attorney fees. This option is obviously attractive to both sides, and most special education disputes end this way. One catch is that the school district has the upper hand because parents generally cannot afford the next step.

That step is "going to due process," formally presenting the case before a hearing officer, with witnesses, exhibits, and other trappings of a trial. Though parents can go to due process without counsel, it is dangerous to do so. The school district will have well-paid (at taxpayer expense) attorneys who know the rules of evidence, the process of cross-examination, and all the maneuvers necessary to take down the parents' case.[48] Retaining an attorney improves the parents' chances but is also a gamble. In 1986, Congress authorized courts to award reasonable attorney fees to parents—but only when they prevail.[49] If parents fight and lose, they will owe thousands to their lawyers.

School districts have built-in expert witnesses in the form of teachers and staff. They also have full access to all relevant information about a proposed placement and often deny parents access to those programs in advance of hearings. When parents' experts can observe children in class, districts can limit their observations.[50] More important, parents have to foot the bill for their experts because of a 2006 Supreme Court decision that IDEA does not authorize reimbursement of witness fees. "While authorizing the award of reasonable attorney's fees, the Act contains detailed provisions that are designed to ensure that such awards are indeed reasonable," Justice Alito wrote for the majority. "The absence of any comparable provisions relating to expert fees strongly suggests that recovery of expert fees is not authorized."[51] It goes without saying that this decision disadvantages all parents, and especially those with modest incomes.

The parents' handicaps do not end there. In the 2005 case of *Schaffer v. Weast*, the Supreme Court held that when a child's IEP is under challenge, the party seeking relief bears the burden of persuasion.[52] In other words, the school district does not have to prove that the IEP is adequate; rather, the parents have to prove that it is *inadequate*. Said parent advocate Wendy

Byrnes: "This decision tips the scale in the district's favor, so that a school district will not be so motivated to work something out."[53] In the decision, the court took no stand on whether state laws could place the burden of persuasion on school districts. Most state laws implicitly or explicitly align with the decision. Only a few states place the burden on the school district.[54]

School districts prevail in most due process hearings.[55] Parents who lose can appeal in federal court.[56] Parents of autistic students did well in court before 2004, but since then, school districts have won most of the cases.[57] A parent will face mounting pressure to settle before the court makes a ruling, because the legal process can drag on and on, and time is on the school district's side. A child is in any one school for only a few years, so services delayed are services denied.[58] And in the long run, there is no long run. IDEA only covers people until their twenty-second birthday: after that, public schools may cut them off. (They do have more limited protections under other laws and programs, which the next chapters will discuss.)

Relatively few cases end in due process decisions: in California, the figure is 3 percent.[59] Although the whole set of procedures—from IEP to mediation to due process—tilts in favor of school districts, parents with education, money, and tenacity still have a fair chance at a good outcome.[60] Fighting with parents imposes costs on schools in the form of time, inconvenience, attorney fees, and—sometimes—bad publicity. (A small number of Internet-savvy parents and students have employed social media shaming to put pressure on district officials.[61]) When parents make clear that they will push back hard, the district may give ground early on. When they cannot do so, the district will take a harder line. School officials often know in advance which parents fall into the latter category. In a practice that Chicago attorney Charles P. Fox calls "educational advocacy redlining," school officials check family addresses, knowing that people in poor neighborhoods will lack the resources to fight.[62] Carmen Carley, a professional advocate for California families seeking services, says parents should put up a formidable front. "Wear a fake diamond ring," she tells mothers who lack a real one. "Make them think you're ready to fight. Don't show them you're weak. Don't show them you're tired."[63]

For parents who agree to an IEP either at the meeting or a mediation session, the document is only the beginning. Once the plan is in place, they have to keep track of compliance. If the school district blatantly fails to carry out its provisions (e.g., by not providing promised speech therapy), parents can file a complaint with their state education agency, which must resolve it within sixty calendar days. A tougher problem arises when the district nominally complies with the IEP but the services are mediocre. Consider a case where the school provides a classroom aide under the terms of an IEP. The aide then spends his day checking sports scores on his smartphone instead of helping the child. How are the parents to know? The teacher might be too preoccupied with other students to notice. The student might not complain, happy that the aide is leaving him alone to daydream. The parents may never witness the aide's negligence. To observe the classroom firsthand, they must first get permission, which means that the aide will know that they are coming and will be on his or her best behavior.

Schools must provide parents with IEP progress reports, which include data on measurable goals, such as success in a task in at least three out of four opportunities. Parents often complain that the data tell them little. One writes of the criteria for mastery and method of evaluation on her son's IEP: "3/4 opportunities and teacher observation. All the way down. Most teachers simply mark in 75-80 percent all the way down for criteria. This pretty much renders the objectives as written in the IEP as useless. Because when progress reports come out, teachers are going to eyeball the objective's progress and make it up as they go out of the air."[64] The challenge for parents is to make sure that the IEP goals are verifiable: that is, they or independent evaluators can see whether the child can perform at the same rate outside the school walls. That is hard to do for tasks that are specific to the classroom, such as interacting with other students in group projects.

The difficulty of monitoring and enforcing IEP compliance stems from the structure of public schools. In large urban areas, the local schools may be part of sprawling bureaucratic structures that are hard to understand and slow to act. In the fall of 2014, hundreds of special education students in New York City had to wait for weeks into the school year for their services. Because of computer glitches and paperwork backlogs, the city's Department of Education held back tutoring, physical therapy, speech therapy, and occupational therapy without telling parents when they would start up.[65] Political scientist James Q. Wilson wrote that schools are "coping organizations," where both the day-to-day activities and their outcomes are hard for outsiders to see.[66] Parents can try to gauge educational outcomes by looking at test scores, but as we shall see momentarily, testing entails serious dilemmas. As for their children's day-to-day activities, they often learn what is going on only after it has gone terribly wrong.

TESTING AND COMMON CORE

The key federal law affecting public schools in general is the Elementary and Secondary Education Act of 1965, which the No Child Left Behind Act (NCLB) of 2001 amended. ESEA and IDEA affect students with disabilities in different ways. ESEA emphasizes holding all students to the same academic standards, while IDEA emphasizes setting individualized learning goals (hence the IEP). The laws can come into tension when IEP goals under IDEA are inconsistent with the grade-level standards under NCLB.[67]

Both laws let eligible students take part in general statewide assessments with accommodations such as getting extra time or taking the test in a separate room. States can also provide alternate assessment for the small number of students who cannot undergo general assessments even with accommodations. In 2014, Louisiana passed legislation authorizing IEP teams in the state to exempt students with disabilities from passing standardized tests in order to move up a grade or receive a high school diploma. IEP teams would instead set "rigorous educational goals" for students to meet.[68] Supporters say the measure will offer more students in special education a better chance at graduating. Critics say that it will merely lower expectations. The U.S. Department of Education sent Louisiana's education superintendent a stern letter warning that the measure could fall afoul of federal law by giving too much leeway to IEP teams.[69]

The NCLB law requires states to break out achievement data by specific groups of students, including those in special education. This requirement "has provided so much good information we never had before about how students with disabilities are really performing," says Lindsay Jones, the director of public policy and advocacy for the National Center for Learning Disabilities.[70] But autism blogger Lisa Rudy sees a problem for students who spend much of their class time in autism support classes.

> While NCLB specifically tests content that is to be taught to ALL students, the Individuals with Disabilities Education Act (IDEA) ensures that each child with a disability is taught according to his or her specific needs and abilities. Because special needs teachers are adhering to the IDEA, it is almost unheard of for a child in an autism support class to be taught how to take a standardized achievement test (although most typical students actually practice the tests in their classes).[71]

In 2009, governors and state school chiefs coordinated a state-led effort to develop the Common Core, a set of academic standards in mathematics and English. These goals outline what students should know and be able to do at the end of each grade. Most states belong to the Common Core State Standards Initiative, though several have voted to repeal or replace the standards. There is much controversy surrounding whether states, school districts, and charter schools will teach curricula grounded in Common Core, as well as how schools will assess and test whether children are learning that content.

In a brief document, Common Core says that disabled students should receive support services but does not spell out what these services are or how schools should provide them.[72] It does not mention autism directly, instead saying that some students with "the most significant cognitive disabilities" will require substantial help. "These supports and accommodations should ensure that students receive access to multiple means of learning and opportunities to demonstrate knowledge, but retain the rigor and high expectations of the Common Core State Standards."[73]

"Unfortunately for students on the spectrum," writes Katherine Beals, "the kinds of tasks we now know are most impaired in autism are also the kinds of tasks that distinguish the Common Core's English and Language Arts Standards from all past standards."[74] With autism, different parts of the brain may not work together smoothly to process information.[75] Autistic people may have great skill at remembering one kind of information (e.g., pictures) but have a hard time relating it to another (e.g., language).[76] Abstract or metaphorical material that is manageable for a typically developing student can be an unnerving challenge for students on the spectrum. Consider this standard for grades 9 and 10: "Determine the meaning of words and phrases as they are used in the text, including figurative and connotative meanings; analyze the cumulative impact of specific word choices on meaning and tone (e.g., how the language evokes a sense of time and place; how it sets a formal or informal tone)." Even a very bright autistic student could falter at this task.

Accommodating this difficulty is a puzzle in itself. School officials might be unaware that an autistic child has this challenge, since it will not necessarily show up in standard IQ tests, which measure simpler skills.[77] So when a high-IQ student botches questions about "figurative and connotative meanings," the officials may infer that he or she is simply not paying attention or working hard enough. If they do see the problem, what then? When Congress passed the original version of IDEA in 1975, lawmakers thought of "accommodations" as wheelchair ramps for paraplegics or Braille for blind people. What kind of accommodations apply when the student's disability involves the subject itself? As Beals asks, "Are we talking about the equivalent of somehow creating accommodations that enable a profoundly deaf child to analyze the tone and beauty in Beethoven's quartets?"[78]

Many ASD people have good math skills, but Common Core math standards can thwart them. The brain processes verbal and quantitative information in different places, so when the links between these regions are underdeveloped—as they are with autism—word problems in math become intimidating. And to teach Common Core concepts, teachers often insist that students break routine calculations into complex multistep processes, which is also a challenge for ASD students. Writes one father of an autistic child:

When consideration is given to the increasing number of ASD children who can no longer excel in the one subject that many of them are good at because language arts objectives must be achieved through math objectives, the effect of Common Core changes greatly. Rather than providing inclusion and support for all children as intended, an increasing number find themselves further marginalized and discouraged; all because they can't master the several methods presented, which is required. Shouldn't a kid be able to use the method that works for them? Yes, in theory. But not so in applied Common Core Standards.[79]

These comments bring us back to the dilemma of difference. Making autistic students take the same tests under the same conditions as nondisabled students will usually work to their detriment. But if Common Core really is the way to prepare for the twenty-first-century economy, as its backers say, then autistic students could lose out by avoiding it. One way around this dilemma is to integrate Common Core standards into IEPs, an aim that is much easier to describe than accomplish. Not only are resources limited, but teachers are struggling with Common Core to begin with. "I think the bigger issue is we struggle with access to the general ed curriculum, period," says special education consultant Carol Kosnitsky. "People aren't coming in confident that they know how to do this, so now it's just another layer on top of not-well-defined practice."[80]

INCLUSION AND ITS DISCONTENTS

IDEA's requirement for the "least restrictive environment" was uncontroversial in the 1970s and has never received much congressional attention since then.[81] During the years before the bill's passage, the mass media had spotlighted scandalous conditions at New York's Willowbrook State School and other institutions for the disabled. The idea of ensuring the least restrictive environment seemed like common sense to just about anyone who had seen the horrific images of children locked in filthy communal rooms. Furthermore, the idea of integration was central to the broader civil rights movement that gave rise to the disability rights movement.

Today only a small share of autistic students are in separate schools or residential facilities, though that portion varies from practically none in Montana, New Mexico, and West Virginia to nearly a third in New Jersey. Separate educational settings are more common in the East than the West.[82] For most children with autism, the "least restrictive environment" is in a regular school, with various mixes of general and special education classes. Research on the results of inclusion is not as extensive as one might want, but there is evidence that well-planned inclusion of autistic students with nondisabled peers does have educational benefits.[83]

Inclusion is tricky, however. General education teachers often may not know much about autism, and even when they do, the variability of autism symptoms is an additional hurdle: by the time the teacher has finally figured out a kid's strengths, weaknesses, and quirks, the school year is over. In one focus group study, special education teachers reported a significant divide between themselves and the general education system. An autism support teacher in Philadelphia noted, "I think a lot of our regular ed teachers as wonderful as they are—they think special education looks different, and it always will."[84]

Inclusion exposes autistic students to bullying by nondisabled peers. In school, bullying involves words or deeds that aggressive children use to intimidate or harm others that they regard as weaker. It can range from blatant physical aggression, to schoolyard taunts, to cyberbullying through social media and other technology. The targets of bullying will suffer lower academic achievement and higher truancy, loneliness, and depression. Students must feel safe in school in order to reach their full academic potential. If bullying is bad enough that a student is not getting meaningful educational benefit from school services, the U.S. Department of Education considers it a denial of the student's right to a free appropriate public education.[85]

Bullies pick on students with disabilities because they are often weaker and more vulnerable. According to the Kennedy Krieger Institute, 63 percent of autistic children had been bullied. And 39 percent had faced bullying in the previous month, compared with just 12 percent of their non-autistic siblings.[86] In fact, students with autism are more likely to undergo bullying than most others with special needs.[87] Although autism is often not apparent to casual observers, peers will eventually pick up on the signs that autistic students are different. Many of them engage in unusual behaviors such as hand-flapping and self-talk, which other kids ridicule. Because they have a hard time reading faces, they might not know when to stop doing or saying things that attract bullying. Limited social skills may prevent them from forming the friendship networks that often protect other students.[88] Like other victims, they may be reluctant or ashamed to tell their parents, who usually have no other way of knowing that the bullying is taking place until it reaches an extreme level.

In the Kennedy Krieger study, *52 percent* of parents of ASD children reported that other kids had intentionally taunted them to trigger a meltdown or other aggressive behavior. "Often kids try to upset her because they find it funny when she gets upset and cries. She is overly emotional, and they seem to get a kick out of this," one mother told researchers. Another parent said:

I'm so glad you asked about other children knowing how to press buttons. That has happened with my son with ASD. . . . Being in a class of gifted children has costs and benefits—kids are more intuitive, which means they can excuse a lot of unusual behavior, but it also means they know exactly how to elicit behaviors when they feel like it. It's never OK for my son to hit, but what happens is kids pick at him until he pops, and often times his target is the teacher! His stress builds up as the kids mess with him, then, if the teacher reprimands him, he loses control, scratching, pulling clothing and hair and trying to bite the teacher.[89]

Safety is also a major problem. About half of autistic children wander or "elope" from adult supervision, and about a third of those children do so at school.[90] Most of the time, adults find them right way, but there have been cases in which parents get the kind of call that they dread. Lori McIlwain, director of the National Autism Association, recalls the time her seven-year-old son slipped out of an unlocked school gate and made his way to a four-lane highway.

> Luckily, a passing driver noticed our son; the driver turned around, just in case. When Connor failed to answer a few basic questions, he was taken to another nearby school. That school called the police. The police had no idea how to deal with Connor: An officer mistook our mostly nonverbal child for a defiant rule-breaker who needed some "tough love." Finally, a staff member at the school reached me, but exactly how long Connor had been missing by the time I got to him, no one could tell me. Connor was hysterical, shaking. I scooped him up in a hug, whispering through my own tears, "You're O.K."[91]

Confidentiality rules, which exist to protect disabled students from stigma, have the unanticipated consequence of making it harder to prevent wandering. "School safety officers do not have any knowledge of whether a student has an IEP," said Johanna Miller, advocacy director at the New York Civil Liberties Union. "We don't advocate that the [education department] shares these records with the cops, but there's a gap in how the adults in the building can protect students with special education needs."[92] Autism parent Lisa Quinones-Fontanez writes:

> Autism is an invisible disability, and it's easy for many autistic kids to pass for "regular." But when there is a population of kids with autism in the same building as "typical" kids, officials should be trained and prepared to act accordingly. Everyone in the building needs to understand what autism is and what it "looks" like. If the Department of Education is not prepared to do that, then maybe they should start creating public schools exclusively for kids with autism and/or special needs.[93]

Similar suggestions have also come from some parents of autistic children who have endured bullying or shunning.[94] Although moving away from inclusivity could help with safety and bullying issues in the short term, it will leave autistic students less prepared for life in mainstream society. "Segregated schools lead to segregated societies," says Ari Ne'eman of the Autistic Self Advocacy Network. "If we have an environment in which autistic people are over there, in that other classroom, in that other environment, it really sends a very clear message that we are not a part of your society."[95]

Schools might not have to choose between reducing inclusion and leaving autistic students open to physical and emotional harm. Broad anti-bullying initiatives can modestly reduce bullying behavior. Improved perimeter security can help keep students from leaving school grounds: in response to the death of an autistic student who wandered from school, New York City passed legislation to evaluate door alarms for elementary schools.[96] The U.S. Department of Justice announced that it would allow the use of existing grant funds to be used to fund voluntary tracking devices through local law enforcement agencies. But neither door alarms nor exhortations to good behavior can provide a complete solution to the dilemma of difference.

DISCIPLINE, RESTRAINT, SECLUSION

Another difficulty with inclusion crops up when autistic children act out in ways that bring them into the disciplinary system. People with autism are no more violent or defiant than anyone else, but their behavior sometimes breaches school norms. There are no national data dealing specifically with autistic students; instead, U.S. Department of Education statistics on disabled students provide a rough proxy. Students who receive special education services represent 12 percent of the student population, 19 percent of students suspended in school, 20 percent of students receiving out-of-school suspension once, 25 percent of students receiving multiple out-of-school suspensions, 19 percent of students expelled, 23 percent of students referred to law enforcement, and 23 percent of students receiving a school-related arrest.[97]

These disciplinary problems are all the more notable in light of legal protections for disabled students. In 1988, the Supreme Court said of IDEA that "Congress very much meant to strip schools of the *unilateral* authority they had traditionally employed to exclude disabled students, particularly emotionally disturbed students, from school"[98] According to this decision, schools cannot punish or expel disabled students for their disability. In 1997 Congress added a "manifestation determination process" to IDEA. When a school is considering an expulsion or a suspension that would last more than ten days, the child's IEP team needs to meet to determine whether the behavior stemmed from disability. For autistic children, the expert opinion of a psychologist or psychiatrist is necessary to make this determination.[99]

Schools often resort to restraint and seclusion to control dangerous misbehavior. Restraint is the restriction of a student's freedom of motion. Physical restraint can range from handholding to headlocks, while mechanical restraint can involve devices such as bungee cords, straps, or even handcuffs. Seclusion is the involuntary isolation of a student (usually for a few minutes but sometimes much longer).[100] Students with disabilities make up *58 percent* of seclusions, and *75 percent* of the cases of restraint.[101] Again, we lack national data distinguishing autism from other disabilities, but a report from Connecticut's Department of Education shows that autism is the top disability among special education students subject to "emergency" restraint or seclusion, accounting for 42 percent of such incidents. More than half of seclusions via an IEP involve autism.[102]

No federal laws specifically restrict restraint and seclusion in public and private schools, and there are widely divergent laws at the state level[103] Thirty-two states require parental notification when disabled students are subject to these measures, but eighteen states and the District of Columbia have no such protection.[104] And even where notification laws are in place, compliance may be spotty.[105] A U.S. Senate report offers some disturbing examples of alleged abuse:

- In December 2011, a Kentucky school district restrained a nine-year-old child with autism in a duffel bag as punishment. The child's mother witnessed him struggling inside the bag while a teacher's aide stood by and did nothing.
- In North Carolina, the mother of a five-year-old girl with autism and other developmental disabilities agreed to the use of restraints only in the event that her daughter became aggressive. She discovered that her daughter had been left alone and strapped to chair, even though she had shown no signs of aggressive behavior. Although the mother believed her daughter was restrained over 90 percent of the time she was at school, the school denied restraining the child on a regular basis. The school eventually released records showing that the IEPs of multiple special education students did not accurately discuss the types of interventions being used or were otherwise incomplete.
- A behavior analyst in Connecticut recommended brief time-outs for an eight-year-old girl with autism and other disabilities. However, when the girl's mother realized that the time-outs had escalated to repeated seclusion in a small cinder-block room, she requested that the school discontinue their use. The behavior analyst opted to continue the seclusion, and the school supported this decision. The mother said that she felt "powerless" to stop them.

The American Association of School Administrators opposes a ban on restraint and seclusion, arguing that abuses are rare and that violent outbursts have sometimes caused serious injury. "We believe the use of seclusion and restraint has enabled many students with serious emotional or behavioral conditions to be educated not only within our public schools, but also in the least restrictive and safest environments possible."[106] A critic of this position might call it an Orwellian argument that restraint equals freedom. But in the rare cases where autistic students do engage in dangerous behavior, schools need some way of controlling it other than sending offenders to a segregated facility. The hard part is making sure that the schools are themselves subject to control, both by higher authorities and parents.

EXIT AND VOICE

According to Albert O. Hirschman, two responses to organizational problems are "exit" and "voice."[107] One can either go elsewhere or agitate for change. For autism parents, exit is hard. If a district does not have a suitable placement, a parent can request an out-of-district placement, which may mean a long commute to an unfamiliar neighborhood. Parents can also move, but housing costs and the need to hold on to current jobs severely limit most people's residential mobility. Parents looking to relocate cannot "shop" for IEPs as one shops for houses, since it is impossible to know what the district will offer until the IEP meeting takes place, which cannot happen until the family lives in the district. There is no database of "good" and "bad" districts for autism services, in part because IEPs are confidential.

Occasionally an IEP provides for private placements when the school district cannot offer the necessary services. Parents can also pull their children from a public school program and get district reimbursement for the private placement, but only if a hearing officer or judge finds that the public program is inappropriate for the child's educational needs and that the private program is appropriate.[108] Such cases are unusual, because few parents want to roll the dice on a lengthy legal process with iffy chances of success. Those with the means may prefer to absorb the tuition cost. "When you get into a fight with a school, it's like a divorce," said one mother of an autistic student. "I'd rather take my energy and money and find an alternative."[109] Some voucher programs do exist, but the money has to come from state and local governments, not federal funds.[110] The federal rule says: "No parentally-placed private school child with a disability has an individual right to receive some or all of the special education and related services that the child would receive if enrolled in a public school."[111] In any case, the numbers are small: fewer than 1 percent of autistic students are parentally placed in private schools.

Voice is just as tough as exit.

In most cases where Americans have complaints about local bureaucracies, they may band together to bring about change, which is the whole idea behind community organizing. Although there are many local groups that provide emotional support, parents of autistic students face constraints in uniting for better schooling. For starters, community organizing typically concentrates on collective goods, things that benefit the whole community (e.g., the establishment of a park or the removal of a toxic waste dump). But by definition, IEPs are individualized, not collective.[112] The provision of good services to one student does not directly benefit anybody else. The parents of such a student have no material incentive to support good services for others: in fact, given that schools have limited resources, they might believe that others could gain only at their own child's expense. Even when parents want to organize, they have a hard time finding one another. The confidentiality of IEPs means that there are no public rosters of special needs parents, so would-be organizers of a parent group have to recruit members by putting announcements online or in the newspaper.[113]

When parents take public action for their children with autism, they are effectively making public disclosure of that condition. And public disclosure is the one thing that many parents of autistic children most want to *avoid*. Even when the other adults are sympathetic, they might not be able to transmit that sympathy to their children. Family therapist Mark Hutten suggests that an autism label is a bull's-eye for bullies. "So, with the exception of siblings, your child's peers (i.e., those about the same age) are best left in the dark about his or her disorder. One parent stated, 'I made the mistake of telling my neighbor that my son was 'a little autistic.' Ever since then, her children have started fights with my son on the bus and in the neighborhood.'"[114]

Parent advocacy faces obstacles at the national level as well. In 2004, when Congress reauthorized the Individuals with Disabilities Education Act, educators sought to ease its procedural burdens—which parents tended to see as an important safeguard. Organizations representing teachers and school districts were well organized with large numbers of professional lobbyists. Groups representing parents of children with autism and other disabilities were at a competitive disadvantage, relying mostly on volunteers who had never worked together before. Autism Speaks did not yet exist, and other autism groups were focusing more on medical issues. In the end, the changes were not as far-reaching as the parents had feared. But as one put it, "We jumped in front of a moving train and we slowed it down. But we didn't stop it."[115] Among other things, the 2004 amendments changed attorney fee rules to make them more favorable to the school districts.[116]

On March 3, 2010, the House of Representatives passed a bill to forbid the use of seclusion and restraint, except in case of imminent danger.[117] The bill did not pass the Senate, however, and subsequent versions failed to make it to the floor of either chamber. Opposition from teachers and school administrators has been strong. Daniel Domenech, the head of the American Association of School Administrators, told ABC News his chief concern with restrictive federal legislation was that it could put teachers in a bind—would they have to risk violating a federal law to handle dangerous situations?[118] The association has also opposed the IDEA Fairness Restoration Act, which would overturn the Supreme Court decision preventing parents from recovering witness fees when they prevail in due process.[119] Despite repeated reintroductions, the legislation has never gained traction in either chamber. These outcomes are consistent with a broader pattern in special education, in which professional groups see it as a grant-in-aid program and support local control, whereas parents see it as a civil rights issue and advocate greater federal action and uniformity. [120]

Another bill has gotten more support among lawmakers and interest groups, however. The IDEA Full Funding Act would increase federal funding for special education to the levels that lawmakers anticipated in the 1970s. The 2014 version would have gradually raised the amount from $11.5 billion in fiscal 2014, which covered about 16 percent of IDEA costs, to $35.6 billion in fiscal 2023, or 40 percent of costs. [121] Chances for passage are not good. Whereas spending for the Autism CARES Act added up to petty cash by federal standards, the amounts in this legislation add up to serious money. The bill would offset the increased spending by raising taxes on the rich, a politically difficult proposition.

Without much prospect of fundamental change in federal policy, parents have to keep looking to their own schools, where decisions come one student at a time, behind closed doors.

Chapter Five

Before, Outside, and After the Classroom

Political scientist Steven M. Teles has coined a term that comes in handy for any discussion of autism services: *kludgeocracy*. In computing, a "kludge" is a system consisting of ill-matched elements or parts made for other applications. Engineers patch it together and hook it up to an existing system in order to solve a new problem. Kludges are complicated, hard to understand, and subject to crashes. Teles says that this description fits much of American public policy: "From the mind-numbing complexity of the health care system . . . our Byzantine system of funding higher education, and our bewildering federal-state system of governing everything from the welfare state to environmental regulation, America has chosen more indirect and incoherent policy mechanisms than any comparable country."[1]

Kludgeocracy is bad for democratic accountability. Instead of clear lines of responsibility, citizens instead find organization charts that resemble spaghetti. Multiple, overlapping, and interlacing programs make it hard to find out who does what, and where to pin blame when things go wrong. More important, complexity hurts people who need help. They must do research merely to find out which programs could benefit them and how they can apply for aid. And then comes the maze of forms and requirements that are necessary to maintain their eligibility.

It is hard to think of a better example of kludgeocracy than autism. Virtually every autism program is an add-on to a program originally designed for something else. As we saw in the previous chapter, the drafters of the Individuals with Disabilities Education Act (IDEA) scarcely gave a thought to autism in 1975. As we shall see in this chapter, autism services under IDEA are a model of rationality compared with the tangle of policies that lie beyond the schoolhouse door. A 2014 consultant's report for the Centers for

Medicare and Medicaid Services said: "Currently, there is no comprehensive, nationwide summary of state services for people with ASD and policies related to people with ASD."[2] The report surveyed state-level offices and departments but acknowledged that there were still gaps in the data. And if policy experts cannot figure out the system, neither can autistic people and their families. In Pennsylvania, the *Hanover Evening Sun* reports on Steve Brown, an autism parent struggling with a state guide to autism services:

> Starting with the 172-page Pennsylvania autism services guide, the one that Steve couldn't help but drag all around the house, finding any of the necessary services for their children is daunting. [The guide is] filled with an alphabet soup of organizations and page after page of complicated instructions.
>
> "You need someone to educate you on this," Steve said. "A typical parent can't just read this and understand it."
>
> When the Browns wanted to apply for a state program, they needed to elicit the help of a caseworker just to walk them through the process, even with the guide.
>
> Applying for federally funded programs can be just as difficult. The long list of acronyms and obscure terms that describe the personal aides available for autistic children through private insurance and Medicaid is likely to leave any parent bewildered.[3]

In this kludgeocracy, an autistic person's lot depends on several things. The first is age, since autistic children get more help than autistic adults. While IDEA guarantees a free appropriate public education (FAPE) only to people between the ages of three and twenty-one, the requirement does not apply to adults. Many other services and supports are also unavailable to people past their school years. "We call it falling off the cliff," says Illinois state representative Patricia Bellock. "We can keep them in school until they're 22. After that, they have nothing for them."[4]

Location and social class make a difference. Two autistic people with the same challenges and abilities will have very different opportunities depending on where they live. And as usual, people with money and education have an edge over people who do not. "Part of what you're seeing here is the more educated and sophisticated you are, the louder you scream and the more you ask for," says an autism specialist at a California center for people with developmental disabilities. After investing in lawyers and experts who could make their way through the autism kludgeocracy, one mother got a generous array of services. "Am I more entitled than someone else?" she says. "No. But that's how the system is set up."[5]

EARLY INTERVENTION

In 1986, Congress added a new part to the Education for all Handicapped Children Act, which four years later would become IDEA. The measure furnished funds to state programs in early intervention services for children from birth to their third birthday.[6] The measure also ensured the right to a free appropriate public education for children from the ages of three to five. Public schools would now have to provide services to preschoolers as well as children at grade level. For children over three, autism would not become a separate eligibility category until the 1990 IDEA legislation. For younger children, however, the early intervention program covered anyone with developmental delays or with a diagnosed condition with a high chance of resulting in such delays. This broader definition remains in place today.

The governor of each state names the "lead agency" for early intervention, and these agencies vary from place to place. In Alaska, the current lead agency is the Department of Health and Social Services, while in Iowa it is the Department of Education. The governor also appoints a state council, including parents of young children with disabilities, to advise the lead agency. Currently, all states and eligible territories are taking part in the program.

Instead of an individualized education program (IEP), the early intervention agency works with the family to create an individualized family service plan (IFSP), which guides the early intervention process. It contains information about the services for the child and often for the family as well. Respite services, for instance, offer temporary care of disabled children so that family members can briefly leave the house for shopping or other personal needs. A coordinator helps the family by overseeing the services in the IFSP. Federal rules require the services to take place in "natural environments" whenever possible, and more than four-fifths of infants and toddlers receive their early intervention services mainly in the home.[7] Families may have to pay for some services, but on a sliding scale that makes the program affordable for those with low incomes. Because of these features, legal scholar Ruth Colker says the program "is probably the best special education program ever adopted in Congress."[8]

Now Part C of IDEA, the program is modest by federal standards, serving fewer than four hundred thousand children and receiving about $439 million in fiscal 2015. Part B of the IDEA, for children and youth ages three to twenty-one, serves more than six million at a cost of $11.5 billion.[9] With such services, autistic children can make gains early in life when potential for change may be greatest.[10] Because the federal government does not publish data on early intervention services by type of disability, we do not know how many autistic children receive them. The number of autistic children in early intervention is probably small, however, and thereby hangs a tale.

As with the original 1975 law, the sponsors of the 1986 law creating the early intervention program gave little thought to autism. A representative of NSAC (now the Autism Society) read a statement to a House committee, but members did not ask him any questions.[11] The House report on the bill indicated what other kinds of disabilities were on their minds: "Downs [sic] Syndrome and other chromosomal abnormalities which are likely to result in mental retardation; severe microcephaly; Cornelia de Lange Syndrome; sensory impairments; Rubenstein-Taybi Syndrome; Fetal Alcohol Syndrome; Epilepsy; and Inborn Errors of Metabolism."[12]

Many such conditions show up early in life, if not during pregnancy. With autism, by contrast, parents usually do not spot the signs until the age of two or so, and health care providers might not see them until later. Early identification requires providers to watch developmental milestones and carry out informal and formal screening. Among the screening tools are questionnaires asking a parent or caregiver about the development of their child at specific ages. One study found that the parents of just one out of every five children aged ten to forty-seven months reported that a provider had asked them to fill out such a questionnaire in the previous year.[13] Red flags do not necessarily spur action. Says Amy Daniels, who heads public health research at Autism Speaks: "There's a lot of questions about what happens to these kids after they screen positive."[14] Even after standardized screenings, one study found, just one-fifth of the children flagged with possible delays got a referral to early intervention and other community resources.[15]

Early intervention encompasses services such as nursing care, which can help children with a broad range of developmental delays. It can also include autism-specific services such as applied behavior analysis (ABA). Although a formal autism diagnosis is not required for the former, it may often be necessary for the latter, which means that parents often confront a bottleneck. Once a pediatrician does make a referral, a child may have to wait for months to get an evaluation at an autism clinic. On average, there is a two-year gap between the first signs and the formal diagnosis.[16] Most children with autism symptoms do not receive a comprehensive evaluation before the age of three.[17]

Parent advocate Irene Tanzman offers an illustration: "In Massachusetts children suspected of having ASD must wait until they receive the 'official diagnosis' from a specialist before they can access autism specialty services. A provisional diagnosis with a positive screen is not enough. It can often take months to get an appointment to receive the 'official diagnosis.'"[18] This example is telling because Massachusetts has plenty of medical professionals and a reputation as one of the better states for autism services.[19] Children in other states fare worse, which means that they probably get just a few months of early intervention before the three-year clock runs out. At that point, they usually lose their family-based intervention and move to a preschool program under the often-adversarial IEP process.

Most school districts provide autistic pre-K students with speech/language and occupational therapies, and many offer various kinds of behavior management programs and learning supports.[20] Some also give limited support for at-home services, but only if they bear some relationship to educational achievement. For the most part, however, parents seeking help outside the classroom setting have to look elsewhere.

OTHER SERVICES

In California, the Department of Developmental Services assists people who have autism and other developmental disabilities. The state runs developmental centers and community facilities, and has contracts with twenty-one nonprofit regional centers, which provide or coordinate services and supports. State law requires regional centers to help developmentally disabled people integrate into mainstream life "regardless of age or degree of disability, and at each stage of life."[21]

A school district might offer FAPE to children without providing the services they need to meet the more extensive California standards. Regional centers work to meet those needs, but the law makes them the "payer of last resort" and requires them to use up all other possible funding sources—including school districts and private medical insurance—before it spends regional center money on services.[22] In practice, experiences vary, as autism mother and advocate Cecilia Chang writes: "My family had a very supportive Regional Center but had to resort to multiple legal proceedings with the school district to have them pick up their portion of the funding responsibility. My good friend had the exact reverse; a very supportive school, but not-so-supportive Regional Center."[23]

In most other states, Medicaid accounts for the bulk of nonschool government help for autistic children. Medicaid passed as part of the Medicare law of 1965. At the time, the media and the political community focused on Medicare, a federal program supporting health care for the elderly. Less attention went to Medicaid, a federal-state program that has traditionally served low-income children, parents, the elderly, and the disabled. At the signing ceremony, President Johnson spoke at length about Medicare but did not mention Medicaid at all.[24] Medicaid has since grown dramatically and now has more enrollees than Medicare.[25]

Medicaid covers about nine million non-elderly people with disabilities.[26] In the program's early years, much of this assistance took the form of institutional care. But because of the broad movement away from institutions—not to mention their high cost to government—Congress in 1981 created the

Medicaid Home and Community-Based Services (HCBS) Waiver. It "waives" some federal requirements to give states more leeway in defining populations that they will serve, such as autistic children, as well as the services they provide. At first, the states were slow to use this new mechanism. In 1990, the Americans with Disabilities Act (ADA) instructed states to avoid the needless institutionalization of disabled people.[27] In the 1999 case of *Olmstead v. L.C.*, the U.S. Supreme Court ruled that ADA required states to place persons with mental disabilities in community settings rather than institutions "when the State's treatment professionals have determined that community placement is appropriate, the transfer from institutional care to a less restrictive setting is not opposed by the affected individual, and the placement can be reasonably accommodated."[28] This decision hastened the shift from institutional to community care. In fiscal 1995, institutions took 70 percent of Medicaid long-term support for people with developmental disabilities. Only 30 percent went to home-based and community services. By fiscal 2012, the proportions had flipped: 70 percent for HCBS, 30 percent for institutions.[29]

Waivers vary widely among states: Mississippi and Florida rank low, while Oregon and Vermont rank high.[30] A state may have multiple waivers, meaning that potential clients (or their parents) have to figure out which ones they can apply for. In 2007, one Texas autism mother wrote that the waivers are confusing.

> Entering each one is like walking into its own little universe. Each one serves a different population: HCS only serves those with an IQ under 70 or with autism (a related disability) and an IQ under 75. CLASS serves those with developmental disabilities, no IQ specification. . . . Texas Home Living is for persons already receiving services funded by general revenue dollars through MHMRA—and this waiver does NOT waive the family income requirement, only the licensing requirement. Not all waivers are available in all counties in Texas. Not all waivers provide identical services or pay the same annual amount (they have different spending caps).[31]

The original idea behind waivers was to serve people who would otherwise end up in institutions. When designing these systems, policymakers were thinking of people with intellectual disabilities, not people with autism. As the example above suggests, eligibility criteria for certain waivers exclude autistic people with average or above-average intelligence.[32] Some states have waivers specifically targeting autism, but most of them are for children, not adults. (We shall shortly return to the lack of services for adults on the spectrum.)

Medicaid is an "entitlement" program, which means that anyone who meets eligibility criteria may sign up. But there is a big exception: services under Medicaid *waivers* are *not* entitlements. In many states, demand for these services greatly exceeds supply, which means that a would-be recipient must wait until a slot opens up—and some of those delays are long.[33] In 2013, 322,273 people with intellectual and developmental disabilities were on these lists, with an average waiting period of fifty months.[34] (There are no separate figures for autistic people.) Again, states vary: some reported that was nobody was waiting, whereas 116,000 were on the Texas list.[35]

Maryland's Medicaid waiver provides respite care, family training, and other services. But Maryland caps the number of children under the Maryland autism waiver at nine hundred. Almost four thousand children are on a waiting list. Autism parent Nora Fitzpatrick writes of testifying on the problem before Maryland legislators:

> My testimony focused on my daughter Rory's therapeutic program, which a Medicaid waiver could enhance outside of what she receives in school, as well as her medical issues in the past few years that have resulted in substantial out-of-pocket expenses for our family. I noted that Rory has been on the autism waiver wait list for five years, and she is only #1,633 out of 3,900 names. There was an audible gasp in the committee room. And that gasp startled me. What's more shocking? That Rory is only at number 1,633 on the list after all these years? Or, that I am surprised that this surprises other people?[36]

Says Ari Ne'eman, president of the Autistic Self Advocacy Network: "[W]ait-lists have become a way of shifting the costs of service provision on family. States know that families of people with disabilities will go to extraordinary lengths to keep loved ones from being institutionalized even without necessary service and supports."[37] And frustrations do not stop at the end of the waiting list. Again, the Maryland waiver provides an illustration. Attorney and autism parent Robert McCarthy writes at the *Washington Post* that his son got no state-financed services until he got off the waiting list. "Then he got very generous services through the waiver program, which basically means the government began paying for what my wife and I previously paid. The catch is that many service providers do not accept Medicaid reimbursements because the rates are low, the procedures are onerous and the reimbursements are delayed."[38]

There is another route to Medicaid services. In 1967, Congress added the Early and Periodic Screening, Diagnostic and Treatment (EPSDT) benefit to provide comprehensive and preventive health care services for children under age twenty-one who are enrolled in Medicaid. By 2014, mostly as the result of lawsuits, ten states were providing behavioral health treatment through this benefit, including ABA coverage.[39] In July of that year, the Centers for Medicare and Medicaid Services (CMS) told states that their EPSDT benefits have to cover all medically necessary care for children with autism through age twenty-one. "This should be of enormous significance to beneficiaries across the country," said Dan Unumb, executive director of

Autism Speaks' Autism Legal Resource Center. "It will dramatically increase access to critical, medically necessary care."[40]

CMS did not endorse ABA in particular, however, stressing that other therapies exist and that states are responsible for determining what services are medically necessary.[41] So although some states acted quickly to expand ABA coverage, it seemed likely that many others would drag their feet. United Cerebral Palsy annually ranks state Medicaid services for people with intellectual and developmental disabilities.[42] The 2014 rankings found that some states had consistently languished at the bottom since 2007, including Arkansas (#47), Illinois (#46), Mississippi (#51), and Texas (#50).

Years of lawsuits and implementation battles still lay ahead. And any expansion of Medicaid services would do little for the majority of autistic people who do not qualify for coverage through EPSDT. They would instead be looking to private health insurance.

MANDATING INSURANCE COVERAGE

As Teles suggests, perhaps no other part of the kludgeocracy is more familiar or vexing than health insurance. Before the Second World War, few Americans had health coverage. When wartime wage controls helped create a labor shortage, employers offered health insurance benefits as one way to attract scarce workers. Not only did the benefits provide a way around wage controls, but unlike wages, they were not subject to income tax or payroll taxes. Employer-sponsored health insurance remained popular after the war and became a central part of the health care system, although it started as an accident of history.

Meanwhile, seemingly unrelated developments ensured that much of the responsibility for regulating this system would fall to state governments. In 1944, the U.S. Supreme Court ruled that insurance was a form of interstate commerce and therefore subject to federal regulation.[43] The general public did not give much thought to the decision, since it appeared in the newspapers on the morning of June 6, also known as D-Day. Insurance companies did pay attention. They worried that the federal government could now use antitrust law to ban anticompetitive practices that had enriched them. They found allies in state officials, who feared that the ruling might jeopardize their ability to tax insurance. Accordingly, the National Association of Insurance Commissioners drafted a bill to exempt insurance from most federal regulation.[44] Senators Pat McCarran (D-NV) and Homer Ferguson (R-MI) sponsored the bill, and an amended version—the McCarran-Ferguson Act—became law in 1945.

Most of the time, state insurance regulation is a case of what James Q. Wilson called "client politics."[45] In this political arena, benefits are concentrated on a handful of special interests and the costs are widely spread at a low per capita rate over many people. The beneficiaries lobby behind the scenes, while the general public has little incentive to organize on the other side, that is, if they ever hear of the policy. The insurance industry has bonded with state lawmakers and regulators, and most of its lobbying involves technical issues that get practically no coverage in the mass media. So the industry usually wins.

Sometimes, however, certain insurance issues do break into the news and the public takes notice. On those rare occasions, lawmakers are more likely to side against the industry because it is unpopular.[46] As health care issues assumed greater prominence in the late 1960s, policy entrepreneurs increasingly drew attention to the idea of insurance mandates for required health coverage for specific treatments, providers, and categories of dependents.[47] Mandates sounded good to the general public, enjoyed political support from the providers, and offered lawmakers a way to claim credit for something that did not show up on the state government balance sheets. From the 1970s to the 1990s, states passed hundreds of new health insurance mandates.[48] Insurance companies generally opposed these measures, arguing that their cost would mean higher premiums for employers and purchasers of individual policies. This argument did not always sway politicians, since they knew that the public would blame premium hikes on the unloved insurance industry, not them.

Insurance companies gave little help to autistic people and refused to cover ABA. By the turn of the century, ABA was about forty years old, but industry insisted on calling it "experimental." In the 1990s, there was some litigation aimed at obtaining insurance coverage in isolated individual cases, but the lawsuits had little broad effect. Autism advocates then turned to the idea of including autism in state mental health parity laws, which require insurers to provide the same level of benefits for mental illness or substance abuse as for other disorders and diseases. These efforts also fell short. Autistic people could get policies that offered mental health benefits, but the policies did not include common autism treatments such as ABA.[49]

We have already seen how Representative Dan Burton (R-IN) raised the national profile of autism through congressional hearings. In 2001, he helped persuade the legislature of his home state to enact an autism insurance mandate. The law's wording was imprecise, and insurers still refused to pay for ABA. In 2006, the state's insurance commissioner issued a regulatory bulletin making clear that ABA was part of the mandate.[50]

South Carolina was the next to pass a mandate. "I'd go to support-group meetings for other moms," said autism parent Lorri Unumb. "They didn't have a house they could sell to pocket the difference, and they didn't have a second salary to sacrifice. I kept thinking, 'This is so unfair.'"[51] Unumb was a law professor at the University of Charleston, so she had the expertise to do something about it. In the summer of 2005, she drafted a bill requiring private insurance companies in South Carolina to include treatment for autism, and over the next two years, she joined with other autism parents to lobby state lawmakers. In June 2007, the bill passed both chambers of the legislature only to run into a veto by Governor Mark Sanford. "At 10:30 at night," she later said, "I had to stay up, call all my autism pals around the state and ask them to show up at the statehouse the next day to see if we could override the veto."[52] They did, and the legislature enacted the bill over Sanford's veto. The legislation was known as Ryan's Law, after Unumb's son.

Why did it take so long for another state to follow Indiana's lead? "If you have a child with autism, you're exhausted all the time," said Unumb. "And the last thing in the world that you have time to do is to take on the insurance industry. That's why it's just persisted this way for so long, it's that the very people who have the motivation to get the coverage just can't do it."[53] In this case, it helped that Unumb and her husband were both lawyers and that South Carolina is a relatively compact state where most citizens can get to the capital in a couple of hours. But the parents had to do it on their own, with no national support.[54]

Things would soon change. Autism Speaks, which had been born in 2005, formed a government relations team in 2007. By the end of the year, it had drafted model insurance legislation and announced a multistate initiative to secure its passage.[55] The organization soon hired Unumb as vice president for state government affairs. In some ways, her efforts to pass Ryan's Law became a template for the organization's lobbying efforts. In state after state, Autism Speaks mobilized parents—mostly mothers—to make their case with state legislators. In testimony and one-on-one conversations, the parents told moving stories about the need for behavior therapy. In some states, advocates put a human face on the legislation by naming the bills after autistic children: voting against "Brandon's Law" or "Steven's Law" would be tougher than voting against an obscure bill number. "This is the hottest trend in mandates we've seen in a long time," said insurance lobbyist J. P. Wieske. "It is hard to fight them."[56]

Legislators said that the stories of the families were especially persuasive. "When things are personal, you work a lot harder," said Michigan Democratic state senator Rebekah Warren of Ann Arbor.[57] The pro-mandate forces had an additional advantage wherever lawmakers and other officials had a direct tie to autism. In Michigan, Republican lieutenant governor Brian Calley, the father of an autistic daughter, helped build bipartisan support for an insurance measure. In New York, the sponsor was Republican state senator Roy McDonald, the grandfather of two autistic children.

Passage was more than a matter of anecdote and sentiment. With the support of the government-affairs professionals at Autism Speaks, mandate advocates were able to make substantive policy arguments. The industry contended that ABA is experimental and that mandates would lead to steep increases in premiums. Autism Speaks provided advocates with information about the scientific basis for ABA, including web links to the relevant research.[58] The organization also engaged a leading independent actuarial firm to develop cost estimates for various state autism insurance bills.[59] According to the estimates, the premium increases would be tiny. Advocates could also point to data showing that the Pennsylvania mandate was associated with a drop in the number of children receiving services under a Medicaid waiver.[60] They could thus make a plausible case that insurance mandates would ease pressure on state budgets.

By the end of 2014, thirty-seven states and the District of Columbia had enacted some form of an autism insurance mandate. Also in that year, the Washington Supreme Court ruled that a major insurer had broken the state's mental health parity law by excluding neurodevelopmental therapies (e.g., ABA) from individual policies.[61] Unlike previous cases under state mental health parity laws, this one had a big effect. The decision prompted the state insurance commissioner to direct all state-regulated private health plans to provide coverage in 2015 and to reconsider all claims denied since 2006 on the basis of a blanket exclusion.

One study has found that the states that have enacted mandates are more prosperous than those that have not.[62] Of the dozen states that had not passed mandates by the end of 2015, eight had median family incomes below the national level.[63] (For much of American history, the South has lagged behind the rest of the country, and five of the non-mandate states—Alabama, Georgia, Mississippi, North Carolina, and Tennessee—were in the Confederacy.) Arguably, this situation compounds the problem of inequality: families in the non-mandate states are poorer to begin with, and the lack of insurance coverage means that parents of autistic children have to pay more out of pocket.

Autism Speaks and other groups have made a major lobbying effort in these remaining states. They have won support from conservative officials who would generally oppose greater government regulation. As noted earlier, Republican Thom Tillis backed an autism mandate when he was speaker of the North Carolina House, and he raised the issue in his successful 2014 race for the U.S. Senate. In Mississippi, Republican secretary of state Delbert Hosemann campaigned for an autism mandate with a lengthy e-mail quoting autism parents.[64] In Georgia, Josh McKoon, a state senator sympathetic to the Tea Party movement, argued that a mandate would be fiscally conservative: "The whole notion that an ounce of prevention is worth a pound of cure comes into play here. Yes, the state is mandating this coverage. But the indirect tax that is levied through the mandate—the taxpayer comes out way ahead."[65]

One important legislative development affects families in every state. Under the Affordable Care Act, most health insurance may not deny, limit, exclude, or charge more for coverage to anyone based on a preexisting condition, including autism. All marketplace health plans and most other private insurance plans must cover preventive services for children without charge. This requirement includes autism screening for children at eighteen and twenty-four months.[66]

So although some states had yet to pass a mandate as 2015 began, many autism advocates thought that events were moving their way. But with kludgeocracy, nothing is ever that smooth.

INSURANCE COVERAGE: THE FINE PRINT

The previous section noted that state governments have primary responsibility for regulating insurance. There is, however, an exception with huge consequences for the coverage of autism treatment. Sixty-one percent of Americans with employer-sponsored health insurance are in a self-funded plan, in which the employer takes direct financial responsibility for enrollees' medical claims.[67] Employers that self-fund typically contract with an insurance company to run the plan. Workers then get cards that bear the name of the insurance company and often look just like those from a traditional plan, so many do not even know that they are in a self-funded plan.[68] Most of the time, the distinction makes little difference—unless the employees are seeking coverage for a family member with autism. The catch is that the *state mandates do not apply to self-funded plans*. A federal law (the Employee Retirement Income Security Act of 1974, or ERISA) exempts self-funded plans from most state insurance laws, including mandated benefits. When South Carolina passed its mandate, the Unumb family was in a self-funded plan, so Ryan could not benefit from Ryan's Law. As lawyers, the Unumbs knew about this exception all along, but for many autism families in states with insurance mandates, it comes as an unpleasant surprise.

Most large employers are self-funders, though some (e.g., Bank of America, Comcast, Nike, and Novartis) have voluntarily included coverage of behavioral health treatment for autism in their employee health plans.[69] To make things more complicated, there is an exception to the exception in state insurance regulation. State and local governments usually self-fund, but they are not subject to ERISA, and some states have specifically required autism coverage for state employees. Still, the great majority of workers in self-funded plans do not have access to autism coverage.

Another limitation of the state mandates stems from the Affordable Care Act. The law seeks to discourage state mandates that exceed its "essential health benefits" requirements. If a state has passed a mandate since 2011 that applies to individual and small group plans, it has to pick up the additional premium cost. In about half of the states, autism coverage is part of essential health benefits, usually because the state mandated coverage before 2012 and thus it became part of that state's "benchmark" plan. Says Lorri Unumb: "For the most part, the states that have passed autism mandates post Dec. 31, 2011, have excluded ACA-compliant plans from the mandate."[70]

The details of insurance mandates vary from state to state. Many have age limits and caps on what insurers have to pay. Because the Affordable Care Act forbids annual dollar limits on essential health benefits, insurers in these states may be able to convert these limits into non-dollar limits (such as a cap on the number of ABA sessions each year).[71] Unumb writes of a visual aid that she and her husband designed: "We set to work designing a double-wheel that would show the 50 states on the big outer wheel and the various types of health insurance on the inner wheel. Only if you're lucky enough while spinning both wheels do you get coverage for the treatments your child needs."[72]

There are no exact figures available, but suppose that we take the total number of autistic people and subtract the following:

- Those in states without mandates;
- Those who live in states with mandates but are under exempt, self-funded plans;
- Those with individual and small group policies to which post-2011 mandates do not apply; and
- Those who have already gone over the various limits and caps.

The remainder surely makes up a minority of the autistic population. For those who still do qualify, the road to coverage has still been treacherous. Pointing to the array of services available under IDEA and state laws, insurers have long held that autism is an educational issue, not a medical one. Autism advocates counter that while it has educational dimensions, its place in the DSM settles its status as a medical issue. One complication, however, is that autistic people get most of their treatments and therapies from providers who are not medical doctors. Behavior analysts, who usually have advanced degrees in psychology or a related field, draw up and supervise treatment plans for providing ABA. Although there is a national organization that credentials behavior analysts (the Behavior Analyst Certification Board), only nineteen states have laws providing for their licensing and certification in their own right.[73] Moreover, the day-to-day delivery of ABA is typically in the hands of therapists or behavior technicians, who need not have any college degree. Insurers have sometimes balked at paying for their services, but as one California court put it: "It appears that ABA, and similar behavior therapies, are somewhat unique among medical treatments in this respect.

While the treatment plan must be created, modified, and supervised by a professional, a paraprofessional may actually deliver the services."[74]

In 2011, New York passed an insurance mandate to great fanfare. The following year, its Department of Financial Services issued a rule requiring that ABA practitioners get a state license to qualify for insurance reimbursement. At the time, New York *had no ABA license*, so the only providers who could qualify were certified behavior analysts who *also* held a New York State license in psychology, psychiatry, or social work.[75] Only a few dozen people met this requirement, and not all of them specialized in autism: accordingly, the rule effectively gutted the mandate. After pressure from autism parents, the legislature had passed legislation to roll back the rule, and the department withdrew it. The legislature then passed another bill for licensing of behavior analysts.

Sometimes the friction comes from other professionals. Shortly after West Virginia enacted a mandate in 2011, its Board of Examiners of Psychologists passed a rule requiring all behavior analysts to be under the supervision of a licensed psychologist at all times. The rule would have stopped ABA for many West Virginians, for as one behavior analyst explained, "There aren't a ton of psychologists in the state who have any training (in autism)."[76] Under threat of a lawsuit and adverse political reaction, the board backed down.

Dealing with insurance companies can be daunting. In a 2014 survey, 55 percent of ABA service providers said that insurance companies' operating restrictions and guidelines implemented by insurance companies were challenging, and thirty-one reported that insurance companies were denying services from board-certified behavior analysts.[77] After Michigan passed its mandate in 2012, Blue Cross-Blue Shield of Michigan required that children get a diagnosis not from their own provider, but from board-certified behavior analysts at approved evaluation centers—of which, in 2012, there were only three in the state. The number has since grown to ten, but for many patients, the wait usually ranges from twelve to eighteen months. "Between Medicaid and Blue Cross, the systems have created a bottleneck that prevents children from accessing services," said the head of a mental health nonprofit.[78]

In New Jersey, parents testified about their problems at a 2013 legislative hearing. Particularly telling was the testimony from parents who were also medical professionals. "I'm a medical doctor and the issues with coding were so involved I had to hire someone to help me," said oral surgeon Meredith Blitz-Goldstein. Pharmacologist Gina Pastino said: "The amount of time that is required is so out of bounds and unreasonable, I've had to take vacation days to take care of some of these things. I can appeal these claims one by one, but at some point something has to change. I am going to go out of my mind."[79]

Once parents get past all the red tape, they often find that providers are scarce. Rural states may be especially short on behavior analysts, who tend to prefer to work in large metropolitan areas that have greater educational and technological resources. If psychiatric help is necessary, it may be hard to get. There is a shortage of child psychiatrists, and insurers are of little help in finding them. When the *New Haven Register* called several doctors' offices listed on Aetna's website as "Psychiatry, child and adolescent," they found none who actually treated preteen children. One doctor said of the rosters of providers issued by insurance companies, "Their lists are never correct."[80] More generally, psychiatrists are less likely than other physicians to accept insurance. A national survey found that barely half said they accepted private insurance and only 43 percent accepted Medicaid.[81]

A related issue involves more than twenty-six thousand military families with autistic children who get coverage of applied ABA and related services through Tricare, the Defense Department's health care system for active duty and retired uniformed service members and their families.[82] In 2014, the department started the Comprehensive Autism Care Demonstration, which reorganized earlier programs and lifted caps on ABA coverage. At the time, the Pentagon also proposed to slash payments for providers. Fearing that behavior analysts would drop Tricare patients, families took part in protests and persuaded lawmakers to object to the payment cuts.[83] The Pentagon then backed off, at least temporarily, pending a review of payment policy. In any case, payments are not the only challenge for military families, who have to deal with constant relocations. They frequently move to places where service providers are few or waiting lists are long. As one mother explained to researchers, it is impossible to maintain therapeutic continuity: "Next year, we'll probably be moving again. To where, I have no idea. . . . You can't really keep any continuity with your therapist, which is an issue because you kind of want that. It would be ideal. Like with nonmilitary families with kids with autism, they can have the same provider, get the rapport going, and make great strides."[84]

ADULTS AND THE CLIFF

When disabled people reach their twenty-second birthday, they no longer qualify for services under IDEA. "We always say at the age of 21 the (school) bus stops coming," says Nina Wall, the director of Pennsylvania's autism services.[85] "They put so much effort and wonderful work into the school experience and for most people all that work all that effort all that wonderful enriching experience just disappears," says autism parent Linda Ster. "They don't even understand it, it's like how come I'm not going to school and I'm sitting at home with mom watching TV all day long."[86]

People in the disability community refer to this point in life as "the cliff." Once autistic people go over the cliff, they have a hard time getting services such as job placement, vocational training, and assistive technology. IDEA entitles students to transition planning services during high school, but afterward, they have to apply as adults and establish eligibility for state and federal help. One study found that 39 percent of young autistic adults received no service at all, and most of the rest got severely limited services. [87]

In 2012, the U.S. Government Accountability Office identified forty-five programs that support employment for people with disabilities. [88] At first blush, this figure may make it seem as if there is a generous menu of options for autistic people, but in fact, most of the programs have a narrow scope or work with other clienteles. (Nineteen of the programs target military veterans, a group that includes few people on the spectrum.) This fragmented system serves mostly to create confusion, like an intricate roadmap where nearly every route comes to a dead end. People with autism and their families often do not know where to turn. [89]

Although employment and training programs are available through Medicaid waivers, few of the waiver programs specifically target autistic adults. Some other state programs exist, and not surprisingly, services are limited and the waiting lists are long. In Pennsylvania, for instance, the only two state-funded programs for autistic individuals over twenty-one are the Adult Autism Waiver and the Adult Community Autism Program. In 2012, the two programs served 456 autistic adults out of an estimated population of 7,000. [90] As for the people who do get access to such programs, there is some evidence that the training and coaching is helpful, but the research is limited and the measurement of outcomes is imprecise. [91]

Compared with young people with other disabilities (speech/language impairment, learning disability, or intellectual disability), young autistic people have the highest risk of being completely disengaged from any kind of postsecondary education or employment, with the figure topping 50 percent for the first two years after high school. [92] As we have seen throughout this book, inequality comes into play. An autistic person who leaves high school and comes from a high-income family is *seventeen times more likely* to find employment than one from a low-income family, all other things being equal. [93]

Supplemental Security Income (SSI) may provide monthly cash payments to people whose disabilities prevent them from having gainful employment. To be eligible, an individual must not have greater than $2,000 in countable assets and must have a limited monthly income. Once a disabled person turns eighteen, the income and assets of family members do not count toward the limit even if the individual still lives at home. In most states, beneficiaries are automatically eligible for medical coverage under Medicaid. Some parents and autistic people may not be fully aware of SSI benefits, and for those who are, the red tape is frustrating.[94]

In the past, federal law posed a problem for families making plans for children with disabilities. For nondisabled children, parents could save up toward vocational training or college tuition through tax-advantaged "529" plans. Financial advisers warned them not to set up such accounts for their disabled children: they might someday need SSI or Medicaid, and the account would breach the $2,000 asset limit. This catch had the perverse effect of making it harder for disabled people to afford the education and training that might enable them to avoid or get off these programs. In 2014, Congress addressed this problem with the Achieving a Better Life Experience (ABLE) Act. The new law enabled people to set up "ABLE accounts" for disabled beneficiaries. As with the existing 529 accounts, earnings on an ABLE account do not count as taxable income for either the contributor or the beneficiary. Within certain limits, assets in an ABLE account and distributions from the account for qualified expenses will no longer count when determining the qualified beneficiary's eligibility for Medicaid, SSI, and other federal means-tested benefits. The ABLE Act is obviously a boon to autistic people whose friends or families can chip in to the accounts. It does less for poor children, who may not have any loved ones who can afford to give.[95]

Getting health care is a quandary for autistic people as they age from adolescence to adulthood. "Once patients move away from their pediatricians, they struggle," says Dr. Christopher Hanks, an autism expert at Ohio State University. "These patients often miss out on important check-ups, immunizations and cancer screenings. It's also important to note that without specialized care, these individuals can have a hard time transitioning into an intimidating world."[96] Coping with change is a challenge, and the switch to a new doctor can be disturbing. Noting that she did not even know who her child's next doctor would be, one mother said: "You think it's hard now. . . . It gets much, much harder for our children [after they turn eighteen]. . . . Our child had no chance to meet this person, no chance in a safe environment with their old doctor to get comfortable with the [new] doctor. Unfortunately [health care] kind of really sucks for our children."[97]

Although pediatricians have made an effort to understand autism, other primary care providers might not be as sensitive to the issue. Another mother said: "Every time we do have to switch doctors, we have to re-educate the doctor [about] our child. He may understand the big picture of Autism, what's on the handouts. But when you're talking about Autism, we're talking about complete individuality with our children. . . . All children with ASD are not going to look the same."[98]

In a statement to a Senate committee, a middle-aged man with autism in the Pacific Northwest addressed overloaded support systems in the field of mental health. "The focus in my region is on mental health and substance abuse recovery, not dealing with developmental disabilities. . . . I have experienced first-hand how little is known about helping individuals with developmental disabilities. Most of us are in mental health systems that often admit they have had little or no training in working with people like me."[99]

Relatively few are living in the large institutions that were once the final destination of so many people with developmental disabilities. The *Olmstead* decision, mentioned earlier, requires placement in "integrated settings" when the individuals are medically cleared, they express a desire for such settings, and the resources are available. *Olmstead* assumed that states would provide long-term services and supports through home- and community-based services. Again, autistic adults often face long waiting lists. State officials reported that an estimated 110,039 people with intellectual and developmental disabilities were waiting for residential services in 2012.[100]

Even when people with disabilities leave institutions or get off the waiting list, their new homes may be troubled. Under the terms of a 2010 settlement with the Justice Department, Georgia agreed to move all disabled people from psychiatric hospitals to community homes. At least three-fourths of the facilities received citations for violating standards of care or have been subject to investigation for patient deaths or abuse and neglect. For 482 people who moved into group homes between 2010 and 2014, forty died, and at least thirty of those deaths were unexpected.[101]

For those who remain at larger residential institutions, the horrors of yesteryear have generally ended. In 2012, however, a ten-year-old video surfaced, showing disturbing images of an electric shock device at the Judge Rotenberg Center in Canton, Massachusetts. Staffers tied one student to a restraint board and shocked him thirty-one times over seven hours, ignoring his screamed pleas to stop. The Rotenberg Center is the only one in the nation that admits to using electric shocks on people with developmental disabilities, including autism. Center officials said that they had stopped using restraint boards but insisted that shocks were necessary in extreme cases to prevent people with severe disorders from hurting themselves or others. Though a majority of the FDA's Neurological Devices Panel said that such devises pose "an unreasonable and substantial risk of illness or injury," the agency had not banned them as of 2014.[102]

OUTCOMES

There has been surprisingly little research on outcomes for autistic adults on such measures as employability, self-sufficiency, and social support—and that thin literature is discouraging.[103] One useful snapshot of the state of autistic America is the 2008 "Living with Autism" study by Easter Seals. Based on a Harris survey of 1,652 parents of children with autism and 917 parents of typically developing children, the study offers some sobering statistics. Relatively few autism parents thought that their children will be able to:

- Make his or her own life decisions (14 percent compared to 65 percent of parents with typically developing children)
- Have friends in the community (17 percent compared to 57 percent of typical parents)
- Have a spouse or life partner (9 percent compared to 51 percent of typical parents)
- Be valued by their community (18 percent compared to 50 percent of typical parents)
- Participate in recreational activities (20 percent compared to 50 percent of typical parents)

The study found that many parents report they're "financially drowning." Seventy-four percent of parents of children with autism fear their children will not have enough financial support after they die, while only 18 percent of typical parents share this fear. Seventy-six percent worry about their child's future employment, when only 35 percent of typical parents share this fear.[104] Others, like Robert McCarthy, point to the kludgeocracy: "As a lawyer in Montgomery County, I handle a great many cases involving disabled children and adults, and even I frequently get confused by the process. Imagine an average parent trying to navigate the disjointed system that exists."[105] Autism blogger Kristina Chew writes of her adolescent son:

> A number of agencies at the state and federal levels (Departments of Developmental Disabilities, Medicaid, Social Security) oversee programs that Charlie is "eligible" for. The problem is, he may not be able to get a spot in the program or group home that best accommodates his needs. In New Jersey, the waiting list for housing for individuals with developmental disabilities has over 8,000 people on it. The estimated wait time to get a residential placement is 15 years. As a state worker once explained to me, the only reason someone gets off the list is because of "an emergency"—the sudden illness or death of his or her parents.[106]

Another autism mother and blogger follows up with this sobering reflection on mortality: "As a parent, anytime that autism is mentioned in conjunction with your child, one of your initial thoughts is 'I can't die.' It's horrible. You can't die, you have to live one day longer than your child because who is going to look after your child the same way you do?"[107] But someday, every autism parent will die. And soon, the current large generation of autistic youths will become an equally large generation of autistic adults.

Chapter Six

The Future

In 1858, Abraham Lincoln said: "If we could first know where we are, and whither we are tending, we could better judge what to do, and how to do it."[1] There is much that we do not know about the past and present of autism, so we should tread lightly in forecasting its future. But with varying degrees of confidence, we can make some guesses about things to come.

The number of people with a stake in the issue is going to mount. I am not saying that there will be a true increase in the prevalence of autism. As we saw in chapter 3, it is unclear how much of the apparent change involves awareness and diagnostic standards. Even if there has been a true increase in recent decades, there is no way of knowing whether it will go on. But the rise in the number of autism diagnoses and educational determinations will translate into a growing population of people who have lived with the autism label, and who think of themselves as autistic. Most in this category will have family members and other people who are close to them. They may be guardians or caregivers, or they may just be friends and relatives with a deep concern. Either way, autism will be part of their lives, too. Overall, the share of Americans who know someone with autism will surely top the 39 percent recorded in 2008. One study found that 60 percent of respondents in Northern Ireland knew someone with autism in their own family, circle of friends, or coworkers.[2] There is no reason to think that the figure would be lower in the United States.

In certain ways, new generations of autistic people will be better off than those in the past, when schools could bar them completely and many ended up in hellholes like Willowbrook. Americans are more accepting of disabilities than they were in the days when Franklin D. Roosevelt had to hide his paralysis from the electorate.[3] Laws such as the Americans with Disabilities Act mean that autistic people have access to opportunities that were once off-limits to them. Because of these changes in attitudes and policies, more have been able to get an education and benefit from behavior therapies.

"Better than the past" is different from "satisfactory." Problems lie ahead, in part because of past successes. Autistic adults are now often in a position to seek employment, only to find that their deficits in communication and social skills limit their job prospects. They are theoretically free to live wherever they want, but when they cannot find work, their actual choices are few. Amid their rising numbers, there will be more demand for services related to autism, especially as their parents grow too old to help.

In any upcoming policy debates, autistic people will have more political resources than they did in the twentieth century. Decades ago, they were isolated from the people around them, and they had no way of knowing that there were others like them all over the country. Today they are not alone. They understand who they are, and thanks in part to social media, they are better able to reach one another. Together with their friends and relatives, they could be an increasingly significant force in public policy debates. We may expect them to press for legislative and judicial action in areas such as housing, employment, and higher education.[4]

Scientific and medical advances are trickier to forecast. For decades, the media have regularly reported autism "breakthroughs" that later withered under scrutiny. Nevertheless, scientific knowledge of autism is moving forward, if only bit by bit. New discoveries and technologies are bound to raise ethical issues, and much more than in the past, autistic people will be weighing in on them. Research may reduce certain areas of uncertainty, but it will not make autism politics any simpler or less contentious.

TSUNAMI: AUTISM, AGING, AND DEMOGRAPHICS

Two demographic trends will influence autism politics in the coming decades. First, the identified autistic population will get bigger, particularly in the adult range. Service providers refer to this coming change as a "tsunami," after a large ocean wave that is barely visible when it moves over deep water but packs great power when it hits land. Second, the general population will be getting older just as the autism tsunami arrives, complicating the policy response.

In the 2012–2013 school year, about half a million students between the ages of three and twenty-one received services for autism under IDEA. By the year 2031, all of them will have passed their twenty-second birthday, which means that they will have "aged out." Joining them will be a number of autistic people who were in school during the 2012–2013 year but were not receiving IDEA services.[5] It is likely that many people in the latter group will eventually get an official label, as more and more people are getting a diagnosis of autism during adulthood. (Here I mean assessments by professionals, not casual self-identification.) A Danish study found that people diagnosed between the ages of twenty-one and sixty-five account for about 9 percent of the new cases, a proportion that has increased over time.[6] It bears repeating that such statistics do not necessarily tell us about true changes in prevalence. "If the incidence [in adults] is increasing, it just has to do with recognition of cases that have been missed up to that age," says leading autism expert Eric Fombonne. "It cannot be that you develop autism at age 50."[7]

Figures from Pennsylvania give additional hints about the future of autism. The state's Department of Public Welfare reports that the number of adults with autism receiving services was 6,113 in 2011, an increase of 334 percent since the state's original 2005 count. As more children grow to adulthood and more adults receive diagnoses, the department reckons the figure to top 36,000 by 2020, and 73,592 by 2030.[8]

There will still be a budgetary impact. Just as the increase in educational determinations caused an upsurge in special education spending, the growth of the identified adult population will affect spending on adult services. When today's autistic schoolchildren grow up, says one estimate, the annual cost to governments for their care will reach $18 billion in current dollars— on top of the cost for adults already in the system. According to the same analysis, some 200,000 additional full-time workers will be necessary for this new wave of autistic adults—again, over and above current staff.[9]

Do not take such estimates as gospel. On the one hand, they might be too pessimistic. Many people who today have an autism label would have a different label in the past, so at least some of the apparent increase in autism service spending may represent a shift from other categories, such as intellectual disability. Moreover, the rising generation of autistic people has grown up since the expansion of educational services in the 1990s. Children who benefited from intensive early intervention are just now entering adulthood, and the long-term effects of these interventions will be clear in the years ahead.[10] Whether or not they lose the autism diagnosis, they could have better outcomes than past generations, so they might not need the same level of adult services. A number of them will have jobs, so they will be paying taxes and contributing to the economy in other ways.

On the other hand, the estimates could be *understating* the challenge. One study found that although autism symptoms and behaviors often improve during adolescence, progress slows after high school. The slowdown is especially severe for youths from disadvantaged families, suggesting that higher-income families might be arranging jobs or educational opportunities that keep their children's progress on track.[11] In the future, therefore, a lot of autistic adults may still need a lot of help. And that help could be more expensive, especially for more severely impaired people who require assistance with daily activities. The huge baby boom generation is now enter-ing old age, so the number of Alzheimer's patients will soar.[12] Competition for suitable workers could drive up the costs of care.[13] And those costs will rise just as overall government budgets are getting tighter. The aging of the baby boom generation will mean fewer workers paying taxes and more sen-iors drawing benefits, simultaneously squeezing revenues and expenditures at all levels of government.[14] "People assume the state will be there to help with their child," financial planner John Nadworny says, "but that's a really risky bet."[15]

Right now, parents take on much of the caregiving responsibility. A 2014 study looked at the living arrangements of autistic people aged twenty-one to twenty-five. Compared with young adults with other disabilities (learning disabilities, intellectual disabilities, or emotional disturbances), those with autism were more likely to have lived with a parent or guardian (87 percent) and less likely ever to have lived independently (16 percent) since leaving high school.[16] One California regional center serves five thousand adult cli-ents who live with their parents. "And every one of those clients will age," says the center's executive director. "People who grew up in our system are now middle-aged, and their parents are older." Adds Frances Gracechild, the executive director of Sacramento's Resources for Independent Living, "We have this phenomenon of aging parents with increasing need for support themselves, and they're still taking care of their grown developmentally dis-abled children. It's quite a burden to meet when you're facing your 70s."[17]

A special needs trust is one way parents can offer their adult autistic children a degree of security. Such a trust enables disabled people to have an unlimited amount of assets available for their benefit. Like ABLE accounts, special needs trusts do not disqualify their beneficiaries from SSI and other programs. The catch is that they are not the beneficiaries' property and they require trustees to run them. Parents usually act as the trustees while they are alive and well, and they name "contingent trustees" to take over in case of their own disability or death. The work is demanding, and one parent asks rhetorically: "How do you ask even a close family member to shoulder what we have taken on?"[18]

The trusts also have other problems, which will become more prominent as more aging parents take advantage of them. For one thing, some trustees turn out to be untrustworthy. Former surrogate judge Kristin Booth Glen says: "The problem is if the trust is for a person with a significant intellectual disability and the person who created the trust, the parent, or whoever, is dead, and the trustee is not acting appropriately, who is going to challenge it? Not the person with the significant intellectual disability who has a serious communicative disorder and is in an institution."[19] Federalism also comes into play, because the regulation of these trusts falls within the jurisdiction of state governments. Families may have to revise them if they move across state lines. Special needs trusts are subject to taxation, and they can be costly and time-consuming to set up and maintain. State legislators will have to address these problems in the years ahead.

Special needs trusts do little to resolve the problem of inequality, since poor people do not have many assets to pass along in the first place. The wealth gap appears to be widening. Between 2000 and 2011, median net worth rose for the top 40 percent of households and fell for the bottom 60 percent.[20] The median wealth of white households was ten times that of Hispanic households in 2013, compared with eight times the wealth in 2007.[21] The Hispanic population is growing faster than the white population, so there will also be an increasing number of Hispanic people with autism. Compared with non-Hispanic whites, they are more likely to be poor and less likely to have received an early diagnosis and good schooling.[22] The upshot is that there will be many more Hispanic adults with autism who are in serious need.

HIGHER EDUCATION AND EMPLOYMENT

Alongside these demographic changes are economic and labor trends that will pose challenges for autistic people.

By most measures of economic well-being, young college graduates surpass their peers with less schooling. And this disparity is greater than in earlier generations.[23] To some extent, then, the fate of autistic people hinges on their ability to get college degrees. About a third of autistic high school graduates eventually go on to some kind of postsecondary education, at least for a while.[24] That rate is higher than one might have expected years ago, but lower than for all other disability groups except intellectual disabilities or multiple disabilities.[25] The numbers are increasing, largely because early identification and intervention have enabled autistic students to advance farther than before. "Behavioral therapy at an early age has really opened doors," said a Ventura College instructor who has worked with ASD students for many years.[26] The ABLE Act will also reduce some of the economic barriers to college attendance. Unfortunately, we know very little about autistic students' completion rates or the quality of their education.

We do know that autistic students suffer high levels of depression, anxiety, and social isolation.[27] We also know that their difficulties can affect their academic performance. (Group projects can be hard.) They have to cope with these problems without the protection of an IEP, since the Individuals with Disabilities Education Act does not apply to higher education. The Americans with Disabilities Act (ADA) and Section 504 of the Rehabilitation Act of 1973 provide for certain accommodations (for instance, extra time for tests), but the student has to seek them. According to Jane Brown

Thierfeld, codirector of an organization of professionals who assist autistic students, for every student receiving special services, there are one or two on that same campus who have not come forward.[28]

Once again, we see the dilemma of difference. When students do not disclose their autism, their work could suffer because they are passing up accommodations and supports that they need. When they do disclose, however, they reasonably worry that administrators and faculty members will look at them differently.[29] They might wonder: will asking for extra time on an exam affect what the professor says about me on a letter of recommendation?

Some colleges go beyond legal requirements in providing special services to autistic students, thereby raising another dilemma of difference. A supportive environment might help students make it through senior year, but does such a setting prepare them for the not-always-supportive world beyond? Though college is not nearly as regimented as grade school or high school, it still offers students a great deal of structure in the form of academic calendars, catalogs, dorm rooms, and cafeterias, among others. The transition to an adult life without these things is tough enough for any graduating student, and it is especially difficult for autistic students who have relied on additional help and guidance. Finding work and organizing their everyday lives usually proves to be a tough challenge.[30]

The continued growth in white-collar and service-sector employment (where job descriptions routinely stress interpersonal skills) creates obstacles for people with deficits in social communication.[31] As one autistic person told the *Huffington Post*, "The conveyor belt of traditional employment puts you at a huge disadvantage with high-functioning autism, because you talk the way you do, and that's an automatic strike one."[32] In the workplace as in college, disclosure involves the dilemma of difference. Writes Katherine Bouton, an author with a hearing impairment: "If you announce your condition, you risk being stigmatized; if you keep it a secret, you risk poor performance reviews or even being fired."[33] In a report on barriers to self-sufficiency among the disabled, the Senate Committee on Health, Education, Labor, and Pensions mentioned the problems of several autistic adults.[34] These accounts are worth quoting at length:

- A young man with autism learned that revealing his disability would often cause more problems for him rather than allow him to work with his supervisors to develop accommodations. When describing disclosing his autism to his manager he said, "I once disclosed to a manager confidentially because I thought it would make things easier, only to have her tell the rest of the management team and have them 'very concerned' about it. This was the one job I had a union rep, and he told them it had nothing to do with my job and that was not something she was supposed to go around telling everyone, not that that did much at that point. I did get the message to stop telling people."

- One middle-aged man with autism said, "I have had more 15-minute interviews than I can count with people who were impressed with my credentials on paper but were crestfallen to find they belonged to me. Most recently, I failed in a group interview process even though the director personally recruited me."

- A young woman with autism also highlighted the lack of understanding regarding accommodations and prejudice for those who request accommodations. She said, "[If you] need an accommodation like working in a quiet corner with less bright lighting . . . you're almost guaranteed to not get hired."

If such cases end up in court, autistic plaintiffs might have a steeper climb than people with other disabilities. When paraplegics seek ramps to accommodate their wheelchairs, they can often count on the understanding of judges and juries. Autistic people, by contrast, have an "invisible" disability, and the accommodations that they seek may seem odd to people unfamiliar with the condition. One autistic worker at a rehabilitation center refused to drive a company van because she smelled deodorant in it, which she could not stand. A supervisor scolded her, and the resulting argument led to her firing. A court found that the altercation was a personality clash and that her sensory issues did not result in a substantial limitation under the Americans with Disabilities Act.[35] Legal expert Daniela Caruso writes: "It is clear that autism advocacy has changed the judicial discourse on autism, but the reality of integrating this particular disability in the workforce remains plagued by the endemic fuzziness of ADA standards, exponentially complicated by the fuzziness of autism science itself."[36]

Some businesses make an extra effort to hire autistic people, and voluntary organizations provide autistic adults with coaching and job search help: one particularly innovative group is the Autism Job Club of the San Francisco Bay Area.[37] Such initiatives could have a lasting impact on the people who take part. One study found that autistic adults who are in jobs with a greater degree of independence have greater reductions in autism and are more likely to gain greater self-sufficiency in daily living.[38] So far, these programs benefit only a sliver of the adult autistic population, but they will probably reach many more in the years ahead.

DANGERS

As more people with an autism label head out into the larger world, they are likely to run into many dangers, some stemming from the beliefs and prejudices of nondisabled people.

There is no evidence linking autism to planned violence, but in recent years, mass shootings by young men have led commentators in the mainstream media and on the Internet to suggest such a connection. After the 2007 Virginia Tech massacre, for instance, news reports said that the shooter was on the spectrum. The speculation made little sense to anyone who understood autism. Whereas autistic people have language delays and deficits, the killer had learned English as a second language—and learned it well enough to major in the subject in college. Later on, it turned out that he had an entirely different problem, a social anxiety disorder.[39] Adam Lanza, who committed the Sandy Hook massacre in 2012, may have had an Asperger's diagnosis, but his father emphasized that his behavior stemmed from the psychiatric illnesses that he also had.[40] Nevertheless, the media speculated about Lanza's place on the spectrum, which worried autism parents. One mother of an autistic child wrote: "This is the first time I'm truly afraid for him. Afraid of what may happen to my son with autism at the hands of a stranger; a stranger who has chosen to buy into the media-fueled misinformation that individuals diagnosed with an Autism Spectrum Disorder are dangerous and capable of horrendous acts of terror and violence."[41]

Some media accounts claim that people with autism are seven times more likely than nondisabled people to come into contact with the police. This figure is an urban myth, deriving from a misreading of an old article about people with intellectual and learning disabilities.[42] A recent literature review concludes that people with autism spectrum disorder "do not seem to be disproportionately over-represented in the criminal justice system.[43] Nevertheless, more autistic adolescents and adults are out in the world, and their interactions with law enforcement can go very wrong.

Autistic people may have poor eye contact or engage in repetitive behaviors, which may strike police officers as suspicious. They also might be slow to react to police commands, which can cause a routine stop to spin out of control. In Greenville, South Carolina, one news account tells of an autistic man named Tario Anderson: "Officers said they saw Anderson walking on the sidewalk and tried to question him. They said when they put a spotlight on Anderson, he put his hands in his pockets, started walking the other way and eventually started running from them. He was shocked with a Taser and arrested because he didn't follow the officers' commands."[44] Anderson is also African American, which adds another dimension to the story. In the wake of incidents in which African Americans had died at the hands of white police officers, one father wrote of his autistic son: "What if my son pulling back from a cop is seen as an act of aggression? What if a simple repetitive motion is mistaken for an attempt at physical confrontation? If a cop is yelling at my son and he doesn't respond because he doesn't understand, what's stopping the cop from murdering my boy in cold blood?"[45]

In response to such concerns, many police departments have trained officers and other first responders how to spot signs of autism and respond accordingly.[46] Some organizations have also published identification cards that ASD adults can carry in order to defuse potential conflicts. Virginia provides for an autism designation on driver's licenses and other state-issued identification cards. Once again, however, the dilemma of difference comes into play. One autistic Virginian worries: "Great, so if I get into an accident, who's the cop going to believe, the guy with the autistic label or the guy without it?" Clinical psychologist Michael Oberschneider is concerned about the understanding level of first responders: "I think many people still think of Rain Man or, more recently, the Sandy Hook Shooter, when they think of autism even though very few people on the autistic spectrum are savants or are homicidal and dangerous."[47]

A related dilemma involves children. In some communities, parents seek the posting of "Autistic Child" signs, similar to the "Blind Child" or "Deaf Child" signs that appear in many places. The idea is to enable motorists to spot children who may be wandering or who are unaware of traffic dangers. Such signs pose two problems. First, because of the variability of autism symptoms, it might be hard for motorists to know which children are autistic and how to respond to a particular autistic child. Second, signs might backfire badly by drawing the attention of child predators. "I totally sympathize with the impulse," says one autism advocate. "The No. 1 cause of death for children with autism is drowning and traffic accidents. . . . I am more worried about singling their kids out and making them vulnerable to people who aren't trustworthy."[48]

People with disabilities are victims of violent crime three times as often as people without disabilities.[49] The Bureau of Justice Statistics does not report separately on autistic victims, but it does note that the victimization rate is especially high among those whose disabilities are cognitive. A small-sample study of Americans and Canadians found that adults with autism face a greater risk of sexual victimization than their peers. Autistic respondents were more than twice as likely to say that they had been the victim of rape and over three times as likely to report unwanted sexual contact.[50]

Sometimes family members commit crimes against autistic people, including murder. In 2013, the mother and the caregiver of fourteen-year-old Alex Spourdalakis allegedly killed him by stabbing him four times in the chest. They had undergone great difficulty in dealing with his health issues, which had been the subject of a video by Andrew Wakefield.[51] A few months later, a Michigan mother named Kelli Stapleton blogged about her struggles with her sometimes-violent autistic fourteen-year-old daughter: "I have to admit that I'm suffering from a severe case of battle fatigue."[52] Shortly afterward, she tried to kill herself and her daughter by lighting charcoal grills in a closed van during a supposed campaign trip. A sheriff's deputy found them unconscious. The mother suffered little harm, but the daughter was in a coma for three days and ended up with brain damage.

In both cases, and others like them, some in the media felt sorry for the suspects, arguing that the struggle with autism had pushed them to the breaking point. Television's Dr. Phil ran a segment titled "Kelli Stapleton: A Mother's Worst Nightmare," calling her "one of the most desperate human beings I had ever talked to."[53] Self-advocates and their allies responded strongly, arguing that sympathizing with alleged perpetrators amounts to devaluing the lives of the victims. The Autistic Self Advocacy Network (ASAN) said that "Dr. Phil offered an abusive and murderous parent a platform, with no regard for the consequences to her victim—or the potential copycat effects."[54]

What if a disabled person *wants* to die? Oregon, Vermont, and Washington have legalized physician-assisted suicide, and a 2014 survey found that 54 percent of physicians agree with such laws, up from 46 percent in 2010.[55] Among the general public, approval is even higher, at 74 percent.[56] Support for legalizing assisted suicide may reflect experiences with loved ones who have struggled through pain and incapacitation with no hope of getting better. Disability rights groups, however, are leery of "right to die" laws, believing that the real issue is another kind of right. "The difference is your health or disability status. Then suddenly suicide is a rational decision," says Diane Coleman, president and CEO of Not Dead Yet, a disability rights organization. "We think equal rights should also mean equal rights to suicide prevention."[57] Advocates of the laws say that their goal is to uphold personal autonomy and reduce suffering, not eradicate disability per se. Groups such as ASAN counter that this distinction is without a difference, since many nondisabled people *equate* disability with suffering. As for autonomy, they argue that many behavior therapies teach autistic people to be compliant. "As a result, many Autistic adults are in the habit of going along with whatever their doctors, therapists, and guardians feel is right," says Kate Ryan of ASAN.[58]

CHANGING ATTITUDES, CHANGING POLITICS

In spite of these disturbing issues, we should not assume widespread hostility toward autistic people. To the contrary: although polling numbers on the subject are meager, some signs point toward increasing goodwill. For one thing, more positive depictions of autism are showing up in popular culture.

Tom Angleberger, author of a wonderful series of comic novels for older children, says that he is on the spectrum, like the central character of the books: "In many ways I feel like the kids that read the book are understanding Dwight, even if they don't realize exactly what his condition is."[59] The television series *Parenthood* depicted an adolescent coming to grips with Asperger's. On the FX crime series *The Bridge*, Diane Kruger played a detective who was on the spectrum. In preparing for the role, she consulted extensively with autistic blogger Alex Plank. Kruger said of her character: "She is very good at her job because she's obsessive when it comes to murder and serial killers. Part of that is because she is on the [autism] spectrum and crime is her passion. . . . People look up to her because she has the ability to focus."[60] Claire Danes won an Emmy for portraying Temple Grandin in a 2010 television movie. In the film's climactic speech, she says: "Everyone worked hard to make sure that I was engaged. They knew that I was different, but not less."

Support from the general public will be an important political asset for autistic people. Another will be their sheer numbers, since a larger population of identified autistic adults will mean more autistic voters and activists. In 2013, the Youth Transitions Collaborative conducted the first-ever national survey of the political views of people with disabilities, their families, and caregivers.[61] (Unfortunately, the published survey data did not separate the responses of the disabled people and nondisabled caregivers.) More than eight in ten respondents said that having a record of supporting services and programs for people with disabilities would affect their vote choice. Eighty-seven percent said they would consider voting against a candidate they otherwise supported who was in favor of cuts to services, and 45 percent said they definitely would.

For most of the issue's history, the "disease frame" dominated public deliberation about autism. From this viewpoint, autism is an illness that we must fight and cure. Another perspective—that autism is a difference or disability that requires accommodation—appears to be gaining ground as more self-advocates join the political fray. One small indication of this shift came when lawmakers changed the name of the Combating Autism Act to the Autism CARES Act. "It was a sign that Congress and many of the autism advocacy organizations that argued in favor of that rhetoric within the legislation lacked any respect for the views of autistic adults," said Ari Ne'eman, president of the Autistic Self Advocacy Network. "Autistic people and a growing number of our families do not see ourselves as something to be combated."[62]

Another signal was a 2013 public apology by Easter Seals for a message using the disease frame: "On Tuesday, we sent you an email about autism and we owe you an apology. We called autism an epidemic and some of you called us out on our language. You're right. Autism is not an epidemic.

Autism is not a public health crisis."[63] In the same vein, *Los Angeles Times* journalist Michael Hiltzik walked back from language that he used in a 2014 story. "I have been taken to task, properly, for referring to autism above as 'a terrible condition for its sufferers and their families.' That's a narrow and ill-informed way of looking at a condition that many people on the autism spectrum feel has benefited their lives."[64]

Those who regard autism as a difference favor a change in research priorities. Autistic author John Elder Robison argues that that the current emphasis on genetics is misplaced:

> I'm a big believer in science, and I absolutely understand that genetics may one day solve the riddle of why some people have spontaneous genetic mutations that lead to severe intellectual disability. It's led to some important discoveries and it will surely be key to more. But how many individuals who live with intellectual disability today will be helped by that? How many autistic job seekers will get a job, thanks to that work? How many autistic kids who wander dangerously will suddenly become safe? How many autistics that suffer from anxiety or gastric distress will suddenly relax in comfort? Those are a few of the very real issues autistic people are actually thinking about now, and genetics isn't one of the answers on tomorrow's table.[65]

Instead he proposes a focus on practical applications to help autistic people in the near term. The medical community could learn better ways to ease co-occurring conditions such as depression, seizure disorders, sleep disorders, and intestinal distress. Engineers could find more solutions to things that many autistic people cannot do naturally. Handheld tablets now enable formerly nonverbal people to communicate, and other technologies could help them read expressions. "Computers can improve anyone's quality of life," he says, "but we stand to benefit more than most from applied technology."[66]

As the ranks of autistic adults continue to increase, we might expect support for this perspective to grow. We should not expect unanimity in the autism community, however. For one thing, some autistic people have a different view. Autistic novelist Jonathan Mitchell has stirred deep controversy by saying, "I hate it. It's a horrible disability. I wish there were a cure."[67] For another thing, the parent perspective will remain significant, and there will still be many parents who love their children without loving their autism. Jody Allard, the mother of two autistic children, has serious disabilities herself. "I do not believe that my self-worth is found in my fingers or my genes, and I have no trouble reconciling the fact that I am both abnormal and worthwhile," she writes. "Perhaps this is why I simply do not understand the push for autism to be considered just another variation of normal. Or something to be merely accepted, without searching for treatment, prevention or even a cure."[68]

SCIENCE AND THE FUTURE

Early on, this book contrasted the simple model of the policy process with the messy reality of autism. In the simple model, science settles many issues by answering factual questions. In the real world, as we have seen, scientific findings are often ambiguous, incomplete, and subject to diverse interpretations. Furthermore, advances in science can raise as many questions as they resolve. No one knows for sure what scientists will learn about autism in the decades to come, but their discoveries could create new conflicts and issues.

Start with the very idea of autism.[69] In the 1940s, Leo Kanner saw it as a specific and rare disorder. By the 1990s, we were talking about an "autism spectrum." Now scientists are suggesting that it will turn out to be a set of related but distinct conditions. "We believe a better term to use is 'the autisms,' or 'the autism spectrum disorders' (that is, plural)," geneticist Stephen W. Scherer says. "There are many different forms of autism. In other words, autism is more of a collection of different disorders that have a common clinical manifestation."[70] Suppose, then, that new findings in genetics and brain science allow us to identify these autisms more clearly. Suppose further that, because of this research, DSM-6 or DSM-7 replaces "autism spectrum disorder" with a group of diagnoses. This change would probably benefit autistic people by allowing for better targeting of behavioral, educational, and medical interventions. People with "type A" autism would get one course of treatment, while people with "type B" would get another, and so on.

Politically, there might be a downside. Notwithstanding many disputes over strategy, tactics, and policy, the autism label provides people across the spectrum with a shared identity. Autistic people with graduate degrees believe that they have something in common with nonverbal autistic people who score low on IQ tests. Their parents also feel a sense of kinship. They may fight among themselves, but they have been through many of the same struggles and sometimes wear caps proclaiming "Proud Autism Dad" or "Keep Calm, I'm an Autism Mom." "The autisms" could strain these ties by leading people in each group to see themselves as fundamentally different from the others. To the extent that each group needs different kinds of intervention, there could also be competition for scarce funding in research and treatment.

Even more divisive issues could arise from discoveries in genetics. Although DNA tests for autism still lie in the future, we already know that having one child with autism means a greater chance that subsequent children will have it, too.[71] Families of children with autism are well aware of this finding, and they are about one-third less likely than other families to have more children.[72] "Reproductive stoppage," however, is not their only option. As we saw in chapter 3, autism prevalence is greater among boys than girls. Accordingly, autism parents could try in vitro fertilization in order to choose the sex of their next baby and opt for a female embryo to lessen the chance of autism.[73] There are no data on how many families take this route, but a number of fertility clinics mention the autism issue on their websites, suggesting that there is interest among potential clients.[74]

Consider the next possible step for in vitro fertilization. Suppose that scientists refine pre-implantation screening so that they could tell whether a particular embryo's genetic makeup entails a high probability of autism. If so, then doctors would presumably discard it in favor of another embryo that they would implant in the mother's womb. Some say that we need to debate the use of such techniques to screen for autism.[75] Ethicist Wesley J. Smith disagrees: "That is like saying allowing eugenic cleansing for racial features is a debate we need have: Both are invidiously discriminatory and have no place in an enlightened, *equality-believing* society."[76]

When a pregnancy is under way, doctors can detect certain kinds of disorders, but neither amniocentesis nor any other prenatal test can currently tell us whether a fetus will become autistic. Suppose that such a test did exist. "The best case use of a prenatal test at the moment would be if you could say to a parent, your child has got an 80 percent likelihood of autism and so once the baby's born, we would like to keep a close eye on that child in case they need extra support like speech therapy or social skills training or some sort of behavioral approach," says leading autism scientist Simon Baron-Cohen.[77] But would the "best case use" be the most common? When amniocentesis indicates Down syndrome, most mothers choose abortion.[78] A study of autism parents in Taiwan found that just over half would abort if a prenatal test indicated that their next child would be autistic.[79] We cannot be sure what the figures would be if such tests were available in the United States, but it seems likely that a large share of autism pregnancies would end in abortion.

The politics of the issue would be complicated, to say the least. For decades, the broader disability rights movement has had an uneasy relationship with the movement to curb abortion. On the one hand, selective abortion angers disability rights activists, with some using terms such as "eugenics" and "genocide." On the other hand, many of these activists also believe that the right to control one's own body is a thread that connects disability rights and abortion rights.[80] The growing ranks of identified autistic adults could be as conflicted as their elders in the disability rights movement. But it is also possible that they could change the issue's political landscape by coming down heavily on one side or the other. Expect pro-life and pro-choice groups to vie for their support.

Most people can easily see how genetic testing and abortion lead to bitter arguments. But newcomers to the autism world are often surprised that there are also deep divides over the search for a "cure." I put the word in quotation marks for a couple of reasons. First, scientists still have not come up with a final and comprehensive definition of autism. The various editions of the DSM have offered evolving lists of symptoms, but there is still no consensus on autism's underlying biology. Identifying a set of "autisms" might lend some clarity, but until then, it is very hard to cure something when you cannot say exactly what the "something" is.

Second, although scientists have yet to draft a roadmap to the condition, they do understand that it is not something narrow and specific that they can simply cut out, as with a tumor. Instead, it seems to involve multiple brain structures and nearly every neurological process.[81] If this understanding is correct, "curing" autism would essentially mean rewiring the whole brain. Philosopher Jami Anderson says the implications are grotesque, given that personal identity has roots in brain structure. "Indeed, the autistic person's very being—who they are (their memories, their desires, wishes, hopes, plans) and what they can become—would be altered by this so-called *cure*."[82] But R. Eric Barnes and Helen McCabe are less willing to reject a cure: "Drastic alterations in personality don't inherently make a treatment wrong. Curing a drug addict will drastically alter her personality, but this does not make it unethical. Of course, this does not imply that it is right to treat PWA [people with autism] in ways that will drastically alter their personality, only that a drastic effect on personality is not adequate reason to shun a cure."[83]

Of course, this discussion is speculative, since we do not know if such a "cure" is possible or what it would look like if it were. And so we end where we started, with uncertainty.

WHAT WE NEED TO KNOW

A key question in autism policy evaluation is simple to pose, hard to answer: How do autistic people benefit? How much better off are they as a result of government action? While there are studies of the short-term impact of various therapies, there is surprisingly little research about the long term, which is really what autistic people and their families care about. As we saw in chapter 4, few studies have focused on the educational attainment of autistic youths. For instance, we do not know much about what happens to them in high school, apart from the kinds of classes that they take.[84] One study searched the autism literature from 1950 through 2011 and found just thirteen rigorous, peer-reviewed studies evaluating psychosocial interventions for autistic adults. The effects of were largely positive, though the main finding of the review is that there is a need for further development and evaluation of treatments for adults.[85]

Paul M. Shattuck and Anne M. Roux note that large businesses mine "Big Data" to measure performance and improve quality. "We need a correspond-

ing measurement revolution for ASD services, including employment supports. An abundance of opportunities exist for collaborating with community
agencies to create practice-based evidence. Scientists with advanced training
in measurement and analysis methods are uniquely positioned to be useful in
this endeavor."[86] They propose more research on social networks, workplace
policies, and the ways in which successful employment programs benefit
businesses and communities, as well as those on the autism spectrum.

Nearly every page of this book has suggested unanswered questions.
Some may not even be answerable. Without a time machine, for instance, we
will probably never have any good way to measure autism prevalence in past
decades.

But there is a big research question that does not require devices from
science fiction: what do autistic people themselves think about autism policy
and politics? Activists in this field have contributed greatly to our understanding of the subject. What is missing is the voice of the rank and file.

One survey found that autistic respondents rejected the idea of a cure but
also accepted efforts to address the deficits that go along with the condition.[87] It is hard to know whether these findings are representative of autistic
opinion, however, since the sample was self-selected and its demographic
characteristics did not match those of the autistic population as a whole.
More survey research is necessary. Granted, such research will be very difficult because of the practical hurdles to sampling autistic people. Diagnoses
and educational determinations are confidential, and many respondents
would require assistive devices in order to answer questions.

Still, the effort is worth making. After decades of talking about autism as
a deficit of communication, people who make and study policy should listen
as autistic people speak for themselves.

Appendix

A Timeline of Autism Policy and Politics

1910

Swiss psychiatrist Eugen Bleuler introduces the term *autism*.

1943

American psychiatrist Leo Kanner publishes "Autistic Disturbances of Affective Contact," identifying autism as a childhood psychiatric disorder.

1944

Austrian pediatrician Hans Asperger publishes an article on "autistic psychopathy" in childhood. It will not be available in English until 1991.

1949

Leo Kanner writes "Problems of Nosology and Psychodynamics of Early Childhood Autism," in which he identifies a "maternal lack of genuine warmth" in autism cases. He says that autistic children "were kept neatly in refrigerators which did not defrost." This phrase is the birth of the idea of "refrigerator mothers."

1950

Representatives of state associations of parents of mentally retarded children meet in Minneapolis to found the Association for Retarded Children of the United States, later the Association for Retarded Citizens and then "the Arc."

1954

In *Brown v. Board of Education of Topeka* (347 U.S. 483), the U.S. Supreme Court rules that separate schools for black and white children are inherently unequal and unconstitutional. This decision becomes a catalyst for the African American civil rights movement, which in turn becomes a template for the disability rights movement.

1959

Scientific American publishes "Joey: A Mechanical Boy," Bruno Bettelheim's case study of an autistic boy who acted like a machine. Bettelheim draws attention to the mother's "total indifference."

1960

Leo Kanner brings the "refrigerator mother" theory to a broader audience when he tells *Time* magazine that autism is often the product of parents "just happening to defrost enough to produce a child."

1961

President Kennedy appoints a special President's Panel on Mental Retardation.

The June 17 issue of the *Saturday Evening Post* carries an article by Rosalind Oppenheim, "They Said Our Child Was Hopeless," about her autistic son's struggle with autism. "We pray and work, too, for the estimated 500,000 mentally handicapped children who are receiving no treatment and have not even had diagnosis because there is no place to get it."

1962

British psychiatrist Lorna Wing founds the National Autistic Society in the United Kingdom.

1963

President Kennedy, in an address to Congress, calls for a reduction in the number of people confined to residential institutions, and he asks that methods be found "to retain in and return to the community the mentally ill and mentally retarded, and there to restore and revitalize their lives through better health programs and strengthened educational and rehabilitation services." Though JFK does not use the word, he is calling for deinstitutionalization.

Congress passes the Mental Retardation Facilities Construction Act of 1963 (P.L. 88-164—later the Developmental Disabilities Act), authorizing federal support for the construction of mental retardation research centers, university-affiliated training facilities, and community service facilities for children and adults with mental retardation.

1964

Dr. Bernard Rimland publishes *Infantile Autism: The Syndrome and Its Implications for a Neural Theory of Behavior.* The book details the clinical features of autism, along with evidence that it is a biological disorder.

1965

Bernard Rimland and Ruth Christ Sullivan found the National Society for Autistic Children, later the Autism Society of America.

Lyndon Johnson signs the Elementary and Secondary Education Act (P.L. 89-10), deepening the federal role in education policy, and the Social Security Amendments of 1965 (P.L. 89-97), creating Medicare and Medicaid.

Psychologist Ole Ivar Lovaas develops applied behavior analysis. The May 7 issue of *Life* gives it national publicity in "Screams, Slaps, and Love: A Surprising, Shocking Treatment Helps Far-Gone Mental Cripples."

1967

Bernard Rimland founds the Autism Research Institute in San Diego.

Bruno Bettelheim publishes *The Empty Fortress: Infantile Autism and the Birth of the Self.* "Throughout this book," he writes, "I state my belief that the precipitating factor in infantile autism is the parent's wish that his child should not exist."

1969

California assemblyman Frank Lanterman introduces Assembly Bill 225, the Lanterman Mental Retardation Services Act, extending regional center services throughout California.

1970

President Richard Nixon signs the Elementary and Secondary Education Act Amendments of 1970 (P.L. 91-230), creating the Education of the Handicapped Act (EHA). Part B authorizes grants to states for the education of children with disabilities. EHA also establishes several competitive grant programs such as personal preparation, research, and demonstration.

President Nixon also signs the Developmental Disabilities Services and Facilities Construction Amendments of 1970 (P.L. 91-517), containing the first legal definition of "developmental disabilities."

1971

In *PARC v. Pennsylvania*, the U.S. District Court for the Eastern District of Pennsylvania enjoins Pennsylvania from applying any statute that would postpone, deny access, or terminate a free appropriate public education to any child with mental retardation. The consent decree also includes important language on the "least restrictive environment."

1972

In *Mills v. Board of Education*, the U.S. District Court for the District of Columbia rules that no child should be excluded from public school on the basis of any DC policy or rule unless the child is offered an alternative educational program suited to meet his or her needs. Further, the court rules that each child is entitled to a free appropriate public education regardless of the degree of disability. Like *PARC v. Pennsylvania*, this case provides a template for the Individuals with Disabilities Education Act.

The parents of residents at the Willowbrook State School file suit (*New York ARC v. Rockefeller*) to end the appalling conditions at that institution. A television broadcast from the facility outrages the general public. This press exposure, together with the lawsuit and other advocacy, eventually moves thousands of people from the institution into community-based living arrangements.

1973

President Nixon signs the Rehabilitation Act of 1973 (P.L. 93-112). Section 504 says: "No otherwise qualified handicapped individual in the United States, shall, solely by reason of his handicap, be excluded from the participation in, be denied the benefits of, or be subjected to discrimination under any program or activity receiving federal financial assistance."

Assemblyman Frank Lanterman authors Assembly Bill 846 expanding the regional center mandate to include other developmental disabilities. In addition to persons with mental retardation, the centers are now mandated to serve people with cerebral palsy, epilepsy, autism, and other neurological handicapping conditions closely related to mental retardation.

Marian Wright Edelman founds the Children's Defense Fund.

1975

Congress passes the Education for All Handicapped Children Act (PL 94-142) (EAHCA) requiring public schools receiving federal funds to provide disabled students a free appropriate public education in the least restrictive setting.

The Developmental Disabilities Assistance and Bill of Rights Act (P.L. 94-103) creates a "bill of rights" for persons with developmental disabilities, funds services for persons with developmental disabilities, adds a new funding authority for university-affiliated facilities, and establishes a system of protection and advocacy organizations in each state. It lists autism by name as one of the disabilities mandated to be served.

The Association of Persons with Severe Handicaps is founded by special education professionals in response to PARC and other right-to-education cases. This organization calls for the end of aversive behavior modification and the closing of all residential institutions for people with disabilities.

1977

American psychiatrist Susan Folstein and British psychiatrist Michael Rutter publish a study of autistic twins, providing evidence that autism has a genetic basis.

1980

The third edition of the *Diagnostic and Statistical Manual* (DSM-III) includes autism.

1981

British psychiatrist Lorna Wing introduces the term *Asperger's syndrome.*

As part of an omnibus spending bill, Congress creates the Medicaid Home and Community-Based Services Waiver.

1982

In *Board of Education of the Hendrick Hudson Central School District, Westchester County, et al., Petitioners v. Amy Rowley, by her parents, Rowley et al. Respondent* (458 U.S. 176), the U.S. Supreme Court narrows the scope of EAHCA. "The Act's legislative history shows that Congress sought to make public education available to handicapped children, but did not intend to impose upon the States any greater substantive educational standard than is necessary to make such access to public education meaningful."

1984

In *Smith v. Robinson* (468 U.S. 992), the U.S. Supreme Court rules that a handicapped child cannot receive an award of attorney's fees upon prevailing in an action to secure a free appropriate public education (FAPE). It also asserts that a child cannot claim Section 504 as the basis for FAPE.

1985

The U.S. Supreme Court rules, in *Burlington School Committee v. Massachusetts Dept. of Education* (471 U.S. 359 (1985)), that schools must pay the expenses of disabled children enrolled in private programs during pending litigation under the EAHCA, if the courts rule such placement was needed to provide the child with an appropriate education in the least restrictive environment.

Margaret Bauman and Thomas Kemper publish a study that, for the first time, links specific brain abnormalities with autism.

1986

Congress passes PL 99-660, the National Childhood Vaccine Injury Act, to limit the liability of vaccine makers due to vaccine injury claims. The law creates the National Vaccine Injury Compensation Program, setting up a claim procedure involving the U.S. Court of Federal Claims.

The Handicapped Children's Protection Act (P.L. 99-372) overturns *Smith v. Robinson* and authorizes courts to award reasonable attorney fees to parents who prevail in due process proceedings and court actions under part B of the Education of the Handicapped Act.

Congress passes the 1986 Amendments (P.L. 99-457) to the EAHCA. It extends the guarantee to a FAPE to children with disabilities, ages three to five, establishes early intervention programs (EIP) for infants and toddlers with disabilities, ages zero to two, and provides for an individualized family service plan (IFSP) for each family with an infant or toddler with disabilities.

1988

The Civil Rights Restoration Act (P.L. 100-259) amends the Rehabilitation Act's definition of an individual with a disability and defines coverage of Section 504 as broad (e.g., extending to an entire university) rather than narrow (e.g., extending to just one department of the university) when federal funds are involved.

The movie *Rain Man*, starring Tom Cruise as Charlie Babbitt and Dustin Hoffman as his autistic brother Raymond, introduces the subject of autism to millions.

1989

Michael Rutter, Ann LeCouteur, and Catherine Lord publish an assessment for people suspected of having autism, called the Autism Diagnostic Interview (ADI).

1990

President George H. W. Bush signs the Americans with Disabilities Act (P.L. 101-336) in a ceremony on the White House lawn including thousands of disability rights activists. The law is the most sweeping disability rights measure to date. It mandates that local, state, and federal governments and programs be accessible, that businesses with more than fifteen employees make "reasonable accommodations" for disabled workers, and that public accommodations such as restaurants and stores make "reasonable modifications."

The Individuals with Disabilities Education Act Amendments (IDEA) (P.L. 101-476) renames the Education of the Handicapped Act and reauthorizes programs under the act to improve support services to students with disabilities, especially in the areas of transition and assistive technology. Autism becomes a separate category in IDEA for special education.

Doreen Granpeesheh founds the Center for Autism and Related Disorders.

Bruno Bettelheim commits suicide.

1994

The fourth edition of the *Diagnostic and Statistical Manual* (DSM-IV) lists five pervasive developmental disorders: autistic disorder, Asperger's disorder, Rett's disorder, childhood disintegrative disorder, and pervasive developmental disorder-not otherwise specified (PDD-NOS).

The National Alliance for Autism Research is established by Karen and Eric London.

1995

Portia Iversen and Jonathan Shestack found Cure Autism Now.

1996

The Mental Health Parity Act of 1996 (P.L. 104-204) includes a provision that prohibits insurance companies from having lower lifetime caps for treatment of mental illness compared with treatment of other medical conditions.

1997

The Individuals with Disabilities Education Act Amendments of 1997 (P.L. 105-17) includes the first major changes to part B since enactment in 1975, extends the early intervention program, and includes a significant streamlining of the discretionary programs.

Richard Pollak reveals in *The Creation of Dr. B.*, the Bruno Bettelheim biography, that the "refrigerator mother" and "undemonstrative father" theory was not backed by sufficient evidence.

1998

Dr. Andrew Wakefield and others publish a controversial study in *The Lancet* about bowel symptoms of MMR-vaccinated children diagnosed with autism spectrum disorders.

1999

Two studies in *The Lancet* conclude that there is no link between MMR shots and autism.

In *Olmstead v. L.C. ex rel. Zimring* (527 U.S. 581 (1999)), the U.S. Supreme Court rules that the Americans with Disabilities Act requires placement of mentally disabled patients in "integrated settings" when they are medically cleared for such settings, they express a desire for such settings, and the necessary resources are available.

2000

President Clinton signs the Children's Health Act (P.L. 106–310), founding the Interagency Autism Coordinating Committee (IACC). The bill also calls for the National Institutes of Health (NIH) to establish centers of excellence in autism research and strengthens federal autism surveillance activities to track the prevalence of autism.

The Coalition for Safe Minds is founded.

The NIH estimates that autism affects one in five hundred children.

Andrew Wakefield tells the House Government Reform and Oversight Committee that there is "compelling evidence" of a link between vaccines and autism.

2001

NIH estimates that autism affects one in 250 children.

Representatives Christopher Smith (R-NJ) and Mike Doyle (D-PA) propose the Congressional Autism Caucus.

2002

The Federal Vaccine Injury Compensation Program receives compensation requests in which parents claim that some vaccines are causing autism.

2003

The U.S. Centers for Disease Control and Prevention (CDC) finds there is no direct link between thimerosal and autism.

The National Autism Association is founded.

Michael Carley founds the Global and Regional Asperger Syndrome Partnership.

2004

The Lancet announces a partial retraction of the 1998 paper, on grounds of "a fatal conflict of interest"—the *Sunday Times* has reported that Dr. Wakefield received £55,000 from the Legal Aid Board for research to support legal action by parents who claimed that their children had been harmed by MMR.

2005

Autism Speaks is founded.

2006

There are about three hundred thousand children diagnosed with autism in the United States, according to the CDC.

Ari Ne'eman and Scott Michael Robertson found the Autistic Self Advocacy Network.

President Bush signs P.L. 109-416, the Combating Autism Act of 2006.

Autism Speaks merges with the National Alliance for Autism Research.

2007

CDC now estimates that autism affects one in 150 U.S. children.

The Senate designates April as National Autism Awareness Month.

Autism Speaks completes merger with Cure Autism Now.

2010

Special masters appointed by the Court of Federal Claims soundly reject the claim that vaccines cause autism.

Britain's General Medical Council bans Andrew Wakefield from the practice of medicine. *The Lancet* retracts his 1998 article on vaccines.

2012

CDC now estimates that autism affects one in eighty-eight U.S. children.

2013

In the fifth edition of the *Diagnostic and Statistical Manual* (DSM-5) autism spectrum disorder encompasses Asperger's disorder, childhood disintegrative disorder, and pervasive developmental disorder-not otherwise specified (PDD-NOS).

2014

CDC now estimates that autism affects one in sixty-eight U.S. children.

President Obama signs the Autism CARES Act (P.L.) 113-157, a reauthorization of the Combating Autism Act. The name change reflects objections from self-advocates.

President Obama signs tax legislation (P.L.113-295) that includes the ABLE Act, providing for tax-advantaged disability savings accounts.

2014–2015

A measles outbreak draws negative attention to the anti-vaccine movement.

Notes

PREFACE

1. Lydia Brown, "The Significance of Semantics: Person-First Language: Why It Matters," *Autistic Hoya*, August 4, 2001. Online: autisticadvocacy.org/identity-first-language/.
2. Kathie Snow, "A Few Words about People-First Language," *Disability Is Natural*. Online: www.disabilityisnatural.com/images/PDF/pfl-sh09.pdf.

1. INTRODUCTION

1. Andrew Solomon, *Far from the Tree: Parents, Children, and the Search for Identity* (New York: Scribner, 2012), 222.
2. Deborah Stone, *Policy Paradox: The Art of Political Decision Making*, 3rd ed. (New York: W.W. Norton, 2013), 34–36.
3. Ariane V. S. Buescher, Zuleyha Cidav, Martin Knapp, and David S. Mandell, "Costs of Autism Spectrum Disorders in the United Kingdom and the United States," *JAMA Pediatrics*, published online June 9, 2014. Online: autismsciencefoundation.org/sites/default/files/Costs%20of%20Autism%20JAMA%20June%202014.pdf. The figure is the sum of the estimates for children ($61 billion) and adults ($175 billion) with autism in the United States under the assumption that 40 percent have intellectual disabilities. If that percentage is higher, so is the aggregate cost.
4. Comments of Ari Ne'eman, Interagency Autism Coordinating Committee, meeting transcript, July 16, 2010. Online: iacc.hhs.gov/events/2010/transcript_071610.pdf.
5. Susan E. Levy, David S. Mandell, and Robert T. Schultz, "Autism," *The Lancet* 374 (November 2009): 1627–38.
6. Greg Boustead, "IMFAR 2013: Autism or 'Autisms'?" Simons Foundation Autism Research Initiative, May 6, 2013. Online: sfari.org/sfari-community/community-blog/2013/imfar-2013-autism-or-autisms.
7. Research is under way to develop such screening tools. Lauren M. Turner Brown et al., "The First Year Inventory: A Longitudinal Follow-Up of 12-Month-Old to 3-Year-Old Children," *Autism* 17 (September 2013): 527–40. Online: aut.sagepub.com/content/17/5/527.

8. Terisa P. Gabrielsen et al., "Identifying Autism in a Brief Observation," *Pediatrics* 135 (February 2015): e330–e338. Online: pediatrics.aappublications.org/content/early/2015/01/07/peds.2014-1428.full.pdf+html.

9. In 2009, 48 percent did so, which was actually more than double the level of 2002. Linda Radecki et al., "Trends in the Use of Standardized Tools for Developmental Screening in Early Childhood: 2002–2009," *Pediatrics* 128, no. 1 (July 1, 2011): 14–19.

10. Amy Sudhinaraset and Alice Kuo, "Letter: Parents' Perspectives on the Role of Pediatricians in Autism Diagnosis," *Journal of Autism and Developmental Disorders* 43 (March 2013): 747–48. Online: link.springer.com/content/pdf/10.1007%2Fs10803-012-1591-z.pdf.

11. Nancy D. Wiseman, *The First Year: Autism Spectrum Disorders: An Essential Guide for the Newly Diagnosed Child* (Cambridge, MA: Da Capo Lifelong Books, 2009), xx.

12. Jon Baio, "Prevalence of Autism Spectrum Disorder among Children Aged 8 Years—Autism and Developmental Disabilities Monitoring Network, 11 Sites, United States, 2010," *Morbidity and Mortality Weekly Report Surveillance Summaries* 63 (March 28, 2014): 1–21. Online: www.cdc.gov/mmwr/preview/mmwrhtml/ss6302a1.htm.

13. David Mitchell, introduction to *The Reason I Jump*, by Naoki Higashida, trans. K. A. Yoshida and David Mitchell (New York: Random House, 2013), x.

14. Jane Gross, "For Siblings of the Autistic, a Burdened Youth," *New York Times*, December 10, 2004. Online: www.nytimes.com/2004/12/10/health/10siblings.html.

15. Catherine Maurice, *Let Me Hear Your Voice* (New York: Ballantine Books, 1994), 145.

16. Tom Fields-Meyer, *Following Ezra* (New York: New American Library, 2011), 46–47.

17. Mari-Jane Williams, "Advice for Parents of Children Just Diagnosed with Autism, From Those Who've Been There," *Washington Post*, July 30, 2014. Online: www.washingtonpost.com/news/parenting/wp/2014/07/30/advice-for-parents-of-children-just-diagnosed-with-autism-from-those-whove-been-there.

18. Nancy De Gennaro, "Autism 24/7: Parents Find Paperwork a Puzzle," *Daily News Journal* [Murfreesboro, TN], March 14, 2013. Online: www.dnj.com/interactive/article/20130317/LIFESTYLE/303170032/Autism-24-7-Parents-find-paperwork-puzzle.

19. For one glossary of related terms, see San Mateo County Office of Education, "Glossary of Special Education Terminology." Online: www.smcoe.org/learning-and-leadership/special-education-local-plan-area/glossary-of-special-education-terminology.html.

20. Gary S. Mayerson, "Autism in the Courtroom," in *Handbook of Autism and Developmental Disorders*, 4th ed., ed. Fred R. Volkmar et al. (Hoboken, NJ: John Wiley & Sons, 2014), 1036–50, at 1040.

21. Taylor Lower, "As Autism Diagnoses Increase, Therapy and Treatment Services Strive to Keep Up," *The Missourian*, October 28, 2014. Online: www.columbiamissourian.com/a/179346/as-autism-diagnoses-increase-therapy-and-treatment-services-strive-to-keep-up.

22. Deborah Fein et al., "Optimal Outcome in Individuals with a History of Autism," *Journal of Child Psychology and Psychiatry* 54 (February 2013): 195–205. Online: onlinelibrary.wiley.com/doi/10.1111/jcpp.12037/pdf.

23. Benedict Carey, "Some with Autism Diagnosis Can Overcome Symptoms, Study Finds," *New York Times*, January 16, 2013. Online: www.nytimes.com/2013/01/17/health/some-with-autism-diagnosis-can-recover-study-finds.html.

24. Deanna L. Sharpe and Dana Lee Baker, "Financial Issues Associated with Having a Child with Autism," *Journal of Family and Economic Issues* 28 (June 2007): 247–64.

25. Guillermo Montes and Jill S. Halterman, "Association of Childhood Autism Spectrum Disorders and Loss of Family Income," *Pediatrics* 121 (April 2008): 821–26.

26. Laura Schieve et al., "The Relationship between Autism and Parenting Stress," *Pediatrics* 119, Supplement 1 (February 1, 2007): S114–S121. Online: pediatrics.aappublications.org/content/119/Supplement_1/S114.full.

27. Liz Collin, "Family Struggles with Complex System of Autism Care," WCCO-TV, November 5, 2014. Online: minnesota.cbslocal.com/2014/11/05/family-struggles-with-complex-system-of-autism-care.

28. Gael I. Orsmond et al., "Social Participation among Young Adults with an Autism Spectrum Disorder," *Journal of Autism and Developmental Disorders* (April 2013). Online: link.springer.com/content/pdf/10.1007%2Fs10803-013-1833-8.pdf.

29. Julie Lounds Taylor and Marsha Mailick Seltzer, "Employment and Post-Secondary Educational Activities for Young Adults with Autism Spectrum Disorders during the Transition to Adulthood," *Journal of Autism and Developmental Disorders* 51 (May 2011): 566–74. Online: www.waisman.wisc.edu/family/pubs/Autism/2010_Post_high_school_activities.pdf.

30. Lisa Croen et al., "Psychiatric and Medical Conditions among Adults with ASD," paper presented at the International Meeting for Autism Research, May 15, 2014. Online: imfar.confex.com/imfar/2014/webprogram/Paper17783.html.

31. "The Myth of Passing," *Musings of an Aspie: One Woman's Thoughts about Life on the Spectrum*, October 24, 2013. Online: musingsofanaspie.com/2013/10/24/the-myth-of-passing/.

32. John Elder Robison, "John Robison at IMFAR: On Autism Rights, Ethics, & Priorities," *The Thinking Person's Guide to Autism*, May 23, 2014. Online: www.thinkingautismguide.com/2014/05/john-robison-at-imfar-on-autism-rights.html.

33. Ido Kedar, "Out of the Closet," *Ido in Autismland*, June 23, 2014. Online: idoinautismland.com/?p=242.

34. Higashida, *The Reason I Jump*, 47–48.

35. Fields-Meyer, *Following Ezra*, 232.

36. Temple Grandin and Richard Panek, *The Autistic Brain: Thinking across the Spectrum* (New York: Houghton Mifflin Harcourt, 2013), 37.

37. People with Rett's disorder have small hands and feet and experience a slowdown in head growth. People with fragile X syndrome have distinctive facial characteristics. But Rett's and fragile X account for only a small proportion of people with ASD.

38. Catherine Rice, "Prevalence of Autism Spectrum Disorders—Autism and Developmental Disabilities Monitoring Network, 14 Sites, United States, 2002," *Morbidity and Mortality Weekly Report—Surveillance Summaries* 56 (February 9, 2007): 12–28. Online: www.cdc.gov/mmwr/pdf/ss/ss5601.pdf. An *incidence* rate is the number of *new* cases divided by the number of persons at risk. A *prevalence* rate is the *total* number of cases divided by the total population.

39. Catherine Rice, "Prevalence of Autism Spectrum Disorders—Autism and Developmental Disabilities Monitoring Network, United States, 2006," *Morbidity and Mortality Weekly Report—Surveillance Summaries* 58 (December 18, 2009): 1–20. Online: www.cdc.gov/mmwr/preview/mmwrhtml/ss5810a1.htm.

40. Jon Baio, "Prevalence of Autism Spectrum Disorders—Autism and Developmental Disabilities Monitoring Network, 14 Sites, United States, 2008," *Morbidity and Mortality Weekly Report—Surveillance Summaries* 61 (March 12, 2012): 1–19. Online: www.cdc.gov/mmwr/preview/mmwrhtml/ss6103a1.htm.

41. Stephen J. Blumberg et al., "Changes in Prevalence of Parent-Reported Autism Spectrum Disorder in School-aged U.S. Children: 2007 to 2011–2012," *National Health Statistics Reports* 65 (March 20, 2013): 1–11. Online: www.cdc.gov/nchs/data/nhsr/nhsr065.pdf/.

42. We could measure a "true increase" by measuring autism among a random sample of people at time A, then rerunning the test at time B, using exactly the same measurement and sampling technique.

43. Blumberg, "Changes in Prevalence," 5.

44. Iva Hertz-Picciotto and Lora Delwiche, "The Rise in Autism and the Role of Age at Diagnosis," *Epidemiology* 20 (January 2009): 84–90.

45. Michael Rutter and Anita Thapar, "Genetics of Autism Spectrum Disorders," in *Handbook of Autism and Developmental Disorders*, 4th ed., ed. Fred R. Volkmar et al. (Hoboken, NJ: John Wiley & Sons, 2014), 411–23.

46. Audrey F. Burgess and Steven E. Gutstein, "Quality of Life for People with Autism: Raising the Standard for Evaluating Successful Outcomes," *Child and Adolescent Mental Health* 12 (May 2007): 80–86.

47. Paul T. Shattuck and Anne M. Roux, "Commentary on Employment Supports Research," *Autism* 19 (February 2014): 246–47. Online: aut.sagepub.com/content/19/2/246.full.

48. Martin Landau, "Redundancy, Rationality, and the Problem of Duplication and Overlap," *Public Administration Review* 29 (July/August 1969): 346–58. Online: www.jstor.org/stable/973247.

49. The preferred term is now "intellectual disability." This book mentions "mental retardation" only in historical context.

50. *Board of Education of Hendrick Hudson School District v. Rowley*. 458 US 176. Online: supreme.justia.com/us/458/176/case.html.

51. Jody Heymann et al., " Constitutional Rights to Health, Public Health and Medical Care: The Status of Health Protections in 191 Countries," *Global Public Health* 8 (2013): 639–53. Online: www.tandfonline.com/doi/pdf/10.1080/17441692.2013.810765. The closest thing in federal law is the Emergency Medical Treatment and Labor Act (EMTALA), which requires Medicare-participating hospitals with emergency departments to stabilize emergency patients regardless of their ability to pay.

52. All state constitutions mention education, and some explicitly call it a right. Molly A. Hunter, "State Constitution Education Clause Language," Pennsylvania Bar Association Constitutional Review Commission. Online: pabarcrc.org/pdf/Molly%20Hunter%20Article.pdf.

53. Ruth Colker, *Disabled Education: A Critical Analysis of the Americans with Disabilities Act* (New York: New York University Press, 2013), 17–22.

54. See the excellent discussion of rights in Dana Lee Baker, *The Politics of Neurodiversity: Why Public Policy Matters* (Boulder, CO: Lynne Rienner, 2011).

55. Martha Minow, *Making All the Difference* (Ithaca, NY: Cornell University Press, 1990), 20.

56. Alexis de Tocqueville, *Democracy in America*, ed. J. P. Mayer and trans. George Lawrence (Garden City, NY: Doubleday, 1969), 270.

57. Eloise Pasachof, "Special Education, Poverty, and the Limits of Private Enforcement," *Notre Dame Law Review* 86, no. 4 (2011): 1413–93. Online: ndlawreview.org/wp-content/uploads/2013/06/Pasachoff.pdf.

58. Sarah DeWeerdt, "Researchers Call for Open Access to Autism Diagnostic Tools," Simons Foundation Autism Research Initiative, June 24, 2013. Online: sfari.org/news-and-opinion/news/2013/researchers-call-for-open-access-to-autism-diagnostic-tools.

59. Association of Professional Behavior Analysts, "APBA 2009 Professional Employment Survey Results," www.apbahome.net/survey-report-johnston.pdf.

60. Autism Health Insurance Project, "37 States Now Have Autism Health Insurance Mandates," June 18, 2014. Online: www.autismhealthinsurance.org/37-states-now-require-autism-health-insurance-mandates.

61. E. E. Schattschneider, *The Semi-Sovereign People* (New York: Holt, Rinehart and Winston, 1960), ch. 1.

62. Thomas Insel, "The Four Kingdoms of Autism," National Institute of Mental Health Director's Blog, February 26, 2013. Online: www.nimh.nih.gov/about/director/2013/the-four-kingdoms-of-autism.shtml.

63. President Barack Obama, "Remarks on Science and Technology," April 2, 2013. Online: www.presidency.ucsb.edu/ws/?pid=103411.

64. Anushka Mehrotr, "Autism Rights Activist Urges Students to Recognize 'Neurodiversity,'" *Cornell Daily Sun*, February 12, 2014. Online: cornellsun.com/blog/2014/02/12/autism-rights-activist-urges-students-to-recognize-neurodiversity/.

65. James Terminello, "Opinion: Expanded Definition of 'Autism' Goes Astray," *South Jersey Times*, May 5, 2013. Online: www.nj.com/south-jersey-voices/index.ssf/2013/05/opinion_expanded_definition_of.html.

66. Paul A. Offit, *Autism's False Prophets* (New York: Columbia University Press, 2008), xvii.

67. I am grateful to Jeremy Shane for this insight.

68. Susan Senator, "Autism Is Hard Enough—Let's Not Make It Harder with a Fight," *Cognoscenti*, January 15, 2014. Online: cognoscenti.wbur.org/2014/01/15/autism-speaks-protest-susan-senator.

2. A SHORT HISTORY OF AUTISM

1. As late as 1956, a plurality of whites thought that white and black students should go to separate schools. See NORC data in William G. Mayer, *The Changing American Mind: How and Why American Public Opinion Changed between 1960 and 1988* (Ann Arbor: University of Michigan Press, 1992), 369.

2. Aaron Wildavsky, *Speaking Truth to Power: The Art and Craft of Policy Analysis* (New Brunswick, NJ: Transaction, 1987), 3.

3. Bertram S. Brown, "A Task Force with a Goal," *Journal of Autism and Childhood Schizophrenia* 1 (January 1971): 1.

4. Roland Kuhn and Charles H. Cahn, "Eugen Bleuler's Concepts of Psychopathology," *History of Psychiatry* 15, no. 3 (2004): 361–66.

5. Adam Feinstein, *A History of Autism: Conversations with the Pioneers* (Malden, MA: Wiley-Blackwell, 2010), 10.

6. A native speaker of German, Kanner may have known of Asperger's work, but experts disagree about the extent to which it influenced his writing.

7. Leo Kanner, "Autistic Disturbances of Affective Contact," *Nervous Child* 2 (1943): 217–50. Online: neurodiversity.com/library_kanner_1943.html.

8. Leo Kanner, "Problems of Nosology and Psychodynamics of Early Infantile Autism," *American Journal of Orthopsychiatry* 19 (July 1949): 419.

9. Natalie Jaffe, "L.I. Staff Gets Through to Autistic," *New York Times*, February 22, 1966, 25.

10. "Mental Illness: The Trance Children," *Time*, August 1, 1969. Online: www.time.com/time/magazine/article/0,9171,901192,00.html.

11. James Q. Simmons III, Stanley J. Leiken, O. Ivar Lovaas, Benson Schaeffer, and Bernard Perloff, "Modification of Autistic Behavior with LSD-25," *American Journal of Psychiatry* 122 (May 1966): 1201–11.

12. Jeff Sigafoos, Vanessa A. Green, Chaturi Edrisinha, and Giulio E. Lancioni, "Flashback to the 1960s: LSD in the Treatment of Autism," *Developmental Neurorehabilitation* 10 (January–March 2007): 79.

13. Nowadays, the preferred term is "intellectually disabled." At certain points, however, this book uses the earlier term because of historical context.

14. As noted above, a more recent figure is one in eighty-eight, but I am using a more conservative assumption here.

15. I am indebted to Fred Lynch for this insight. Data are author's calculations from Matthew Sobek, "New Statistics on the U.S. Labor Force, 1850–1990," *Historical Methods* 34 (Spring 2001): 71–87, Table 1.

16. Roy Richard Grinker, *Unstrange Minds: Remapping the World of Autism* (New York: Basic Books, 2007), 73.

17. Leo Kanner, "Problems of Nosology," 425.

18. Laura Schreibman, *The Science and Fiction of Autism* (Cambridge, MA: Harvard University Press, 2005), 81.

19. "Frosted Children," *Time*, April 26, 1948. Online: www.time.com/time/magazine/article/0,9171,798484,00.html.

20. "Medicine: The Child Is Father," *Time*, July 25, 1960. Online: autismedsp5310s20f10.pbworks.com/f/Time-The+Child+Is+Father.pdf.

21. Bruno Bettelheim, "Joey: A Mechanical Boy," *Scientific American* 200 (March 1959): 117–26. Online: www.weber.edu/wsuimages/psychology/FacultySites/Horvat/Joey.PDF.

22. Bettelheim, "Joey: A Mechanical Boy," 117–18.

23. Feinstein, *A History of Autism*, 34, 48.

24. Bruno Bettelheim, *The Empty Fortress: Infantile Autism and the Birth of the Self* (New York: Simon and Schuster, Free Press, 1967), 125.

25. Richard Pollak, *The Creation of Dr. B: A Biography of Bruno Bettelheim* (New York: Simon and Schuster, Touchstone, 1997), 270–72.

26. Katherine DeMaria Severson, James Arnt Aune, and Denise Jodlowski, "Bruno Bettelheim, Autism, and the Rhetoric of Scientific Authority," in Mark Osteen, ed., *Autism and Representation* (New York: Routledge, 2008), 65–77.

27. Mitzi Waltz, *Autism: A Social and Medical History* (New York: Palgrave Macmillan, 2013), 106.

28. Eric Schopler and Robert J. Reichler, "Parents as Cotherapists in the Treatment of Psychotic Children," *Journal of Autism and Childhood Schizophrenia* 1 (January–March 1971): 87–102.

29. Bernard Rimland, "Freud Is Dead: New Directions in the Treatment of Mentally Ill Children," in Eddie H. Williams, James F. Magary, and Fred A. Moore, eds., *Ninth Annual Distinguished Lectures Series in Special Education and Rehabilitation* (Los Angeles: University of Southern California Press, 1971), 40.

30. Bernard Rimland, "The History of the Autism Research Institute and the Defeat Autism Now! Project," in Stephen M. Edelson and Bernard Rimland, eds., *Treating Autism: Parent Stories of Hope and Success* (San Diego: Autism Research Institute, 2003), 14.

31. Don Moser and Alan Grant, "Screams, Slaps, and Love: A Surprising, Shocking Treatment Helps Far-Gone Mental Cripples," *Life*, May 7, 1965, 90–101. Online: neurodiversity. com/library_screams_1965.pdf.

32. Bernard Rimland, "A Risk/Benefit Perspective on the Use of Aversives," *Journal of Autism and Childhood Schizophrenia* 8 (March 1978): 100–104, at 100–101.

33. John F. Kennedy, "Special Message to the Congress on Mental Illness and Mental Retardation." February 5, 1963. Online: www.presidency.ucsb.edu/ws/?pid=9546.

34. 29 U.S.C. 794. Online: www.law.cornell.edu/uscode/text/29/794.

35. Richard K. Scotch, *From Good Will to Civil Rights: Transforming Federal Disability Policy*, 2nd ed. (Philadelphia: Temple University Press, 2001), 24–25, 49–50.

36. Dora Zames Fleischer and Frieda Zames, *The Disability Rights Movement: From Charity to Confrontation*, updated ed. (Philadelphia: Temple University Press, 2011), 51–56.

37. Joseph M. Shapiro, *No Pity: People with Disabilities Forging a New Civil Rights Movement* (New York: Three Rivers Press, 1994), 165.

38. *Pennsylvania Association for Retarded Citizens (PARC) v. the Commonwealth of Pennsylvania* 343 F. Supp 279 (E.D. PA 1972). Online: www.pilcop.org/wp-content/uploads/2012/04/PARC-Consent-Decree.pdf.

39. *Mills v. Board of Education of the District of Columbia*, 348 F.Supp. 866 (D. DC 1972). Online: www.leagle.com/decision/19721214348FSupp866_11090.xml/MILLS%20v. %20BOARD%20OF%20EDUCATION%20OF%20DISTRICT%20OF%20COLUMBIA.

40. *Brown v. Board of Education*, 347 U.S. 483, 493.

41. U.S. Senate, Committee on Labor and Public Welfare, S. Rept. 94-168, June 2, 1975, 6. Online: files.eric.ed.gov/fulltext/ED112561.pdf.

42. Ruth Christ Sullivan, "The Politics of Definitions: How Autism Got Included in the Developmental Disabilities Act," *Journal of Autism and Developmental Disorders* 9 (June 1979): 221–31.

43. Shapiro, *No Pity,* 74–84.

44. Beth Haller, "Paternalism and Protest: The Presentation of Deaf Persons in the *New York Times* and *Washington Post,*" paper presented at the Annual Meeting of the Association for Education in Journalism and Mass Communication, Montreal, Quebec, Canada, August 5–8, 1992. Online: files.eric.ed.gov/fulltext/ED351698.pdf.

45. Trudy Steuernagel, "Increases in Identified Cases of Autism Spectrum Disorders: Policy Implications," *Journal of Disability Policy Studies* 16 (Winter 2005): 138–146, at 140.

46. H.Rept. 101-544, (June 18, 1990), 5.

47. *Congressional Record* (daily), October 15, 1990, H9632.

48. R. E. Kendell et al., "Diagnostic Criteria of American and British Psychiatrists," *Archives of General Psychiatry* 25 (August 1971): 123–30. Online: www.wpic.pitt.edu/research/biometrics/Publications/Biometrics%20Archives%20PDF/400-1971%20Kendell,%20 Coop.,%20Gour.,%20Cope.,%20Shar.,%20&%20Gurl.0001.pdf.

49. D. L. Rosenhan, "On Being Sane in Insane Places," *Science* 179 (January 19, 1973): 250–58. Online: faculty.wiu.edu/CB-Dilger/s13/483/vp/article.pdf.

50. Travis Thompson, "Autism Research and Services for Young Children: History, Progress and Challenges," *Journal of Applied Research in Intellectual Disabilities* 26 (March 2013): 81–107. Online: onlinelibrary.wiley.com/doi/10.1111/jar.12021/pdf.

51. Lorna Wing, "Asperger's Syndrome: A Clinical Account," *Psychological Medicine* 11 (February 1981): 115–29. Online: www.mugsy.org/wing2.htm.

52. Margaret Bauman and Thomas L. Kemper, "Histoanatomic Observations of the Brain in Early Infantile Autism," *Neurology* 35 (June 1985): 866–74.

53. Feinstein, *A History of Autism*, 207.

54. Feinstein, *A History of Autism*, 121.

55. Gil Eyal et al., *The Autism Matrix* (New York: Polity, 2010), 125.

56. O. Ivar Lovaas et al., "Some Generalization and Follow-Up Measures on Autistic Children in Behavior Therapy," *Journal of Applied Behavior Analysis* 6 (Spring 1973): 131–65. Online: www.ncbi.nlm.nih.gov/pmc/articles/PMC1310815.

57. O. Ivar Lovaas, "Behavioral Treatment and Normal Educational and Intellectual Functioning in Young Autistic Children," *Journal of Consulting and Clinical Psychology* 55 (February 1987): 3–9. Online: rsaffran.tripod.com/lovaas1987.html.

58. Catherine Maurice, *Let Me Hear Your Voice* (New York: Ballantine Books, 1994).

59. Eyal, *The Autism Matrix*, 101.

60. Eyal, *The Autism Matrix*, 139–40.

61. Barbara J. Nelson, *Making an Issue of Child Abuse* (Chicago: University of Chicago Press, 1984), 56–57.

62. In 2008, Professor Stanley Fish illustrated the persistence of this misunderstanding when he likened autistic people to the mutant superheroes of *X-Men*. Stanley Fish, "Norms and Deviations: Who's to Say?" *New York Times Opinionator Blog*, June 1, 2008, at opinionator. blogs.nytimes.com/2008/06/01/norms-and-deviations-whos-to-say.

63. Schreibman, *The Science and Fiction of Autism*, 45–46.

64. Gary Greenberg, *The Book of Woe: The DSM and the Unmaking of Psychiatry* (New York: Blue Rider Press, 2013), 187.

65. Grinker, *Unstrange Minds*, 140.

66. Tim Page, *Parallel Play: Growing Up with Undiagnosed Asperger's* (New York: Doubleday, 2009).

67. For a comprehensive review of prevalence estimates, see: J. G. Williams, J. P. T. Higgins, and C. E. G. Brayne, "Systematic Review of Prevalence Studies of Autism Spectrum Disorders," *Archives of Disease in Childhood* 9 (January 2006): 8–15. Online: www.ncbi.nlm. nih.gov/pmc/articles/PMC2083083.

68. Perry A. Zirkel, "Autism Litigation under the IDEA: A New Meaning of 'Disproportionality'?" *Journal of Special Education Leadership* 24 (September 2011): 92–103, at 92. Online: blogs.edweek.org/edweek/speced/Zirkel%20Article%20on%20Autism%20Litigation%20Dis proportional.PDF.

69. Morton Ann Gernsbacher, Michelle Dawson, and H. Hill Goldsmith, "Three Reasons Not to Believe in an Autism Epidemic," *Current Directions in Psychological Science* 14 (April 2005): 55–58, at 57. Online: cdp.sagepub.com/content/14/2/55.full.pdf+html.

70. Deborah Stone, *Policy Paradox: The Art of Political Decision Making*, 3rd ed. (New York: W.W. Norton, 2013), 198.

71. Allen Frances, *Saving Normal* (New York: William Morrow, 2013), 148.

72. James R. Laidler, "US Department of Education Data on 'Autism' Are Not Reliable for Tracking Autism Prevalence," *Pediatrics* 116 (July 2005): e120–e124, at e123. Online: pediatrics.aappublications.org/content/116/1/e120.full.

73. Angela S. Colson, "Framing Autism Causes and Prevalence: A Content Analysis of Television Evening News Coverage—1994 through April 2010" (master's thesis, Georgia State University, 2010). Online: scholarworks.gsu.edu/cgi/viewcontent.cgi?article=1062&context= communication_theses.

74. Sandy Kleffman, "Bewildering Increase in Child Autism Cases: Rash of Diagnoses Raises Numerous Questions," *Contra Costa Times*, February 26, 2000, A1.

75. Tracy Connor, "What's Causing Rise in Autism Cases?—Authorities Baffled by Sudden 'Epidemic,'" *New York Post*, October 10, 2000, 8.

76. For a skeptical view of "the geek syndrome," see Lizzie Buchen, "Scientists and Autism: When Geeks Meet," *Nature* 479 (November 2, 2011): 25–27. Online: www.nature.com/news/2011/111102/full/479025a.html.

77. Steve Silberman, "The Geek Syndrome," *Wired*, December 2001. Online: archive.wired.com/wired/archive/9.12/aspergers_pr.html.

78. U.S. Centers for Disease Control and Prevention, "Prevalence of Autism in Brick Township, New Jersey, 1998: Community Report," April 2000. Online: www.cdc.gov/ncbddd/developmentaldisabilities/documents/brick-report.pdf.

79. Representative Chris Smith, "Autism: A National Public Health Crisis," n.d. Online: chrissmith.house.gov/specialfeatures/autismspecialfeature.htm.

80. House Committee on Government Reform, *Autism: Present Challenges, Future Needs—Why the Increased Rates?* 106th Cong, 2d sess., April 6, 2000. Online: www.gpo.gov/fdsys/pkg/CHRG-106hhrg69622/html/CHRG-106hhrg69622.htm.

81. Susan Dominus, "The Crash and Burn of an Autism Guru," *New York Times*, April 20, 2011. Online: www.nytimes.com/2011/04/24/magazine/mag-24Autism-t.html.

82. Frank Warren, "The Role of the National Society in Working with Families," in *The Effects of Autism on the Family*, ed. Eric Schopler and Gary B. Mesibov (New York: Plenum Press, 1984), 99–115.

83. Open Secrets, "Autism Society of America," 2009. Online: www.opensecrets.org/lobby/clientsum.php?id=D000047521&year=2009.

84. Karen Reznek, "LISTSERV 25th Anniversary: LISTSERV Stories," May 17, 2011. Online: www.lsoft.com/news/listservstory.asp.

85. Eric London, "A Psychiatrist's Journey from Parent to Founder of Research Advocacy Organization." *Psychiatric Times*, November 1, 1997. Online: www.psychiatrictimes.com/psychiatrists-journey-parent-founder-research-advocacy-organization.

86. Trudy Steuernagel and Irene Barnett, "U.S. Health Social Movements and Public Policy: Autism and Alzheimer's Disease," paper presented at the annual meeting of the Midwest Political Science Association, Chicago, April 12–15, 2007. Online: citation.allacademic.com//meta/p_mla_apa_research_citation/1/9/8/5/5/pages198556/p198556-1.php.

87. U.S. Congress, House, Committee on Commerce, Subcommittee on Health and the Environment, *Children's Health: Building toward a Better Future*, 106th Congress, 1st session, October 12, 1999.

88. Csar G. Sciorano, "Ms. Russo Goes to Washington," *USA Today*, October 13, 1999, 2D.

89. Brooke Weberling McKeever, "News Framing of Autism: Understanding Media Advocacy and the Combating Autism Act," *Science Communication* 35 (April 2013): 213–40. Online: scx.sagepub.com/content/35/2/213.

90. Jack Walker, "The Origins and Maintenance of Interest Groups in America," *American Political Science Review* 77 (June 1983): 390–406.

91. Center for Responsive Politics, lobbying database, "Autism Speaks." Online: www.opensecrets.org/lobby/clientsum.php?id=D000047522.

92. Meredith Wadman, "Autism Speaks, the United States Pays Up," *Nature* 449 (August 9, 2007): 628–29. Online: www.nature.com/nature/journal/v448/n7154/full/448628a.html.

93. Jane Gross and Stephanie Strom, "Autism Debate Strains a Family and Its Charity," *New York Times*, June 18, 2007. Online: www.nytimes.com/2007/06/18/us/18autism.html.

94. See Katie Wright's posts at www.ageofautism.com/katie-wright.

95. Meredith Wadman, "Autism's Fight for Facts: A Voice for Science," *Nature* 479 (November 2, 2011): 28–31. Online: www.nature.com/news/2011/111102/full/479028a.html.

96. Rob Ring, "Vaccines and Autism," Autism Speaks, February 2015. Online: www.autismspeaks.org/science/policy-statements/information-about-vaccines-and-autism.

97. Lydia N. Bierer, "Online Community Building by Autistic Adults" (Ph.D. dissertation, University of Texas at Austin, 2013). Online: repositories.lib.utexas.edu/bitstream/handle/2152/21735/BIERER-DISSERTATION-2013.pdf.

98. Joseph F. Kras, "The 'Ransom Notes' Affair: When the Neurodiversity Movement Came of Age," *Disability Studies Quarterly* 30, no. 1 (2010). Online: dsq-sds.org/issue/view/43.

99. Claudia Wallis, "'I Am Autism': An Advocacy Video Sparks Protest," *Time*, November 6, 2009. Online: content.time.com/time/health/article/0,8599,1935959,00.html.

100. School of Psychology, Florida Institute of Technology, "First National Public Opinion Survey: Americans' Knowledge and Understanding of Autism, 2008," October 3, 2008. Online: www.thescottcenter.org/documents/doc_mgr/875/Highlights%20of%20survey%202008. pdf.

101. Hillary Clinton, "Remarks at the Autism Event with Sally Pederson in Sioux City, Iowa," November 24, 2007. Online: www.presidency.ucsb.edu/ws/?pid=77079.

102. John McCain, "Address Accepting the Presidential Nomination at the Republican National Convention in Saint Paul," September 4, 2008. Online: www.presidency.ucsb.edu/ws/? pid=78576.

103. "Presidential Candidates Debate on Autism," *Schafer Autism Report*, August 30, 2008. Online: groups.yahoo.com/neo/groups/-AuTeach/conversations/messages/3368.

104. Huma Khan, "Sharron Angle in 2009: People Have to Pay for Autism Mandate," ABC News, September 24, 2010. Online: abcnews.go.com/Politics/2010_Elections/sharron-angle-2009-people-pay-autism-mandate/story?id=11720472.

105. Daniel Strauss, "Hagan GOP Challenger Promotes Autism Group That Touted Obamacare in Ad Attacking the Law," *Talking Points Memo*, January 3, 2014. Online: talkingpointsmemo.com/dc/hagan-gop-challenger-promotes-autism-group-that-touted-obamacare-in-ad-attacking-the-law.

106. Mark Binker, "New Ad Emphasizes Tillis' Work on Autism Despite Bill's Failure," WRAL-TV, September 23, 2014. Online: www.wral.com/new-ad-emphasizes-tillis-work-on-autism/14008389.

107. Amy Harmon, "Nominee to Disability Council Is Lightning Rod for Dispute on Views of Autism," *New York Times*, March 27, 2010. Online: www.nytimes.com/2010/03/28/health/policy/28autism.html.

3. MEDICINE, SCIENCE, AND MATH

1. Richard Nelson, "*The Moon and the Ghetto* Revisited," *Science and Public Policy* 38 (November 2011): 681–90. Online: spp.oxfordjournals.org/content/38/9/681.full.pdf+html.

2. According to a July 1999 Gallup poll, only about 6 percent of the American public believed the hoax theory. Frank Newport wrote: "Although, if taken literally, 6% translates into millions of individuals, it is not unusual to find about that many people in the typical poll agreeing with almost any question that is asked of them—so the best interpretation is that this particular conspiracy theory is not widespread." Frank Newport, "Landing a Man on the Moon: The Public's View," Gallup, July 20, 1999. Online: www.gallup.com/poll/3712/Landing-Man-Moon-Publics-View.aspx.

3. Paul A. Offit, *Autism's False Prophets* (New York: Columbia University Press, 2008), 235–37.

4. Baron William Thomson Kelvin, *Popular Lectures and Addresses* (London: Macmillan, 1889), 73.

5. Gareth Williams, *Paralysed with Fear: The Story of Polio* (New York: Palgrave Macmillan, 2013), 36.

6. Nicholas Lange, "Perspective: Imaging Autism," *Nature* 491 (November 1, 2012): S17. Online: www.nature.com/nature/journal/v491/n7422_supp/full/491S17a.html.

7. Thomas Insel, "Transforming Diagnosis," *National Institute of Mental Health Director's Blog*, April 29, 2013. Online: www.nimh.nih.gov/about/director/2013/transforming-diagnosis.shtml.

8. Sarah DeWeerdt, "Culture: Diverse Diagnostics," *Nature* 491 (November 1, 2012): S18–S19. Online: www.nature.com/nature/journal/v491/n7422_supp/full/491S18a.html.

9. Allen Frances, "America's False Autism Epidemic," *New York Post*, April 24, 2012. Online: nypost.com/2012/04/24/americas-false-autism-epidemic.

10. Roy Richard Grinker, *Unstrange Minds: Remapping the World of Autism* (New York: Basic Books, 2007), 130.

11. Malinda L. Pennington, Douglas Cullinan, and Louise B. Southern, "Defining Autism: Variability in State Education Agency Definitions of and Evaluations for Autism Spectrum Disorders," *Autism Research and Treatment* (2014), Article ID 327271. Online: www.hindawi.com/journals/aurt/2014/327271/cta/.

12. For an exhaustive review of prevalence studies, see Alison Presmanes Hill, Katherine E. Zuckerman, and Eric Fombonne, "Epidemiology of Autism Spectrum Disorders," in *Handbook of Autism and Developmental Disorders*, 4th ed., ed. Fred R. Volkmar et al. (Hoboken, NJ: John Wiley & Sons, 2014), 57–96.

13. Marshall University, "West Virginia Autism Spectrum Disorders Registry." Online: www.marshall.edu/atc/wvasd-registry.

14. Candace Nelson, "State's Autism Registry Facing Difficulties in Reporting," *Charleston Daily Mail*, April 29, 2013. Online: www.charlestondailymail.com/News/201304280133.

15. Felice Freyer, "R.I. Autism Registry to Be Created with $1.2-Million Grant," *Providence Journal*, August 16, 2013. Online: www.providencejournal.com/breaking-news/content/20130816-r.i.-autism-registry-to-be-created-with-1.2-million-grant.ece.

16. Young Shin Kim et al., "Prevalence of Autism Spectrum Disorders in a Total Population Sample," *American Journal of Psychiatry* 168 (September 2011): 904–12. Online: ajp.psychiatryonline.org/article.aspx?articleid=116570.

17. Dorothy Bishop, "How Common Is Autism?" *The Guardian*, June 7, 2011. Online: www.theguardian.com/science/blog/2011/jun/07/how-common-autism-diagnosis.

18. Jon Baio, "Prevalence of Autism Spectrum Disorder among Children Aged 8 Years— Autism and Developmental Disabilities Monitoring Network, 11 Sites, United States, 2010," *Morbidity and Mortality Weekly Report Surveillance Summaries* 63 (March 28, 2014): 1–21. Online: www.cdc.gov/mmwr/preview/mmwrhtml/ss6302a1.htm.

19. David Mandell and Luc Lecavalier, "Should We Believe the Centers for Disease Control and Prevention's Autism Spectrum Disorder Prevalence Estimates?" *Autism* 18 (July 2014): 482–84. Online: aut.sagepub.com/content/18/5/482.full.

20. Ibid.

21. Marissa King and Peter Bearman, "Diagnostic Change and the Increased Prevalence of Autism," *International Journal of Epidemiology* 38 (October 2009): 1224–34. Online: ije.oxfordjournals.org/content/38/5/1224.full.

22. Irva Hertz-Picciotto and Lora Delwiche, "The Rise in Autism and the Role of Age at Diagnosis," *Epidemiology* 20 (January 2009): 84–90, at 89. Online: www.ncbi.nlm.nih.gov/pmc/articles/PMC4113600.

23. Hill, Zuckerman, and Fombonne, "Epidemiology of Autism Spectrum Disorders," 86–88.

24. Katherine E. Zuckerman et al., "Pediatrician Identification of Latino Children at Risk for Autism Spectrum Disorder," *Pediatrics* 132 (September 2013): 445–53. Online: pediatrics.aappublications.org/content/132/3/445.full.

25. Allen Frances, "Two Fatal Technical Flaws in the DSM-5 Definition of Autism," *Huffington Post*, May 25, 2013. Online: www.huffingtonpost.com/allen-frances/two-fatal-technical-flaws_b_3337009.html.

26. Matthew J. Maenner, "Potential Impact of DSM-5 Criteria on Autism Spectrum Disorder Prevalence Estimates," *JAMA Psychiatry* 71 (March 2014): 292–300. Online: archpsyc.jamanetwork.com/article.aspx?articleid=1814891.

27. John Elder Robison, *Look Me in the Eye: My Life with Asperger's* (New York: Three Rivers Press, 2008), 237.

28. Gary Greenberg, *The Book of Woe: The DSM and the Unmaking of Psychiatry* (New York: Blue Rider Press, 2013), 196.

29. Carol A. Bernstein, "DSM-5: A Year in Review and the Year Ahead," *Psychiatric News*, August 20, 2010. Online: psychnews.psychiatryonline.org/doi/full/10.1176%2Fpn.45.16.psychnews_45_16_008.

30. Luke Y. Tsai, "Asperger's Disorder Will Be Back," *Journal of Autism and Developmental Disorders* 43 (December 2013): 2914–42. Online: link.springer.com/article/10.1007/s10803-013-1839-2.

31. To this day, some leading autism scientists are also autism parents. Liz Szabo, "Autism Scientists Search for Help, for Their Own Kids' Sakes," *USA Today*, May 22, 2012. Online: usatoday30.usatoday.com/news/health/story/2012-05-21/Autism-parent-researchers/55118382/1.

32. Chloe Silverman, *Understanding Autism: Parents, Doctors, and the History of a Disorder* (Princeton: Princeton University Press, 2011), 157–58.

33. U.S. Government Accountability Office, "Federal Autism Activities: Funding for Research Has Increased, but Agencies Need to Resolve Surveillance Challenges," GAO-06-700, July 2006. Online: www.gao.gov/new.items/d06700.pdf.

34. Ibid.

35. U.S. Government Accountability Office, "Federal Autism Activities: Better Data and More Coordination Needed to Help Avoid the Potential for Unnecessary Duplication," GAO 14-16, November 2013. Online: www.gao.gov/assets/660/659147.pdf.

36. U.S. Department of Health and Human Services, Interagency Autism Coordinating Committee, "2010 Autism Spectrum Disorder Research Portfolio Analysis Report," July 2012, p. 53. Online: iacc.hhs.gov/portfolio-analysis/2010/2010_portfolio_analysis.pdf.

37. U.S. Department of Health and Human Services, Interagency Autism Coordinating Committee, "IACC/OARC Autism Spectrum Disorder Publications Analysis: The Global Landscape of Autism Research," July 2012. Online: iacc.hhs.gov/publications-analysis/july2012/chapter-one.shtml#chapter-one-themes.

38. S. 843 (109th Congress), the Combating Autism Act of 2006, passed the House by voice vote and the Senate by unanimous consent. www.govtrack.us/congress/bills/109/s843. H.R. 2005 (112th Congress), the Combating Autism Reauthorization Act of 2011, passed both houses by voice vote. www.govtrack.us/congress/bills/112/hr2005. H.R. 4631 (113th Congress), the Autism CARES Act of 2014, passed the House by voice vote and the Senate by unanimous consent. www.govtrack.us/congress/bills/113/hr4631.

39. Tom W. Smith, "Trends in National Spending Priorities 1973–2012," National Opinion Research Center, March 8, 2013, p. 31. Online: www.norc.org/PDFs/GSS%20Spending%20Priorities.pdf.

40. National Institutes of Health, "Estimates of Funding for Various Research, Condition, and Disease Categories (RCDC)," March 7, 2014. Online: report.nih.gov/categorical_spending.aspx.

41. Meredith Wadman, "Autism Speaks, the United States Pays Up," *Nature* 449 (August 9, 2007): 628–29. Online: www.nature.com/nature/journal/v448/n7154/full/448628a.html.

42. U.S. Government Accountability Office, "Federal Autism Activities: Better Data and More Coordination Needed to Help Avoid the Potential for Unnecessary Duplication," GAO-14-16, November 20, 2013. Online: www.gao.gov/products/GAO-14-16.

43. U.S. Congress, House of Representatives, Committee on Oversight and Government Reform, "Examining the Federal Response to Autism Spectrum Disorders," May 20, 2014. Online: oversight.house.gov/hearing/examining-federal-response-autism-spectrum-disorders.

44. H.R. 4631 (113th Congress), The Autism Collaboration, Accountability, Research, Education, and Support Act of 2014. Online: beta.congress.gov/bill/113th-congress/house-bill/4631/text.

45. William J. Clinton, "Statement on Signing the Children's Health Act of 2000," October 17, 2000. Online: www.presidency.ucsb.edu/ws/?pid=1197.

46. "Senator Hillary Rodham Clinton to Serve as Honorary Chair for Fifth Annual Westchester-Fairfield Walk for Autism Research on Sunday, June 4," Autism Speaks, May 16, 2006. Online: www.autismspeaks.org/about-us/press-releases/senator-hillary-rodham-clinton-serve-honorary-chair-fifth-annual-westchest-0.

47. George W. Bush, "Statement on Signing the Combating Autism Act of 2006," December 19, 2006. Online: www.presidency.ucsb.edu/ws/?pid=24388.

48. Autism Caucus: Coalition for Autism Research and Education Information. Online: doyle.house.gov/issue/autism-caucus.

49. Paul Bedard, "Cantor: Shift $100m Presidential Campaign Money to Autism," *Washington Examiner*, April 2, 2013. Online: washingtonexaminer.com/cantor-shift-100m-presidential-campaign-money-to-autism/article/2526052.

50. Sarah Zhang, "Autism Ads Raise Ire, Pulled Off Buses," *Seattle Times*, July 8, 2013. Online: seattletimes.com/html/localnews/2021356716_autismadsxml.html.

51. Michael John Carley, testimony before the House Committee on Oversight and Government Reform, November 22, 2012. Online: oversight.house.gov/wp-content/uploads/2012/11/Carley-Testimony-Bio-TNT.pdf.

52. According to ASAN, about three-quarters of the spending on services research actually went to preexisting practitioner training programs. Melody Latimer, "ASAN Expresses Concern Regarding New HHS Report on Autism Research," Autistic Self Advocacy Network, July 10, 2012. Online: autisticadvocacy.org/2012/07/asan-expresses-concern-regarding-new-hhs-report-on-autism-research.

53. Mark Roth and Julia Rendleman, "Mysteries of the Mind: Dealing with the Different Worlds of Autism," *Pittsburgh Post-Gazette*, October 6, 2013. Online: www.post-gazette.com/news/science/2013/10/06/Mysteries-of-the-Mind-Dealing-with-the-different-worlds-of-autism/stories/201310060004.

54. U.S. Department of Health and Human Services, Interagency Autism Coordinating Committee, "Strategic Plan for Autism Spectrum Disorder Research, 2013 Update," April 2014. Online: iacc.hhs.gov/strategic-plan/2013/IACC_2013_Strategic_Plan.pdf.

55. Ibid., pp. 57–58.

56. Sally Satel and Scott O. Lilienfeld, *Brainwashed: The Seductive Appeal of Mindless Neuroscience* (New York: Basic Books, 2013).

57. Gary Marcus, "The Trouble with Brain Science," *New York Times*, July 11, 2014. Online: www.nytimes.com/2014/07/12/opinion/the-trouble-with-brain-science.html.

58. Susan Folstein and Michael Rutter, "Infantile Autism: A Genetic Study of 21 Twin Pairs," *Journal of Child Psychology and Psychiatry* 18 (September 1977): 297–321. Online: onlinelibrary.wiley.com/doi/10.1111/j.1469-7610.1977.tb00443.x/pdf.

59. Sven Sandin et al., "The Familial Risk of Autism," *JAMA* 311 (May 7, 2014): 1770–77. Online: jama.jamanetwork.com/article.aspx?articleid=1866100; Trent Gaugler et al., "Most Genetic Risk for Autism Resides with Common Variation," *Nature Genetics* 46 (August 2014): 881–85. Online: www.nature.com/ng/journal/v46/n8/pdf/ng.3039.pdf.

60. Katharina Dworzynski, "How Different Are Girls and Boys above and below the Diagnostic Threshold for Autism Spectrum Disorders?" *Journal of the American Academy of Child and Adolescent Psychiatry* 51 (August 2012): 788–97. Online: tinyurl.com/mew2poj.

61. Devanand Manoli and Nirao Shah, "How Gender Influences the Autism Brain," Simons Foundation Autism Research Initiative, August 27, 2013. Online: sfari.org/news-and-opinion/viewpoint/2013/how-gender-influences-the-autism-brain.

62. Janie F. Shelton, "Neurodevelopmental Disorders and Prenatal Residential Proximity to Agricultural Pesticides: The CHARGE Study," *Environmental Health Perspectives,* June 23, 2014 (advance publication). Online: ehp.niehs.nih.gov/wp-content/uploads/advpub/2014/6/ehp.1307044.pdf.

63. Andrea L. Roberts et al., "Perinatal Air Pollutant Exposures and Autism Spectrum Disorder in the Children of Nurses' Health Study II Participants," *Environmental Health Perspectives* 121 (August 2013): 978–84. Online: ehp.niehs.nih.gov/wp-content/uploads/121/8/ehp.1206187.pdf; Heather E. Volk et al., "Residential Proximity to Freeways and Autism in the CHARGE Study," *Environmental Health Perspectives* 119 (June 2011): 873–77. Online: ehp.niehs.nih.gov/wp-content/uploads/119/6/ehp.1002835.pdf.

64. Gustavo C. Román et al., "Association of Gestational Maternal Hypothyroxinemia and Increased Autism Risk," *Annals of Neurology* 74 (November 2013): 733–42. Online: onlinelibrary.wiley.com/doi/10.1002/ana.23976/full.

65. Lior Brimberg et al., "Brain-Reactive IgG Correlates with Autoimmunity in Mothers of a Child with an Autism Spectrum Disorder," *Molecular Psychiatry* 18 (November 2013): 1171–77. Online: www.nature.com/mp/journal/v18/n11/full/mp2013101a.html.

66. Simon G. Gregory et al., "Association of Autism with Induced or Augmented Childbirth in North Carolina Birth Record (1990–1998) and Education Research (1997–2007) Databases,"

JAMA Pediatrics 167 (October 2013): 959–66. Online: archpedi.jamanetwork.com/article.aspx?articleid=1725449.

67. Michael W. Kuzniewicz et al., "Prevalence and Neonatal Factors Associated with Autism Spectrum Disorders in Preterm Infants," *Journal of Pediatrics* 164 (January 2014): 20–25. Online: www.jpeds.com/article/S0022-3476(13)01142-6/abstract?cc=y.

68. Eileen A. Curran et al., "Research Review: Birth by Caesarean Section and Development of Autism Spectrum Disorder and Attention-Deficit/Hyperactivity Disorder: A Systematic Review and Meta-Analysis," *Journal of Child Psychology and Psychiatry* (October 27, 2014). Online: onlinelibrary.wiley.com/doi/10.1111/jcpp.12351/pdf.

69. L. C. Reynolds et al., "Maternal Obesity and Increased Risk for Autism and Developmental Delay among Very Preterm Infants," *Journal of Perinatology*, May 8, 2014 (advance publication). Online: www.nature.com/jp/journal/vaop/ncurrent/full/jp201480a.html; Pål Surén et al., "Parental Obesity and Risk of Autism Spectrum Disorder," *Pediatrics* 133 (May 2014): e1128–e1138. Online: pediatrics.aappublications.org/content/early/2014/04/02/peds.2013-3664.full.pdf+html.

70. John McGrath et al., "A Comprehensive Assessment of Parental Age and Psychiatric Disorders," *JAMA Psychiatry* 71 (March 2014): 301–9. Online: archpsyc.jamanetwork.com/article.aspx?articleid=1814892; Selma Idring et al., "Parental Age and the Risk of Autism Spectrum Disorders: Findings from a Swedish Population-Based Cohort," *International Journal of Epidemiology* 43 (February 2014): 107–15. Online: ije.oxfordjournals.org/content/43/1/107.full.pdf+html.

71. Andrea L. Roberts et al., "Women's Posttraumatic Stress Symptoms and Autism Spectrum Disorder in Their Children," *Research in Autism Spectrum Disorders* 8 (June 2014): 608–16. Online: www.sciencedirect.com/science/article/pii/S1750946714000427.

72. Phuong Lien Tran et al., "Smoking during Pregnancy and Risk of Autism Spectrum Disorder in a Finnish National Birth Cohort," *Paediatric and Perinatal Epidemiology* 27 (May 2013): 266–74. Online: onlinelibrary.wiley.com/doi/10.1111/ppe.12043/full.

73. Rebecca A. Harrington et al., "Prenatal SSRI Use and Offspring with Autism Spectrum Disorder or Developmental Delay," *Pediatrics* 133 (May 2014): e1241–e1248. Online: pediatrics.aappublications.org/content/133/5/e1241.

74. Virginia Hughes, "The Sexual Politics of Autism," *National Geographic*, July 11, 2014. Online: phenomena.nationalgeographic.com/2014/07/11/the-sexual-politics-of-autism; Eva Gillis-Buck and Sarah S. Richardson, "Autism as a Biomedical Platform for Sex Difference Research," *BioSocieties* advance copy (2014). Online: scholar.harvard.edu/files/srichard/files/gillis-buck_and_richardson_autism_2014.pdf.

75. John J. Pitney Jr., "IVF, Autism, and Headlines," *Autism Policy and Politics*, July 2, 2013. Online: www.autismpolicyblog.com/2013/07/ivf-autism-and-headlines.html; "Autism and IVF: More Contradictory Headlines," *Autism Policy and Politics*, July 3, 2013. Online: www.autismpolicyblog.com/2013/07/autism-and-ivf-more-contradictory.html.

76. Harris Interactive, "National Consumers League 2013 Vaccine Study," November 21, 2013. Online: www.slideee.com/slide/national-consumers-league-2013-vaccine-study.

77. "Notice to Readers: Thimerosal in Vaccines: A Joint Statement of the American Academy of Pediatrics and the Public Health Service," *Morbidity and Mortality Weekly Report*, July 9, 1999. Online: www.cdc.gov/mmwr/preview/mmwrhtml/mm4826a3.htm.

78. Lyn Redwood and William T. Redwood, letter to Dr. Neal Halsey, December 30, 1999. Online: www.vaccinationnews.org/DailyNews/July2001/LtrToHalseyFromRedwood.htm.

79. Seth Mnookin, *The Panic Virus: A True Story of Medicine, Science, and Fear* (New York: Simon and Schuster, 2011), 140–41.

80. U.S. Congress, House of Representatives, Committee on Government Reform, "Autism: Present Challenges, Future Needs—Why the Increased Rates?" April 6, 2000. Online: www.gpo.gov/fdsys/pkg/CHRG-106hhrg69622/html/CHRG-106hhrg69622.htm.

81. Ibid.

82. Andrew Wakefield et al., "Ileal-Lymphoid-Nodular Hyperplasia, Non-Specific Colitis, and Pervasive Developmental Disorder in Children," *The Lancet* 351 (February 28, 1998): 637–41. Online: www.thelancet.com/journals/lancet/article/PIIS0140673697110960/fulltext.

83. Ibid.

84. C-SPAN, "Autism and Childhood Vaccines," April 6, 2000. Online: www.c-span.org/video/?156441-1/autism-childhood-vaccines; Philip J. Hilts, "House Panel Asks for Study of a Vaccine," *New York Times*, April 7, 2000. Online: www.nytimes.com/2000/04/07/us/house-panel-asks-for-study-of-a-vaccine.html.

85. The program aired on November 12, 2000. Nielsen ratings for the week are in Frazier Moore, "The Viewers Speak: ABC Wins the Week," Associated Press, November 14, 2000. Online: members.tripod.com/nielsen_ratings/001106-12-2.shtml.

86. Robert F. Kennedy Jr., "Vaccinations: Deadly Immunity—Government Cover-Up of a Mercury/Autism Scandal," *Rolling Stone*, July 20, 2005. Online: www.globalresearch.ca/vaccinations-deadly-immunity/14510.

87. David Kirby, *Evidence of Harm* (New York: St. Martin's, 2005), 418.

88. Dan Olmsted, "The Age of Autism," United Press International. Online: www.vaccinationnews.org/age-autism.

89. John J. Pitney, Jr., "Gossip and Autism," April 6, 2010. Online: www.autismpolicyblog.com/2010/04/gossip-and-autism.html.

90. Joelle Anne Moreno, "Toxic Torts, Autism, and Bad Science: Why the Courts May Be Our Best Defense against Scientific Relativism," *New England Law Review* 40 (Winter 2006): 409–18, at 410. Online: www.nesl.edu/userfiles/file/lawreview/vol40/2/Moreno.pdf.

91. Edward Wyatt, "ABC Drama Takes on Science and Parents," *New York Times*, January 23, 2008. Online: www.nytimes.com/2008/01/23/arts/television/23ston.html.

92. Carolyn Maloney, "New, Thorough Study of Possible Mercury-Autism Link Proposed by Rep. Maloney," March 30, 2006. Online: maloney.house.gov/media-center/press-releases/new-thorough-study-possible-mercury-autism-link-proposed-rep-maloney.

93. *Congressional Record* (daily), August 3, 2006, S8772.

94. Benedict Carey, "Into the Fray over the Cause of Autism," *New York Times*, March 4, 2008. Online: www.nytimes.com/2008/03/04/us/politics/04autism.html.

95. Michael Dobbs, "Dr. Obama and Dr. McCain," *Washington Post*, April 22, 2008. Online: voices.washingtonpost.com/fact-checker/2008/04/dr_obama_and_dr_mccain.html.

96. School of Psychology, Florida Institute of Technology, "First National Public Opinion Survey."

97. It also said: "Some members of the public are convinced that the current data are sufficient to demonstrate that vaccines do not play a causal role in autism and argue against using limited autism research funds to do additional vaccine studies when many other scientific avenues remain to be explored. At the same time, those who believe that prior studies of the possible role of vaccines in ASD have been insufficient argue that investigation of a possible vaccine/ASD link should be a high priority for research (e.g., a large-scale study comparing vaccinated and unvaccinated groups)." Interagency Autism Coordinating Committee, "The 2010 Interagency Autism Coordinating Committee Strategic Plan for Autism Spectrum Disorder Research," January 19, 2010. Online: iacc.hhs.gov/strategic-plan/2010/IACC_2010_Strategic_Plan.pdf.

98. Elizabeth McBreen, "Insel: IACC Has Lost the Trust of the Autism Community," *Spectrum*, April/May 2010. Online: web.archive.org/web/20110110202038/http://www.spectrumpublications.com/index.php/news/insel_iacc_has_lost_the_trust_of_the_autism_community.

99. Steven Novella, "IACC Statement on Autism Research," *NeuroLogica Blog*, November 12, 2009. Online: theness.com/neurologicablog/index.php/iacc-statement-on-autism-research. Grossman is the president and CEO of the Autism Society of America. Redwood is the vice president of SafeMinds.

100. Sarah Kurchak, "I'm Autistic, and Believe Me, It's a Lot Better Than Measles," *Medium*, February 6, 2015. Online: medium.com/the-archipelago/im-autistic-and-believe-me-its-a-lot-better-than-measles-78cb039f4bea.

101. Matt Carey, "Why Won't the Government Fund Vaccine/Autism Research?" LeftBrain/RightBrain, July 15, 2014. Online: leftbrainrightbrain.co.uk/2014/07/15/why-wont-the-government-fund-vaccineautism-research.

102. Offit, *Autism's False Prophets*, 45.

103. Brent Taylor et al., "Autism and Measles, Mumps, and Rubella Vaccine: No Epidemiological Evidence for a Causal Association," *The Lancet* 353 (June 12, 1999): 2026–29. Online: www.sciencedirect.com/science/article/pii/S0140673699012398.

104. Simon Murch et al., "Retraction of an Interpretation," *The Lancet* 363 (March 6, 2004): 750. Online: www.thelancet.com/journals/lancet/article/PIIS0140-6736(04)15715-2/fulltext.

105. Brian Deer, "MMR Doctor Andrew Wakefield Fixed Data on Autism," *The Times*, February 8, 2009. Online: www.thesundaytimes.co.uk/sto/public/news/article148992.ece.

106. General Medical Council, Fitness to Practise Panel Hearing, January 28, 2010. Online: www.rescuepost.com/files/facts-wwsm-280110-final-complete-corrected.pdf.

107. "Retraction—Ileal-Lymphoid-Nodular Hyperplasia, Non-Specific Colitis, and Pervasive Developmental Disorder in Children," *The Lancet*, February 2, 2010. Online: download. thelancet.com/flatcontentassets/pdfs/S0140673610601754.pdf.

108. Margaret A. Maglione et al., "Safety of Vaccines Used for Routine Immunization of US Children: A Systematic Review," *Pediatrics* 134 (August 2014). Online: pediatrics. aappublications.org/content/early/2014/06/26/peds.2014-1079.full.pdf+html.

109. "Vaccines Are Not Associated with Autism: An Evidence-Based Meta-Analysis of Case-Control and Cohort Studies," *Vaccine* 32 (June 17, 2014): 3623–29. Online: www. sciencedirect.com/science/article/pii/S0264410X14006367.

110. *King v. Secretary of Health and Human Services* Case No. 03-584V. Special Master Hastings, March 12, 2010. Online: www.uscfc.uscourts.gov/sites/default/files/opinions/ Hastings.King%20Decision.pdf.

111. Kerry Lauerman, "Correcting Our Record," *Salon*, January 16, 2011. Online: www. salon.com/2011/01/16/dangerous_immunity.

112. National Conference of State Legislatures, "States with Religious and Philosophical Exemptions from School Immunization Requirements," February 1, 2015. Online: www.ncsl. org/research/health/school-immunization-exemption-state-laws.aspx.

113. Chelsea Rice, "On the Front Lines of the Vaccine Debate, Pediatricians Play Both Sides," *Boston Globe*, December 15, 2014. Online: www.boston.com/health/2014/12/15/the-front-lines-the-vaccine-debate-pediatricians-play-both-sides/Kk3ZrEIdSqr5Gc4HxjfcDl/story. html.

114. Ranee Seither et al., "Vaccination Coverage among Children in Kindergarten—United States, 2013–14 School Year," *Morbidity and Mortality Weekly Report*, October 17, 2014. Online: www.cdc.gov/mmwr/preview/mmwrhtml/mm6341a1.htm.

115. Rosemary Parker, "Vaccination Waivers Put Hundreds of Michigan Communities at Risk of Disease Outbreaks," MLive.com, December 10, 2014. Online: www.mlive.com/news/ index.ssf/2014/12/michigan_vaccinations_risk_imm.html.

116. Centers for Disease Control and Prevention, "Measles Cases and Outbreaks." Online: www.cdc.gov/measles/cases-outbreaks.html.

117. U.S. Centers for Disease Control and Prevention, "Measles Cases in the United States Reach 20-Year High," May 29, 2014. Online: www.cdc.gov/media/releases/2014/p0529-measles.html.

118. Tracy A. Lieu et al., "Geographic Clusters in Underimmunization and Vaccine Refusal," *Pediatrics* 135 (February 2015): 280–89. Online: pediatrics.aappublications.org/content/early/ 2015/01/13/peds.2014-2715.full.pdf+html.

119. Christopher Ingraham, "California's Epidemic of Vaccine Denial, Mapped," *Washington Post*, January 27, 2015. Online: www.washingtonpost.com/blogs/wonkblog/wp/2015/01/ 27/californias-epidemic-of-vaccine-denial-mapped.

120. Rebecca Rosenberg et al., "Survey of Vaccine Beliefs and Practices among Families Affected by Autism Spectrum Disorders," *Clinical Pediatrics* 52 (September 2013): 871–74. Online: cpj.sagepub.com/content/52/9/871.

121. Daniel Kahneman, *Thinking Fast and Slow* (New York: Farrar, Straus, and Giroux, 2011), 130.

122. PBS, *Frontline*, "The Vaccine War," April 27, 2010, www.pbs.org/wgbh/pages/ frontline/vaccines/etc/script.html.

123. Kahneman, *Thinking Fast and Slow*, 142.

124. See Anne Dachel's criticism of Dr. Paul Offit in *The Big Autism Cover-Up: How and Why the Media Is Lying to the American Public* (New York: Skyhorse, 2014), 100–101.

125. "Business and Industry Sector Ratings," Gallup, August 2014. Online: www.gallup.com/poll/12748/Business-Industry-Sector-Ratings.aspx.

126. U.S. Congress, House of Representatives, Committee on Oversight and Government Reform, "1 in 88 Children: A Look into the Federal Response to Rising Rates of Autism," November 29, 2013. Online: oversight.house.gov/wp-content/uploads/2013/04/2012-11-29-Ser-No-112-194-FC-Hearing-on-Autism.pdf.

127. Ibid.

128. Christopher E. Clarke, "A Question of Balance: The Autism-Vaccine Controversy in the British and American Elite Press," *Science Communication* 30 (September 2008): 77–107. Online: scx.sagepub.com/content/30/1/77.full.pdf+html.

129. Graham N. Dixon and Christopher E. Clarke, "Heightening Uncertainty around Certain Science: Media Coverage, False Balance, and the Autism-Vaccine Controversy," *Science Communication* 35 (June 2013): 358–82. Online: scx.sagepub.com/content/35/3/358.

130. Curtis Brainard, "Sticking with the Truth," *Columbia Journalism Review*, May 1, 2013. Online: www.cjr.org/feature/sticking_with_the_truth.php.

131. Edward Alan Miller, Antoinette Pole, and Clancey Batemen, "Diagnosis Blog: Checking Up on Health Blogs in the Blogosphere," paper presented at the annual meeting of the Midwest Political Science Association, Chicago, April 2–5, 2009.

132. Seth Mnookin, "A Jenny McCarthy Reader, Pt. 2: Jenny Brings Her Anti-Vaccine Views to Oprah," *PLOS Blogs: The Panic Virus*, July 15, 2013. Online: blogs.plos.org/thepanicvirus/2013/07/15/a-jenny-mccarthy-reader-pt-2-jenny-brings-her-anti-vaccine-views-to-oprah.

133. Anna Kata, "A Postmodern Pandora's Box: Anti-Vaccination Misinformation on the Internet," *Vaccine* 28 (February 17, 2010): 1709–16. Online: www.sciencedirect.com/science/article/pii/S0264410X09019264.

134. Jeanette B. Ruiz and Robert A. Bell, "Understanding Vaccination Resistance: Vaccine Search Term Selection Bias and the Valence of Retrieved Information," *Vaccine* 32 (October 7, 2014): 5776–80. Online: www.sciencedirect.com/science/article/pii/S0264410X14011657.

135. Dr. Sophia Colamarino, testimony before the Subcommittee on Information Policy, Census and National Archives Committee on Oversight and Government Reform, July 29, 2010. Online: oversight.house.gov/wp-content/uploads/2012/01/20100729Colamarino.pdf.

136. Roy Richard Grinker, "Commentary: On Being Autistic, and Social," *Ethos* 38 (March 2010): 172–78, at 175. Online: onlinelibrary.wiley.com/doi/10.1111/j.1548-1352.2010.01087.x/pdf.

137. Jordynn Jack, *Autism and Gender: From Refrigerator Mothers to Computer Geeks* (Urbana: University of Illinois Press, 2014), 77.

138. Anna Kata, "Anti-Vaccine Activists, Web 2.0, and the Postmodern Paradigm—An Overview of Tactics and Tropes Used Online by the Anti-Vaccination Movement," *Vaccine* 30 (May 28, 2012): 3778–89. Online: www.sciencedirect.com/science/article/pii/S0264410X11019086.

139. Anne Dachel, "Dismissed!" *Age of Autism*, April 29, 2010. Online: www.ageofautism.com/2010/04/dismissed.html.

140. Pew Research Center for the People and the Press, "Public Trust in Government: 1958–2014," November 13, 2014. Online: www.people-press.org/2014/11/13/public-trust-in-government.

141. The signs of autism should be clear to a trained professional when the child is two. According to one recent study, the average age of diagnosis is six. Paul T. Shattuck et al., "Timing of Identification among Children with an Autism Spectrum Disorder: Findings from a Population-Based Surveillance Study," *Journal of the American Academy of Child and Adolescent Psychiatry* 48 (May 2009): 474–83.

142. Jenny McCarthy, *Louder Than Words: A Mother's Journey in Healing Autism* (New York: Dutton, 2007), 57–58.

143. Among the first books that parents read after a diagnosis is Maurice's *Let Me Hear Your Voice.* Though mostly a memoir, it contains an extensive discussion of Bettelheim.

144. Brendan Nyhan et al., "Effective Messages in Vaccine Promotion: A Randomized Trial," *Pediatrics* 133 (April 2014). Online: pediatrics.aappublications.org/content/early/2014/02/25/peds.2013-2365.full.pdf+html.

145. Amy Wallace, "Life as a Female Journalist: Hot or Not?" *New York Times*, January 19, 2014. Online: www.nytimes.com/2014/01/20/opinion/life-as-a-female-journalist-hot-or-not.html.

146. Maine Administrators of Services for Children with Disabilities, "Report of the MAD-SEC Autism Task Force," February 2000 (rev. ed.). Online: cc103.wazisolutions.com/aba.

147. Louis P. Hagopian and Samantha L. Hardesty, "Applied Behavior Analysis: Overview and Summary of Scientific Support," Kennedy Krieger Institute, March 2014. Online: www.kennedykrieger.org/patient-care/patient-care-programs/inpatient-programs/neurobehavioral-unit-nbu/applied-behavior-analysis.

148. Margaret A. Maglione et al., "Nonmedical Interventions for Children with ASD: Recommended Guidelines and Further Research Needs," *Pediatrics* 130, Supplement 2 (November 1, 2012): S169–S178. Online: pediatrics.aappublications.org/content/130/Supplement_2/S169.full.pdf+html.

149. Amy S. Weitlauf, "Therapies for Children with Autism Spectrum Disorder: Behavioral Interventions Update," U.S. Agency for Healthcare Research and Quality, August 2014. Online: www.ncbi.nlm.nih.gov/books/NBK241444/.

150. Deborah Fein, "Optimal Outcome in Individuals with a History of Autism," *Journal of Child Psychology and Psychiatry* 54 (February 2013): 195–205. Online: onlinelibrary.wiley.com/doi/10.1111/jcpp.12037/abstract.

151. Martin Knapp and Ariane Buescher, "Economic Aspects of Autism," in *Handbook of Autism and Developmental Disorders*, 4th ed., ed. Fred R. Volkmar et al. (Hoboken, NJ: John Wiley & Sons, 2014), 1089–1106, at 1102.

152. Gregory S. Chasson, Gerald E. Harris, and Wendy J. Neely, "Cost Comparison of Early Intensive Behavioral Intervention and Special Education for Children with Autism," *Journal of Child and Family Studies* 16 (June 2007): 401–413. Online: link.springer.com/article/10.1007/s10826-006-9094-1/fulltext.html.

153. Elizabeth Picciuto, "They Don't Want an Autism Cure," *Daily Beast*, February 25, 2015. Online: www.thedailybeast.com/articles/2015/02/25/they-don-t-want-an-autism-cure.html.

154. Ido Kedar, *Ido in Autismland* (Sharon Kedar, 2012), 58.

155. David M. Allen, "Why Psychotherapy Efficacy Studies Are Nearly Impossible," *Psychology Today*, December 24, 2012. Online: www.psychologytoday.com/blog/matter-personality/201212/why-psychotherapy-efficacy-studies-are-nearly-impossible.

156. U.S. Department of Health and Human Services, Interagency Autism Coordinating Committee, "2010 IACC Autism Spectrum Disorder Research Portfolio Analysis Report," July 2013, p. 18. Online: iacc.hhs.gov/portfolio-analysis/2010/2010_portfolio_analysis.pdf.

157. James M. Perrin et al., "Complementary and Alternative Medicine Use in a Large Pediatric Autism Sample," *Pediatrics* 130, Supplement 2 (November 1, 2012): S77–S82. Online: pediatrics.aappublications.org/content/130/Supplement_2/S77.full; Roger S. Akins et al., "Utilization Patterns of Conventional and Complementary/Alternative Treatments in Children with Autism Spectrum Disorders and Developmental Disabilities in a Population-Based Study," *Journal of Developmental & Behavioral Pediatrics*, 2014; 35 (January 2014): 1–10. Online: journals.lww.com/jrnldbp/Abstract/2014/01000/Utilization_Patterns_of_Conventional_and.1.aspx; Joanna Granich et al., "High Use of Complementary and Alternative Medication among Children with Autism Is Not Associated with the Severity of Core Symptoms," *Journal of Autism* 1 (October 6, 2014). Online: www.hoajonline.com/journals/pdf/2054-992X-1-4.pdf.

158. Sarah E. Hall and Cynthia A. Riccio, "Complementary and Alternative Treatment Use for Autism Spectrum Disorders," *Complementary Therapies in Clinical Practice* 18 (August 2012): 159–63. Online: www.ctcpjournal.com/article/S1744-3881%2812%2900029-1/fulltext.

159. Bernard Rimland, "The History of the Autism Research Institute and the Defeat Autism Now! Project," in Stephen M. Edelson and Bernard Rimland, eds., *Treating Autism: Parent Stories of Hope and Success* (San Diego: Autism Research Institute, 2003), 16.

160. Paul A. Offit, *Do You Believe in Magic? The Sense and Nonsense of Alternative Medicine* (New York: HarperCollins, 2013), ch. 3.

161. Austin Mulloy et al., "Gluten-Free and Casein-Free Diets in the Treatment of Autism Spectrum Disorders: A Systematic Review," *Research in Autism Spectrum Disorders* 4 (July–September 2010): 328–39. Online: www.sciencedirect.com/science/article/pii/S1750946709001111.

162. Nicholas Lofthouse et al., "A Review of Complementary and Alternative Treatments for Autism Spectrum Disorders," *Autism Research and Treatment* (2012), Article ID 87039. Online: www.hindawi.com/journals/aurt/2012/870391.

163. *Thompson v. Western States Medical Center* 535 U.S. 357 (2002). Online: www.law.cornell.edu/supct/html/01-344.ZS.html.

164. Sharon Begley, "How Compounding Pharmacies Rallied Patients to Fight Regulation," *Reuters*, October 16, 2012. Online: www.reuters.com/article/2012/10/16/us-usa-health-meningitis-compounding-idUSBRE89F05Y20121016.

165. Tonya N. Davis et al., "Chelation Treatment for Autism Spectrum Disorders: A Systematic Review," *Research in Autism Spectrum Disorders* 7 (January 2013): 49–55. Online: www.sciencedirect.com/science/article/pii/S1750946712000724.

166. U.S. Food and Drug Administration, "Beware of False or Misleading Claims for Treating Autism," June 19, 2014. Online: www.fda.gov/ForConsumers/ConsumerUpdates/ucm394757.htm.

167. Stephen Barrett, "Regulatory Actions against Chelation Therapists," *Quackwatch*, October 6, 2014. Online: www.quackwatch.com/01QuackeryRelatedTopics/chelationreg.html.

168. Patricia Callahan, "Naperville Doctor Disciplined in Controversial Autism Case," *Chicago Tribune*, December 30, 2014. Online: www.chicagotribune.com/lifestyles/health/ct-autism-anjum-usman-discipline-met-20141229-story.html.

169. Robert Langreth and John Lauerman, "Autism Cures Promised by DNA Testers Belied by Regulators," *Bloomberg News*, December 20, 2012. Online: www.bloomberg.com/news/2012-12-21/autism-cures-promised-by-dna-testers-belied-by-regulators.html.

170. Eric Berger, "A Worthy Endeavor: How Albert Thomas Won Houston NASA's Flagship Center," *Houston Chronicle*, September 14, 2013. Online: www.houstonchronicle.com/news/houston-texas/houston/article/A-worthy-endeavor-How-Albert-Thomas-won-Houston-4815595.php.

171. John F. Kennedy, "Special Message to the Congress on Urgent National Needs," May 25, 1961. Online: www.presidency.ucsb.edu/ws/?pid=8151.

172. Mayada Elsabbagh, "Community Engagement and Knowledge Translation: Progress and Challenge in Autism Research," *Autism* 18 (October 2014): 771–81. Online: aut.sagepub.com/content/18/7/771.

173. Dana Lee Baker, "Use of Science in Autism Policy Development," *Open Journal of Political Science* 3 (January 2013): 1–7. Online: www.scirp.org/journal/PaperDownload.aspx?paperID=27154.

174. Jennifer Jacobs, "Rand Paul Talks in Iowa on 'Petulance' of Obama," *Des Moines Register*, August 4, 2014. Online: www.desmoinesregister.com/story/news/politics/elections/2014/08/04/rand-paul-sioux-city-iowa/13597441.

175. David A. Farenthold and Matea Gold, "For Rand Paul, a Rude Awakening to the Rigors of a National Campaign," *Washington Post*, February 5, 2015. Online: www.washingtonpost.com/politics/for-rand-paul-a-rude-awakening-to-the-rigors-of-a-national-campaign/2015/02/04/af855b5e-ac83-11e4-abe8-e1ef60ca26de_story.html.

176. Steve Silberman, "Exclusive: First Autistic Presidential Appointee Speaks Out," *Wired*, October 6, 2010. Online: www.wired.com/2010/10/exclusive-ari-neeman-qa/all.

177. Jeffrey Howe, "The Language of Autism: Disease or Difference?" *New York Times*, May 14, 2014. Online: parenting.blogs.nytimes.com//2014/05/14/the-language-of-autism-disease-or-difference/.

4. EDUCATION

1. P.L. 94-142, "The Education for All Handicapped Children Act of 1975." Online: www. gpo.gov/fdsys/pkg/STATUTE-89/pdf/STATUTE-89-Pg773.pdf.

2. *Congressional Record*, November 19, 1975, 37413. Several other lawmakers made similar comments. See Karl Boettner, "Attack on the EHA: The Education for All Handicapped Children Act after *Board of Education v. Rowley*," *University of Puget Sound Law Review* 7 (1983): 183–210, at 195, fn. 92. Online: digitalcommons.law.seattleu.edu/cgi/viewcontent.cgi? article=1166&context=sulr.

3. *Brown v. Board of Education* 4347 U.S. 483 (1954), at 495. Online: www.law.cornell. edu/supremecourt/text/347/483#writing-USSC_CR_0347_0483_ZO.

4. Deborah Stone, *Policy Paradox: The Art of Political Decision Making*, 3rd ed. (New York: W.W. Norton, 2013), ch. 2.

5. Martha Minow, *Making All the Difference* (Ithaca, NY: Cornell University Press, 1990), 20.

6. Douglas Rae refers to these concepts as "lot-regarding equality" (identical treatment) and "person-regarding equality" (treatment that takes personal differences into account). Douglas Rae, *Equalities* (Cambridge, MA: Harvard University Press, 1981), 85–93.

7. Eloise Pasachoff, "Special Education, Poverty, and the Limits of Private Enforcement," *Notre Dame Law Review* 86, no. 4 (2011): 1413–94. Online: ndlawreview.org/wp-content/ uploads/2013/06/Pasachoff.pdf.

8. Paul L. Tractenberg, "Education Provisions in State Constitutions: A Summary of a Chapter for the State Constitutions for the Twenty-First Century," Center for State Constitutional Studies. Online: camlaw.rutgers.edu/statecon/subpapers/tractenberg.pdf.

9. Gerald R. Ford, "Statement on Signing the Education for All Handicapped Children Act of 1975," December 2, 1975. Online: www.presidency.ucsb.edu/ws/?pid=5413.

10. Federal Budget Education Project, "Individuals with Disabilities Education Act—Funding Distribution," New America Foundation, April 25, 2014. Online: febp.newamerica.net/ background-analysis/individuals-disabilities-education-act-funding-distribution.

11. U.S. Department of Education, "10 Facts about K–12 Education Funding," September 19, 2014. Online: www2.ed.gov/about/overview/fed/10facts/index.html.

12. Tara A. Lavelle et al., "Economic Burden of Childhood Autism Spectrum Disorders," *Pediatrics* 133 (March 2014): e520–e529. Online: pediatrics.aappublications.org/content/early/ 2014/02/04/peds.2013-0763.abstract.

13. Jay G. Chambers, Jamie Shkolnik, and María Pérez, "Total Expenditures for Students with Disabilities, 1999-2000: Spending Variation by Disability." Special Education Expenditure Project, Center for Special Education Finance, June 2003. Online: csef.air.org/ publications/seep/national/final_seep_report_5.pdf.

14. *Timothy W., Etc., Plaintiff, Appellant, v. Rochester, New Hampshire, School District, Defendant, Appellee*, 875 F.2d 954 (1st Cir. 1989). Online: law.justia.com/cases/federal/ appellate-courts/F2/875/954/179023.

15. Christina Samuels, "Landmark Special Ed. Case Confirming 'Zero Reject' Rule Marks 25 Years," *Education Week*, December 8, 2014. Online: blogs.edweek.org/edweek/speced/ 2014/12/landmark_special_ed_case_confi.html.

16. Jeffrey Meitrodt and Kim McGuire, "Rising Special Ed Cases Are Huge Cost to Minnesota Schools," *Minneapolis Star-Tribune*, March 3, 2013. Online: www.startribune.com/local/ 194572221.html.

17. 34 CFR, 300.8(c)(1). Online: idea.ed.gov/explore/view/p/%2Croot%2Cregs%2C300 %2CA%2C300%252E8%2C.

18. 34 CFR, 300.304. Online: idea.ed.gov/explore/view/p/%2Croot%2Cregs%2C300 %2CD%2C300%252E304%2C.

19. Anthony Rebora, "Keeping Special Ed in Proportion," *Education Week*, October 12, 2011. Online: www.edweek.org/tsb/articles/2011/10/13/01disproportion.h05.html; Jason C. Travers, Matt Tincani, and Michael P. Krezmien, "A Multiyear National Profile of Racial

Disparity in Autism Identification," *Journal of Special Education* 47 (May 2013): 41–49. Online: sed.sagepub.com/content/47/1/41.

20. J. Blacher, S. R. Cohen, and G. Azad, "In the Eye of the Beholder: Reports of Autism Symptoms by Anglo and Latino Mothers," *Research in Autism Spectrum Disorders* 8 (December 2014): 1648–56. Online: www.sciencedirect.com/science/article/pii/S1750946714002098.

21. Saime Tek and Rebecca J. Landa, "Differences in Autism Symptoms between Minority and Non-Minority Toddlers." *Journal of Autism and Developmental Disorders* 42 (September 2012): 1967–73. Online: www.ncbi.nlm.nih.gov/pmc/articles/PMC3402594.

22. Jason C. Travers et al., "Racial Disparity in Administrative Autism Identification across the United States during 2000 and 2007," *Journal of Special Education* 49 (November 2014): 155–66. Online: sed.sagepub.com/content/48/3/155.full.pdf+html.

23. Nirvi Shah, "Group Acts to Address Overidentification of Black Children as Disabled," *Education Week*, January 12, 2012. Online: blogs.edweek.org/edweek/speced/2012/01/a_new_ initiative_hopes_to.html.

24. Malinda L. Pennington, Douglas Cullinan, and Louise B. Southern, "Defining Autism: Variability in State Education Agency Definitions of and Evaluations for Autism Spectrum Disorders," *Autism Research and Treatment* (2014), Article ID 327271. Online: www.hindawi. com/journals/aurt/2014/327271/cta/.

25. U.S. Department of Education, Office of Special Education and Rehabilitative Services *35th Annual Report to Congress on the Implementation of the Individuals with Disabilities Education Act 2013*, May 2014. Online: www2.ed.gov/about/reports/annual/osep/2013/parts-b-c/35th-idea-arc.pdf.

26. Elizabeth Harstad et al., "Disparity of Care for Children with Parent-Reported Autism Spectrum Disorders," *Academic Pediatrics* 13 (July/August 2013): 334–39. Online: www. academicpedsjnl.net/article/S1876-2859(13)00065-X/abstract.

27. 20 USC 1412. Online: www.law.cornell.edu/uscode/text/20/1412.

28. U.S. Department of Education, Institute of Education Sciences, *Digest of Education Statistics*, 2013, Table 204.60. Percentage Distribution of Students 6 to 21 Years Old Served under Individuals with Disabilities Education Act (IDEA), Part B, by educational environment and type of disability: Selected years, fall 1989 through fall 2011. Online: nces.ed.gov/ programs/digest/d13/tables/dt13_204.60.asp.

29. U.S. Government Accountability Office, "Charter Schools: Additional Federal Attention Needed to Help Protect Access for Students with Disabilities." GAO-12-543, June 2012. Online: http://www.gao.gov/assets/600/591435.pdf.

30. Arianna Prothero, "Special Education Charters Renew Inclusion Debate," *Education Week,* September 17, 2014. Online: www.edweek.org/ew/articles/2014/09/17/04specialneeds charters.h34.html.

31. Xin Wei, "Special Education Services Received by Students with Autism Spectrum Disorders from Preschool through High School," *Journal of Special Education* 48 (November 2014): 167–79. sed.sagepub.com/content/48/3/167.full.pdf+html.

32. Ruth Colker, *Disabled Education: A Critical Analysis of the Americans with Disabilities Act* (New York: New York University Press, 2013), 41.

33. Areva Martin, *The Everyday Advocate: Standing Up for Your Child with Autism* (New York: New American Library, 2010), 228.

34. Dani Carlson, "More Autism, Less Special Education," WOOD-TV, May 14, 2013. Online: www.rocketnews.com/2013/05/more-autism-less-special-education.

35. *Board of Education v. Rowley*, 458 US 176, at 177. Online: supreme.justia.com/us/458/ 176/case.html.

36. 20 USC 1400. Online: www.law.cornell.edu/uscode/text/20/1400.

37. *J. L. v. Mercer Island School District* (9th Cir. 2009). Online: cdn.ca9.uscourts.gov/ datastore/opinions/2009/08/06/07-35716.pdf.

38. 20 USC 1414. Online: http://www.law.cornell.edu/uscode/text/20/1414.

39. Robert Crabtree, "Treatment of Applied Behavioral Analysis under IDEA: Has Recent Peer-Reviewed Support for Intensive Behavioral Approaches Given Parents a Right to ABA Services for Children with Autism?" 2010. Online: www.kcslegal.com/assets/Treatment_of_ ABA_under_IDEA.pdf.

40. *Board of Education v. Rowley*, 458 US 176, at 209. Online: supreme.justia.com/us/458/176/case.html.

41. Karen Syma Czapanskiy, "Special Kids, Special Parents, Special Education," *University of Michigan Journal of Law Reform* 47 (Spring 2014): 733–90. Online: http://repository.law.umich.edu/cgi/viewcontent.cgi?article=1109&context=mjlr.

42. Martin, *The Everyday Advocate*, 204.

43. Amy Gould Caraballo, in "30 More Ridiculous Comments Heard at an IEP Meeting." Online: www.friendshipcircle.org/blog/2012/01/26/30-more-ridiculous-comments-heard-at-an-iep-meeting.

44. Mary Wagner et al., "A National Picture of Parent and Youth Participation in IEP and Transition Planning Meetings," *Journal of Disability Policy Studies* 23 (December 2012): 140–55. Online: dps.sagepub.com/content/23/3/140.short?rss=1&ssource=mfc. This study looked at IEPs for all disabilities, not just autism.

45. Lauren Roth, "Florida Parents Seek Help from Special-Education Advocates," *Orlando Sentinel*, January 2, 2012. Online: articles.orlandosentinel.com/2012-01-02/business/os-florida-special-education-advocacy-20111225_1_special-education-advocates-special-education-individualized-education-program.

46. Sue Whitney, "Doing Your Homework: What Type of Training Is Required to Become an Advocate?" Online: www.wrightslaw.com/heath/advocate.guidelines.htm.

47. Sharon Lutz, "Tongue-Tied at IEP Meetings," *The Wrightslaw Way*, December 1, 2011. Online: www.wrightslaw.com/blog/?p=6124.

48. Martin, *The Everyday Advocate*, 251.

49. The Handicapped Children's Protection Act of 1986, P.L. 99-372. Online: www.gpo.gov/fdsys/pkg/STATUTE-100/pdf/STATUTE-100-Pg796.pdf.

50. Council of Parent Attorneys and Advocates, "Make Burden of Proof Fair and Equitable," 2012. Online: www.copaa.org/?page=BOP.

51. *Arlington Central School District Board Of Education v. Murphy* 548 U.S. 291 (2006). Online: www.law.cornell.edu/supct/html/05-18.ZO.html.

52. *Schaffer v Weas*t, 546 U.S. 49 (2005). Online: www.law.cornell.edu/supct/html/04-698.ZS.html.

53. Linda Greenhouse, "Parents Carry Burden of Proof in School Cases, Court Rules," *New York Times*, November 15, 2005. Online: www.nytimes.com/2005/11/15/politics/15scotus.html.

54. Perry A. Zirkel, "Who Has the Burden of Persuasion in Impartial Hearings under the Individuals with Disabilities Education Act?" *Connecticut Public Interest Law Journal* 13 (Fall–Winter 2013). Online: www.law.seattleu.edu/Documents/aljho/resources/Zirkel%20Burden%20of%20Proof%20Article.pdf.

55. One study of California cases found that parents of autistic children had a better rate of success than parents of children with special learning disabilities or mental retardation, but they still prevailed less often than the school districts. Gil Eyal and Allison Mann, "Who Prevails? Comparison of Special Education Due Process Hearings for Autistic, MR and SLD Children," January 2010. Online: works.bepress.com/cgi/viewcontent.cgi?article=1002&context=gil_eyal.

56. Terry Jean Seligmann, "Rowley Comes Home to Roost: Judicial Review of Autism Special Education Disputes," *UC Davis Journal of Juvenile Law and Policy* 9 (Summer 2005): 217–88.

57. Doris Adams Hill and Regina Kearley, "Autism Litigation: Outcomes for 2010, Trends in Decision Making and Changes in Diagnostic Criteria," *Research in Developmental Disabilities* 34 (May 2013): 1843–48. Online: www.sciencedirect.com/science/article/pii/S0891422213000760.

58. Colker, *Disabled Education*, 46.

59. Legislative Analyst's Office, "Overview of Special Education in California," January 3, 2013. Online: www.lao.ca.gov/reports/2013/edu/special-ed-primer/special-ed-primer-010313.aspx.

60. Compared with families of students with other disabilities, families of students with autism are more likely to use mediation and due process. Parents who file are likely to be strong advocates for their child and have greater household incomes. Meghan M. Burke and Samantha

E. Goldman, "Mediation and Due Process in Families of Students with Autism Spectrum Disorder," *Journal of Autism and Developmental Disorders*, November 2014. Online: link. springer.com/article/10.1007/s10803-014-2294-4.

61. Marlene Sokol, "When All Else Fails, Parents of Special-Needs Students Turn to Social Media," *Tampa Bay Times*, September 27, 2014. Online: www.tampabay.com/news/education/k12/when-all-else-fails-parents-of-special-needs-students-turn-to-social-media/2199766.

62. Charles P. Fox, "School District's Gathering Information on Parents," *Special Education Law Blog*, February 9, 2011. Online: blog.foxspecialedlaw.com/2011/02/school-districts-gathering-information-on-parents.html.

63. Alan Zarembo, "Warrior Parents Fare Best in Securing Autism Services," *Los Angeles Times*, December 12, 2011. Online: www.latimes.com/local/autism/la-me-autism-day-two-html-htmlstory.html.

64. "IEP Process: Goals and Objectives," *The Life That Chose Me*, May 6, 2006. Online: specialed.wordpress.com/2006/05/06/iep-process-goals-and-objectives/.

65. Tera Tuten, "Bureaucracy and IEP Compliance," *Soliant Health*, October 14, 2014. Online: blog.soliant.com/therapy-2/bureaucracy-and-iep-compliance.

66. James Q. Wilson, *Bureaucracy: What Government Agencies Do and Why They Do It* (New York: Basic Books, 1991): 168–69.

67. Rebecca R. Skinner and Kyrie E. Dragoo, "The Education of Students with Disabilities: Alignment between the Elementary and Secondary Education Act and the Individuals with Disabilities Education Act," Congressional Research Service, March 13, 2014. Online: kihd.gmu.edu/assets/docs/kihd/AIMVA/2014/Congressional-Research-Service-Paper.pdf.

68. Christina Samuels, "Louisiana Struggles in Allowing IEP Teams to Create Diploma Pathways," *Education Week*, December 18, 2014. Online: blogs.edweek.org/edweek/speced/2014/12/louisiana_struggles_to_impleme.html.

69. Michael K. Yudin, acting assistant secretary of the Office of Special Education and Rehabilitative Services, and Deborah S. Delisle, assistant secretary of the Office of Elementary and Secondary Education, U.S. Department of Education, letter to John White, superintendent of the Louisiana Department of Education, July 2, 2014. Online: www.advocacyinstitute.org/resources/USEDltrLDOEHB1015July2-2014.pdf.

70. Alyson Klein, "Where Do Special Education Groups Stand on Annual NCLB Tests?" *Education Week*, January 7, 2015. Online: blogs.edweek.org/edweek/campaign-k-12/2015/01/where_do_special_education_gro.html.

71. Lisa Jo Rudy, "No Child Left Behind (NCLB) and Autism," About.com, January 24, 2014. Online: autism.about.com/od/termsanddefinitions/g/nclb.htm.

72. Alison DeNisco, "What Does the Common Core Mean for Special Ed?" *District Administration*, December 2014. Online: districtadministration.com./article/what-does-common-core-mean-special-ed.

73. Common Core State Standards Initiative, "Application to Students with Disabilities." Online: www.corestandards.org/assets/CCSSonSWD-AT.pdf.

74. Katherine Beals, "Why Common Core Is All Wrong for High-Functioning Autistic Kids," *Education News*, October 2, 2014. Online: www.educationnews.org/education-policy-and-politics/why-common-core-is-all-wrong-for-high-functioning-autistic-kids.

75. Diane L. Williams and Nancy J. Minshew, "How the Brain Thinks in Autism: Implications for Language Intervention," *ASHA Leader*, April 27, 2010. Online: www.asha.org/Publications/leader/2010/100427/How-The-Brain-Thinks-In-Autism.htm.

76. Temple Grandin, *Thinking in Pictures: My Life with Autism* (New York: Vintage, 2006).

77. Beals, "Why Common Core is All Wrong."

78. Ibid.

79. Jeff Severt, Facebook post, March 26, 2014. Online: www.facebook.com/jeff.severt1/posts/10201895304210800. Also see Liana Heitin, "Common Core Redoes the Math," *Education Week*, November 10, 2014. Online: www.edweek.org/ew/articles/2014/11/12/12cc-overview.h34.html.

80. Christina A. Samuels, "Common Core's Promise Collides with IEP Realities," *Education Week*, October 28, 2013. Online: www.edweek.org/ew/articles/2013/10/30/10cc-iep.h33.html.

81. Ruth Colker, *When Is Separate Unequal? A Disability Perspective* (New York: Cambridge, 2009), 99.

82. Jennifer Kurth, "Educational Placement of Students with Autism: The Impact of State of Residence," *Focus on Autism and Other Developmental Disabilities*, September 3, 2014. Online: foa.sagepub.com/content/early/2014/08/28/1088357614547891.full.pdf+html.

83. Megan P. Martins, Sandra L. Harris, and Jan S. Handleman, "Supporting Inclusive Education," in *Handbook of Autism and Developmental Disorders*, 4th ed., ed. Fred R. Volkmar et al. (Hoboken, NJ: John Wiley & Sons, 2014), 858–70. It is not clear, however, that the *degree* of inclusivity (whether the child spends all day in general education or just a part of it) makes a difference. E. Michael Foster and Erin Pearson, "Is Inclusivity an Indicator of Quality of Care for Children with Autism in Special Education?" *Pediatrics* 130 (Supplement 2, November 2012): S179–S185. Online: pediatrics.aappublications.org/content/130/Supplement_2/S179.full.html.

84. Suzannah Iadarola et al., "Services for Children with Autism Spectrum Disorder in Three, Large Urban School Districts: Perspectives of Parents and Educators," *Autism*, September 5, 2014. Online: aut.sagepub.com/content/early/2014/09/04/1362361314548078.full.pdf+html.

85. Melody Musgrove and Michael K. Yudin, "Dear Colleague: Bullying of Students with Disabilities," U.S. Department of Education, Office of Special Education and Rehabilitative Services, August 20, 2013. Online: www2.ed.gov/policy/speced/guid/idea/memosdcltrs/bullyingdcl-8-20-13.pdf.

86. Connie Anderson, "IAN Research Report: Bullying and Children with ASD," Interactive Autism Network, March 26, 2012; rev. October 7, 2014. Online: www.iancommunity.org/cs/ian_research_reports/ian_research_report_bullying.

87. Judith Hebron and Neil Humphrey, "Exposure to Bullying among Students with Autism Spectrum Conditions: A Multi-Informant Analysis of Risk and Protective Factors," *Autism* 18 (August 2014): 618–30. Online: aut.sagepub.com/content/18/6/618.full.pdf+html.

88. Jessica H. Schroeder et al., "Shedding Light on a Pervasive Problem: A Review of Research on Bullying Experiences among Children with Autism Spectrum Disorders," *Journal of Autism and Developmental Disorders* 44 (July 2014): 1520–34. Online: link.springer.com/article/10.1007/s10803-013-2011-8.

89. Connie Anderson, "IAN Research Report: Bullying and Children with ASD."

90. Connie Anderson et al., "Occurrence and Family Impact of Elopement in Children with Autism Spectrum Disorders," *Pediatrics* 130 (November 2012): 870–77. Online: pediatrics.aappublications.org/content/130/5/870.

91. Lori McIlwain, "The Day My Son Went Missing," *New York Times*, November 12, 2013. Online: www.nytimes.com/2013/11/13/opinion/wandering-is-a-major-concern-for-parents-of-children-with-autism.html.

92. Rebecca White, "Missing Autistic Teen Puts Focus on School 'Mainstreaming,'" Al Jazeera America, November 30, 2013. Online: america.aljazeera.com/articles/2013/11/30/public-school-mainstreamingunderfireinlightofmissingautisticteen.html.

93. Lisa Quinones-Fontanez, "Why NYC Schools Aren't Equipped to Handle Kids with Autism," *Babble*, October 18, 2013. Online: www.babble.com/kid/why-nyc-schools-arent-equipped-to-handle-kids-with-autism.

94. Robert Tomsho, "Parents of Disabled Students Push for Separate Classes," *Wall Street Journal*, November 27, 2007. Online: www.wsj.com/articles/SB119610348432004184.

95. Dina Prichep, "Do Autistic Kids Fare Better in Integrated or Specialized Schools?" National Public Radio, June 2, 2014. Online: www.npr.org/2014/06/02/316462407/do-autistic-kids-fare-better-in-integrated-or-specialized-schools.

96. Office of the Mayor, City of New York, "Mayor de Blasio Signs 'Avonte's Law,'" August 7, 2014. Online: www1.nyc.gov/office-of-the-mayor/news/391-14/mayor-de-blasio-signs-avonte-s-law-#/0.

97. U.S. Department of Education, "Guiding Principles: A Resource Guide for Improving School Climate and Discipline," January 2014. Online: www2.ed.gov/policy/gen/guid/school-discipline/guiding-principles.pdf.

98. *Honig v. Doe*, 484 U.S. 305, 323 (1988). Online: supreme.justia.com/cases/federal/us/484/305.

99. Marcia Eckerd and Andrew Feinstein, "Kids with Asperger's Syndrome, Schools and the Law," *Autism Spectrum News*, Spring 2011. Online: www.mhnews-autism.org/back_issues/ASN-Spring2011.pdf.

100. U.S. Department of Education, "Restraint and Seclusion: A Resource Document," May 2012. Online: www2.ed.gov/policy/seclusion/restraints-and-seclusion-resources.pdf.

101. U.S. Department of Education, Office for Civil Rights, "Civil Rights Data Collection: Data Snapshot (School Discipline)," March 21, 2014. Online: ocrdata.ed.gov/Downloads/CRDC-School-Discipline-Snapshot.pdf.

102. State of Connecticut, Department of Education, *Annual Report on the Use of Physical Restraint and Seclusion, School Year 2013–2014*, December 29, 2014. Online: www.sde.ct.gov/sde/lib/sde/pdf/deps/special/restraint_and_seclusion_annual_report_2013_14.pdf.

103. U.S. Government Accountability Office, "Seclusion and Restraints: Selected Cases of Death and Abuse at Public and Private Schools and Treatment Centers," GAO-09-719T, May 19, 2009. Online: www.gao.gov/new.items/d09719t.pdf.

104. Jessica Butler, "How Safe Is the Schoolhouse? An Analysis of State Seclusion and Restraint Laws and Policies," Autism National Committee, January 20, 2014. Online: www.autcom.org/pdf/HowSafeSchoolhouse.pdf.

105. U.S. Senate, Health, Education, Labor, and Pensions Committee, "Dangerous Use of Seclusion and Restraints in Schools Remains Widespread and Difficult to Remedy: A Review of Ten Cases: Majority Committee Staff Report," February 12, 2014. Online: www.help.senate.gov/imo/media/doc/Seclusion%20and%20Restraints%20Final%20Report.pdf.

106. Sasha Pudelski, "Keeping Schools Safe: How Seclusion and Restraint Protects Students and School Personnel," American Association of School Administrators, March 2012. Online: www.aasa.org/uploadedFiles/Resources/Tool_Kits/AASA-Keeping-Schools-Safe.pdf.

107. Albert O. Hirschman, *Exit, Voice, and Loyalty: Responses to Decline in Firms, Organizations, and States* (Cambridge, MA: Harvard University Press, 1970).

108. *Burlington School Committee. v. Massachusetts Department of Education*, 471 U.S. 359 (1985), at 370. Online: caselaw.lp.findlaw.com/scripts/getcase.pl?court=US&vol=471&invol=359.

109. Jennifer Radcliffe, "More Parents of Special-Needs Children Opt out of Public Schools," *Houston Chronicle*, August 25, 2012. Online: www.chron.com/news/houston-texas/article/More-parents-of-special-needs-kids-fleeing-public-3815655.php.

110. Laura C. Hoffman, "Special Education for a Special Population: Why Federal Special Education Law Must Be Reformed for Autistic Children," *Rutgers Law Record* 39 (2011–2012): 128–60. Online: lawrecord.com/files/39_Rutgers_L_Rec_128.pdf.

111. 34 CFR 34 300.137. Online: www.ecfr.gov/cgi-bin/retrieveECFR?gp=&SID=35b8e1052defd52a81e854959aa60477&n=34y2.1.1.1.1&r=PART&ty=HTML#34:2.1.1.1.1.2.43.35.

112. Colin Ong-Dean, *Distinguishing Disability: Parents, Privilege, and Special Education* (Chicago: University of Chicago Press, 2009), 24–25.

113. For an example, see Jonathan Andrade, "Parents Want to Improve Special Education," *Simi Valley Acorn*, December 26, 2014. Online: www.simivalleyacorn.com/news/2014-12-26/Community/Parents_want_to_improve_special_education.html.

114. Mark Hutten, "Should You Disclose Your Child's Diagnosis to Others?" *My Aspergers Child*, March 2014. Online: www.myaspergerschild.com/2014/03/should-you-disclose-your-childs.html.

115. Brian Friel, "School of Hard Knocks," *National Journal*, November 13, 2004. Online: www.nationaljournal.com/njmagazine/nj_20041113_19.php.

116. Colker, *Disabled Education*, 104.

117. H.R. 4247 (111th Congress): Keeping All Students Safe Act. Online: www.govtrack.us/congress/bills/111/hr4247.

118. Matthew Mosk, Angela M. Hill, and Brian Ross, "Which Congressman Is Blocking Bill That Would Protect Kids with Autism?" ABC News, December 5, 2012. Online: abcnews.go.com/Blotter/congressman-blocking-bill-protect-kids-autism/story?id=17887843.

119. Leslie Finnan, "Sen. Harkin Introduces IDEA Litigation Legislation," *Leading Edge*, March 21, 2011. Online: www.aasa.org/aasablog.aspx?id=18480&blogid=286.

120. Tina Itkonen, *The Role of Special Education Interest Groups in National Policy* (Amherst, NY: Cambria Press, 2009), 170.

121. S. 2789 (113th Congress) IDEA Full Funding Act. Online: www.govtrack.us/congress/bills/113/s2789.

5. BEFORE, OUTSIDE, AND
AFTER THE CLASSROOM

1. Steven M. Teles, "Kludgeocracy: The American Way of Policy," New America Foundation, December 2012. Online: newamerica.net/sites/newamerica.net/files/policydocs/Teles_Steven_Kludgeocracy_NAF_Dec2012.pdf.

2. L&M Policy Research, "Autism Spectrum Disorders (ASD): State of the States of Services and Supports for People with ASD," Centers for Medicare and Medicaid Services, January 24, 2014. Online: www.medicaid.gov/medicaid-chip-program-information/by-topics/long-term-services-and-supports/downloads/asd-state-of-the-states-report.pdf.

3. Amy Stansbury, "Autism: Red Tape Can Tie Families in Knots," *Hanover Evening Sun*, June 10, 2013. Online: www.eveningsun.com/ci_23428799/autisms-red-tape-can-tie-families-knots.

4. Chris Wetterick, "Autism Getting More Attention from Illinois Legislators," *State Journal-Register*, April 22, 2012. Online: www.sj-r.com/top-stories/x1364621768/Autism-getting-more-attention-from-Illinois-legislators.

5. Alan Zarembo, "Warrior Parents Fare Best in Securing Autism Services," *Los Angeles Times*, December 12, 2011. Online: www.latimes.com/local/autism/la-me-autism-day-two-html-htmlstory.html.

6. P.L. 99-457 (1986). Online: www.gpo.gov/fdsys/pkg/STATUTE-100/pdf/STATUTE-100-Pg1145.pdf.

7. U.S. Department of Education, Office of Special Education and Rehabilitative Services *35th Annual Report to Congress on the Implementation of the Individuals with Disabilities Education Act 2013*, May 2014, p. 15. Online: www2.ed.gov/about/reports/annual/osep/2013/parts-b-c/35th-idea-arc.pdf.

8. Ruth Colker, *Disabled Education: A Critical Analysis of the Americans with Disabilities Act* (New York: New York University Press, 2013), 88.

9. Christina Samuels, "Infant and Toddler Special Education Passed Over for Other Initiatives," *Education Week*, December 23, 2014. Online: blogs.edweek.org/edweek/speced/2014/12/infant_and_toddler_special_edu.html; The Early Childhood Technical Assistance Center, Annual Appropriations and Number of Children Served under Part C of IDEA Federal Fiscal Years 1987–2012, October 10, 2014. Online: ectacenter.org/partc/partcdata.asp; U.S. Department of Education, Institute of Education Sciences, *Digest of Education Statistics*, 2014 Tables and Figures, "Children 3 to 21 years old served under Individuals with Disabilities Education Act (IDEA), Part B, by type of disability: Selected years, 1976–77 through 2012–13." Online: nces.ed.gov/programs/digest/d14/tables/dt14_204.30.asp.

10. Fred R. Volkmar, "Editorial: The Importance of Early Intervention," *Journal of Autism and Developmental Disorders*, October 18, 2014. Online: link.springer.com/article/10.1007/s10803-014-2265-9/fulltext.html.

11. U.S. Congress. House. Committee on Education and Labor, "The Education of the Handicapped Amendments of 1986: Hearing before the Subcommittee on Select Education," 99th Cong. 2dt sess., July 24, 1986. Online: babel.hathitrust.org/cgi/pt?id=mdp.39015031745543;view=1up;seq=4.

12. H. Rept. 99-860, September 22, 1986, 7.

13. Catherine E. Rice et al., "Screening for Developmental Delays among Young Children—National Survey of Children's Health, United States, 2007," *Morbidity and Mortality*

Weekly Report, September 12, 2014. Online: www.cdc.gov/mmwr/preview/mmwrhtml/su6302a5.htm.

14. Karen Weintraub, "Autism Treatment for Under-Threes Is Key, but Diagnosis Is Tough," *Connecticut Health I-Team*, April 13, 2014. Online: c-hit.org/2014/04/13/autism-treatment-for-under-threes-is-key-but-diagnosis-is-tough.

15. Ayelet Talmi et al., "Improving Developmental Screening Documentation and Referral Completion," *Pediatrics* 134 (October 2014): e1181–e1188. Online: pediatrics.aappublications.org/content/134/4/e1181.abstract?sid=6b1e6f5c-9c83-4683-8bc7-ce33fa9538c3.

16. Sarah DeWeerdt, "Lack of Training Begets Autism Diagnosis Bottleneck," SFARI, January 13, 2014. Online: sfari.org/news-and-opinion/news/2014/lack-of-training-begets-autism-diagnosis-bottleneck.

17. Jon Baio, "Prevalence of Autism Spectrum Disorder among Children Aged 8 Years—Autism and Developmental Disabilities Monitoring Network, 11 Sites, United States, 2010," *Morbidity and Mortality Weekly Report Surveillance Summaries* 63 (March 28, 2014): 1–21. Online: www.cdc.gov/mmwr/preview/mmwrhtml/ss6302a1.htm.

18. Irene Tanzman, "Autism & Four Road Blockers in the System," *Pulse*, January 16, 2015. Online: www.linkedin.com/pulse/autism-four-road-blockers-system-irene-tanzman.

19. An Autism Speaks survey found the Boston metropolitan area among the ten best places for people with autism. "The 10 Best Places to Live If You Have Autism," Autism Speaks, April 1, 2011. Online: www.autismspeaks.org/about-us/press-releases/10-best-places-live-if-you-have-autism. United Cerebral Palsy ranks the state eighth for overall disability services. United Cerebral Palsy, "The Case for Inclusion," April 18, 2014. Online: http://cfi2014.ucp.org.`

20. Xin Wei, "Special Education Services Received by Students with Autism Spectrum Disorders from Preschool through High School," *Journal of Special Education* 48 (November 2014): 167–79. ed.sagepub.com/content/48/3/167.full.pdf+html.

21. California Welfare and Institutions Code, section 4501. Online: leginfo.legislature.ca.gov/faces/codes_displaySection.xhtml?lawCode=WIC&sectionNum=4501.

22. California Welfare and Institutions Code, section 4659. Online: leginfo.legislature.ca.gov/faces/codes_displaySection.xhtml?lawCode=WIC&sectionNum=4659. In a 2012 survey, California parents reported that school districts were funding 48 percent of treatment (ABA ST, OT, and PT); state regional centers, 22 percent; health insurance companies, 13 percent; and the parents themselves, 17 percent. Autism Society of California, "Autism in California: 2012 Survey," April 2012. Online: www.scdd.ca.gov/res/docs/pdf/Whats_New/ASC_Survey_April_2012.pdf.

23. Cecilia Chang, "Who Pays for Your ABA Program," Spectrum of Hope Foundation, 2011. Online: www.spectrumofhope.org/who-pays.html.

24. Shanna Rose, *Financing Medicaid: Federalism and the Growth of America's Health Care Safety Net* (Ann Arbor: University of Michigan Press, 2013), 2.

25. Ibid., 3.

26. Centers for Medicare and Medicaid Services, "Individuals with Disabilities." Online: www.medicaid.gov/medicaid-chip-program-information/by-population/people-with-disabilities/individuals-with-disabilities.html.

27. Laura Katz Olson, *The Politics of Medicaid* (New York: Columbia University Press, 2010), 142.

28. *Olmstead v. L.C.* 527 US 581, at 587 (1999). Online: supreme.justia.com/cases/federal/us/527/581/case.html.

29. Steve Eiken et al., "Medicaid Expenditures for Long-Term Services and Supports In FFY 2012," Centers for Medicare and Medicaid Services, April 28, 2014. Online: www.medicaid.gov/Medicaid-CHIP-Program-Information/By-Topics/Long-Term-Services-and-Supports/Downloads/LTSS-Expenditures-2012.pdf.

30. Ibid. Also note that the most common waiver authority for HCBS is the Section 1915(c) waiver authority, named for a section=of the Social Security Act. Individuals in these programs need the level of care that an institution normally offers, but support services enable them to live in a community-based setting. A few states use Section 1115 waivers, providing for demonstration projects.

31. Cynthia Singleton, "Medicaid Waiver 101," Greater Lewisville Special Education PTSA, November 2007. Online: lisdseptsa.txpta.org/index.php?module=dynamic_pages& level=main&page=19.

32. Jennifer Hall-Lande, Amy Hewitt, and Charles R. Moseley, "A National Review of Home and Community Based Services (HCBS) for Individuals with Autism Spectrum Disorders," University of Minnesota Institute on Community Integration, December 2011. Online: ici.umn.edu/products../prb/213/default.html.

33. Samuel R. Bagenstos, "The Disability Cliff," *Democracy: A Journal of Ideas* 35 (Winter 2015). Online: www.democracyjournal.org/35/the-disability-cliff.php.

34. Terence Ng et al., "Eligibility and Cost Containment Policies Used In Medicaid HCBS Programs," Henry J. Kaiser Family Foundation, December 22, 2014. Online: kff.org/report-section/medicaid-home-and-community-based-services-programs-2011-data-update-eligibility-and-cost-containment-policies-used-in-medicaid-hcbs-programs.

35. Ibid., table 14 at files.kff.org/attachment/tables-medicaid-home-and-community-based-services-programs-2011-data-update.

36. "The Medicaid Waiting Game: Parents Tell Their Stories," Autism Speaks, March 21, 2014. Online: www.autismspeaks.org/blog/2013/03/21/medicaid-waiting-game-parents-tell-their-stories.

37. Elizabeth Picciuto, "Medicaid Will Give You Money for At-Home Care, but You Might Wait Years," *Daily Beast*, December 2, 2014. Online: www.thedailybeast.com/articles/2014/12/02/medicaid-will-give-you-money-for-at-home-care-but-you-might-wait-years.html.

38. Robert McCarthy, "When Disabled Children Become Adults, Parents Often Are Left with Few Options," *Washington Post*, August 29, 2014. Online: www.washingtonpost.com/opinions/when-disabled-children-become-adults-parents-often-have-few-options/2014/08/29/9bccabe8-2958-11e4-8593-da634b334390_story.html.

39. Children's Defense Fund California, "2014–2015 Budget Recommendation." Online: www.cdfca.org/policy-priorities/assets/documents/applied-behavior-analysis.pdf.

40. Michelle Diament, "Feds Clarify Obligations to Kids with Autism," *Disability Scoop*, July 17, 2014. Online: www.disabilityscoop.com/2014/07/17/feds-clarify-kids-autism/19519.

41. Cindy Mann, director of Center for Medicaid and CHIP Services, "Clarification of Medicaid Coverage of Services to Children with Autism," July 7, 2014. Online: www.medicaid.gov/Federal-Policy-Guidance/Downloads/CIB-07-07-14.pdf.

42. United Cerebral Palsy, "The Case for Inclusion," April 18, 2014. Online: cfi2014.ucp.org/wp-content/uploads/2014/03/Case-for-Inclusion-2014.pdf.

43. *United States v. South-Eastern Underwriters*, 322 U.S. 533 (1944). Online: supreme.justia.com/cases/federal/us/322/533/case.html.

44. Erin K. Powrie, "'Too Big to Fail' Is Too Big: Why the McCarran-Ferguson Exemption to Federal Antitrust Enforcement of Insurance is Past Its Prime," *Rutgers Law Review* 63 (Fall 2010): 359–88, at 367–68. Online: pegasus.rutgers.edu/~review/vol63n1/Powrie_EIC.pdf.

45. James Q. Wilson, "The Politics of Regulation," in *The Politics of Regulation*, ed. James Q. Wilson (New York: Basic, 1980), 367.

46. A 2006 Ipsos survey asked Americans about various business sectors: only the oil and gas industry got worse ratings than insurance. Ipsos Public Affairs, "Individual Insurance Company Reputations Better Than Overall Industry," October 4, 2006. Online: www.ipsos-na.com/download/pr.aspx?id=5727. In 2003 and 2010, Gallup asked respondents to rate various aspects of health care. Whereas nurses, physicians, and hospitals got mostly "good" or "excellent" ratings, health insurance companies got mostly "fair" or "poor" ratings. Gallup, "Healthcare System." Online: www.gallup.com/poll/4708/healthcare-system.aspx.

47. Karmen Hanson, "Mandated Health Insurance Benefits and State Laws," National Conference of State Legislatures, January 2014. Online: www.ncsl.org/research/health/mandated-health-insurance-benefits-and-state-laws.aspx.

48. Miriam Laugesen et al., "A Comparative Analysis of Mandated Benefit Laws, 1949–2002," *Health Services Research* 41 (June 2006). Online: www.ncbi.nlm.nih.gov/pmc/articles/PMC1713218.

49. Lorri Shealy Unumb and Daniel R. Unumb, *Autism and the Law: Cases, Statutes, and Materials* (Durham, NC: Carolina Academic Press, 2011), 56.

50. Ibid., 60–62.

51. David Newton, "Humanitarian Award Winner Inspiring," ESPN NASCAR, December 7, 2012. Online: espn.go.com/racing/nascar/cup/story/_/id/8724473/nascar-lorri-unumb-kind-difference-maker-worth-honoring.

52. Ibid.

53. Justine Redman, "Mom Wins Fight for Autism Insurance," CNN, April 1, 2008. Online: www.cnn.com/2008/HEALTH/conditions/04/01/autism.insurance/index.html.

54. Unumb and Unumb, *Autism and the Law*, 65.

55. Autism Speaks, "Autism Speaks Announces Multi-State Insurance Legislation Campaign," December 27, 2007. Online: www.autismspeaks.org/about-us/press-releases/autism-speaks-announces-multi-state-insurance-legislation-campaign.

56. Carla K. Johnson, "Parents Press States for Autism Insurance Laws," Associated Press, October 20, 2008. Online: news.google.com/newspapers?nid=1988&dat=20081020&id=2IkxAAAAIBAJ&sjid=s6kFAAAAIBAJ&pg=2898,3460786.

57. Sandy Banks Hoffman, "Calley Signs Legislation Mandating Autism Coverage," Associated Press, April 18, 2012. Online: www.deseretnews.com/article/765569752/Calley-signs-legislation-mandating-autism-coverage.html.

58. Autism Speaks, "Applied Behavior Analysis." Online: www.autismspeaks.org/what-autism/treatment/applied-behavior-analysis-aba.

59. Autism Speaks, "Cost Estimates of State Autism Insurance Reform Bills." Online: www.autismspeaks.org/node/214706.

60. Bradley D. Stein et al., "Impact of a Private Health Insurance Mandate on Public Sector Autism Service Use in Pennsylvania," *Journal of the American Academy of Child & Adolescent Psychiatry* 51 (August 2012): 771–79. Online: www.sciencedirect.com/science/article/pii/S0890856712004182.

61. Supreme Court of the State of Washington, *O.S.T. v. Regence Blue Shield*, October 9, 2014. Online: www.courts.wa.gov/opinions/pdf/889406.pdf.

62. Rebecca A. Johnson, Marion Danis, and Chris Hafner-Eaton, "US State Variation in Autism Insurance Mandates: Balancing Access and Fairness," *Autism* 18 (October 2014): 803–14. Online: aut.sagepub.com/content/18/7/803.full.

63. Author's calculation from census data at www.census.gov/hhes/www/income/data/statemedian.

64. Emily LeCoz, "Parents Share Heartbreaking Stories, Support Autism Bill," *Clarion-Ledger*, January 27, 2015. Online: www.clarionledger.com/story/politicalledger/2015/01/27/autism-insurance-proposal-gains-support/22403957.

65. Jim Galloway, "A Bill to Mandate Insurance Coverage for Autism Swims Upstream at the Capitol," *Atlanta Journal-Constitution*, March 12, 2014. Online: www.ajc.com/news/news/state-regional-govt-politics/a-bill-to-mandate-insurance-coverage-for-autism-sw/nfBnG.

66. U.S. Department of Health and Human Services, "The Affordable Care Act and Autism and Related Conditions." Online: www.hhs.gov/autism/factsheet-aca-autism.html.

67. Henry J. Kaiser Family Foundation, "2014 Employer Health Benefits Survey," September 10, 2014. Online: kff.org/report-section/ehbs-2014-section-ten-plan-funding.

68. Lorri Shealy Unumb, letter to families, Autism Speaks, February 2014. Online: www.autismspeaks.org/sites/default/files/docs/gr/erisa_tool_kit_10232014.pdf.

69. Autism Speaks, "Major Employers Voluntarily Introduce Autism Benefits for 2015," January 9, 2015. Online: www.autismspeaks.org/advocacy/advocacy-news/major-employers-voluntarily-introduce-autism-benefits-2015.

70. Michelle Andrews, "Health Law Tempers States' Insurance Mandates," National Public Radio, September 16, 2014. Online: www.npr.org/blogs/health/2014/09/16/348956212/health-law-tempers-states-insurance-mandates.

71. Autism Speaks, "The Affordable Care Act and Autism." Online: www.autismspeaks.org/sites/default/files/docs/gr/ehb.10.31de_0.pdf. Also see Michelle Andrews, "Advocates Worry Conn. Decision Could Undermine Autism Coverage," Kaiser Health News, June 24, 2014. Online: kaiserhealthnews.org/news/michelle-andrews-on-autism-coverage-and-changes-in-connecticut.

72. Lorri Unumb, "On the Road: Autism Insurance Game of Chance;" Autism Speaks, November 22, 2013. Online: www.autismspeaks.org/blog/2013/11/22/road-autism-insurance-game-chance.

73. Behavior Analyst Certification Board, "About the BACB." Online: www.bacb.com/index.php?page=1; Association of Professional Behavior Analysts, "State Laws to License/Certify Behavior Analysts in Their Own Right as of June 23, 2014." Online: www.apbahome.net/pdf/State%20Regulation%20of%20BA%20062314%20V2.png.

74. Court of Appeal, Second District, Division 3, California, *Consumer Watchdog v. Department of Managed Health Care*. B232338, April 23, 2014. Online: caselaw.findlaw.com/ca-court-of-appeal/1664321.html.

75. Ellen Spangelthal, "Proposed Emergency Regulations Threaten Services Protected by Autism Insurance Law," *Summit News*, December 4, 2013. Online: www.summited.org/summit-news/102-proposed-emergency-regulations-threaten-services-protected-by-autism-insurance-law.html.

76. Zack Harold, "Psychologist Board Withdraws Emergency Rule after Lawsuit," *Charleston Daily Mail*, September 27, 2011. Online: www.charlestondailymail.com/News/201109273296.

77. Autism Training Solutions, "State of ABA Service Providers 2014." Online: www.autismtrainingsolutions.com/resources/research/state-aba-service-providers-2014.

78. Rosemary Parker, "Autism Diagnosis Bottleneck Leaving Michigan Kids Stranded without Services," MLive.com, July 26, 2014. Online: www.mlive.com/news/kalamazoo/index.ssf/2014/07/new_autism_diagnosis_bottlenec.html.

79. Susan K. Livio, "N.J. Law Mandating Autism Treatment Coverage Needs Work, Parents and Lawmakers Say," *Newark Star-Ledger*, March 7, 2013. Online: www.nj.com/politics/index.ssf/2013/03/nj_law_mandating_autism_treatm.html.

80. Ed Stannard, "Shortage of Child Psychiatrists Has Families Scrambling for Help," *New Haven Register*, January 20, 2013. Online: www.nhregister.com/general-news/20130119/shortage-of-child-psychiatrists-has-families-scrambling-for-help-3.

81. Tara Bishop et al., "Acceptance of Insurance by Psychiatrists and the Implications for Access to Mental Health Care," *JAMA Psychiatry* 71 (February 2014): 176–81. Online: archpsyc.jamanetwork.com/article.aspx?articleid=1785174.

82. Tom Philpott, "Autism Care Coverage Improves, But Costs Are Still a Worry," *Stars and Stripes*, November 20, 2014. Online: www.stripes.com/news/us/autism-care-coverage-improves-but-costs-are-still-a-worry-1.315180.

83. Tim Devaney, "Pentagon to Delay Autism Spending Cuts," *The Hill*, October 8, 2014. Online: thehill.com/regulation/defense/220215-pentagon-to-delay-autism-spending-cuts.

84. Jennifer M. Davis and Erinn H. Finke, "The Experience of Military Families with Children with Autism Spectrum Disorders during Relocation and Separation," *Journal of Autism and Developmental Disorders*, January 21, 2015. Online: link.springer.com/article/10.1007/s10803-015-2364-2.

85. Jeff Hawkes, "Life after School Poses Challenges for Garden Spot Grad with Autism," Lancaster Online, August 24, 2014. Online: lancasteronline.com/news/local/life-after-school-poses-challenges-for-garden-spot-grad-with/article_072c1490-2955-11e4-aeb8-001a4bcf6878.html.

86. Camille Smith, "What Happens to People with Autism When They Age Out of School?" WBEZ, January 2, 2015. Online: www.wbez.org/news/what-happens-people-autism-when-they-age-out-school-111326.

87. Paul Shattuck et al., "Post–High School Service Use among Young Adults with an Autism Spectrum Disorder," *JAMA Pediatrics* (February 2011): 141–46. Online: archpedi.jamanetwork.com/article.aspx?articleid=384252.

88. U.S. Government Accountability Office, "Employment for People with Disabilities: Little Is Known about the Effectiveness of Fragmented and Overlapping Programs," GAO-12-677, June 2012. Online: www.gao.gov/assets/600/592074.pdf.

89. U.S. Government Accountability Office, "Students with Disabilities: Better Federal Coordination Could Lessen Challenges in the Transition from High School," GAO-12-594, July 2012. Online: www.gao.gov/assets/600/592329.pdf.

90. Amy Stansbury, "Autism: When Autistic Children Are No Longer Children," *Hanover Evening Sun*, June 13, 2013. Online: www.eveningsun.com/news/ci_23454488/when-autistic-children-are-no-longer-children.

91. David B. Nicholas et al., "Vocational Support Approaches in Autism Spectrum Disorder: A Synthesis Review of the Literature," *Autism* 19 (February 2015): 235–45. Online: aut.sagepub.com/content/19/2/235.abstract.

92. Paul T. Shattuck et al., "Postsecondary Education and Employment among Youth with an Autism Spectrum Disorder," *Pediatrics* 129 (June 2012): 1042–49. Online: pediatrics.aappublications.org/content/early/2012/05/09/peds.2011-2864.full.pdf+html.

93. Hsu-Min Chiang, "Factors Associated with Participation in Employment for High School Leavers with Autism," *Journal of Autism and Developmental Disorders* 43 (August 2013): 1832–42. Online: link.springer.com/article/10.1007/s10803-012-1734-2.

94. John M. Keesler, "Applying for Supplemental Security Income (SSI) for Individuals with Intellectual and Developmental Disabilities: Family and Service Coordinator Experiences," *Intellectual and Developmental Disabilities* 53 (February 2015): 42–57. Online: aaiddjournals.org/doi/abs/10.1352/1934-9556-53.1.42.

95. Howard Gleckman, "Are Tax-Free ABLE Accounts the Right Financial Solution for People with Disabilities?" *Forbes*, December 4, 2014. Online: www.forbes.com/sites/beltway/2014/12/04/are-tax-free-able-accounts-the-right-financial-solution-for-people-with-disabilities.

96. Christopher Hanks, "Hospitals Adapting for Adults with Autism," *Live Science*, September 23, 2014. Online: www.livescience.com/47961-adults-with-autism-need-tailored-medicine.html.

97. Nancy C. Cheak-Zamora and Michelle Teti, "'You Think It's Hard Now . . . It Gets Much Harder For Our Children': Youth with Autism and Their Caregiver's Perspectives of Health Care Transition Services," *Autism*, December 11, 2014. Online: aut.sagepub.com/content/early/2014/12/11/1362361314558279.full.pdf+html.

98. Ibid.

99. U.S. Senate Committee on Health, Education, Labor and Pensions, "Fulfilling the Promise: Overcoming Persistent Barriers to Economic Self-Sufficiency for People with Disabilities," majority committee staff report, September 18, 2014. Online: www.help.senate.gov/imo/media/doc/HELP%20Committee%20Disability%20and%20Poverty%20Report.pdf.

100. Sheryl Larson et al., "In-Home and Residential Long-Term Supports and Services for Persons with Intellectual or Developmental Disabilities: Status and Trends through 2012," Residential Information Systems Project, University of Minnesota, 2014. Online: risp.umn.edu/RISP_FINAL_2012.pdf.

101. Alan Judd, "Mentally Disabled Suffer in Moves from Georgia Institutions," *Atlanta Journal-Constitution*, June 21, 2014. Online: dbhdd.org/enews/docs/Mentally%20disabled%20suffer%20in%20moves%20from%20Georgia%20institutions_AJC.pdf.

102. U.S. Food and Drug Administration, Summary of the Neurological Devices Panel Meeting, April 24, 2014. Online: www.fda.gov/downloads/AdvisoryCommittees/Committees MeetingMaterials/MedicalDevices/MedicalDevicesAdvisoryCommittee/NeurologicalDevices Panel/UCM395022.pdf.

103. Audrey F. Burgess and Steven E. Gutstein, "Quality of Life for People with Autism: Raising the Standard for Evaluating Successful Outcomes," *Child and Adolescent Mental Health* 12 (May 2007): 80–86.

104. Easter Seals, "Living with Autism Study," December 16, 2008. Online: www.easterseals.com/site/DocServer/Study_FINAL_Harris_12.4.08_Compressed.pdf?docID=83143.

105. McCarthy, "When Disabled Children Become Adults."

106. Kristina Chew, "My Autistic Child Receives Great Social Services. Adulthood Is Another Story," *The Guardian*, November 29, 2013. Online: www.theguardian.com/commentisfree/2013/nov/29/autism-access-to-social-services-adulthood.

107. Jessi C., "This Is Not a Happy Post," *Deciphering Morgan*, January 22, 2012. Online: www.decipher-morgan.com/2012_01_01_archive.html.

6. THE FUTURE

1. Abraham Lincoln, "House Divided Speech," Springfield, Illinois, June 16, 1858. Online: www.nps.gov/liho/historyculture/housedivided.htm.

2. Karola Dillenburger et al., "Awareness and Knowledge of Autism and Autism Interventions: A General Population Survey," *Research in Autism Spectrum Disorders* 7 (December 2013): 1558–67. Online: www.sciencedirect.com/science/article/pii/S175094671300175X.

3. Roosevelt's efforts to conceal his disability were so successful that, out of thirty-five thousand still photos at his presidential library, only two show him in a wheelchair. Hugh Gregory Gallagher, *FDR's Splendid Deception* (New York: Dodd, Mead, 1985).

4. Gary S. Mayerson, "Autism in the Courtroom," in *Handbook of Autism and Developmental Disorders*, 4th ed., ed. Fred R. Volkmar et al. (Hoboken, NJ: John Wiley & Sons, 2014), 1049.

5. Between 12 and 20 percent of autistic students do not get an IEP. Elizabeth Harstad et al., "Disparity of Care for Children with Parent-Reported Autism Spectrum Disorders," *Academic Pediatrics* 13 (July/August 2013): 334–39. Online: www.academicpedsjnl.net/article/S1876-2859(13)00065-X/abstract. Some of the children who were not receiving IDEA services in 2012–2013 might qualify for them later during their schooling.

6. Christina Mohr Jensen et al., "Time Trends over 16 Years in Incidence-Rates of Autism Spectrum Disorders across the Lifespan Based on Nationwide Danish Register Data," *Journal of Autism and Developmental Disorders* 44 (August 2014): 1808–18. Online: link.springer.com/article/10.1007/s10803-014-2053-6.

7. Laura Geggel, "Rising Awareness May Explain Spike in Autism Diagnoses," *Medical Xpress*, March 25, 2014. Online: medicalxpress.com/news/2014-03-awareness-spike-autism.html.

8. Pennsylvania Department of Public Welfare, "Pennsylvania Autism Census Update 2014," 2014. Online: www.paautism.org/Portals/0/Docs/Census/Census%20Update%202014%20Final.pdf.

9. "The Economic Impact of Autistic Children Entering the Adult Population, 2014–2028," Sage Crossing Foundation, March 15, 2013. Online: www.sagecrossingfoundation.org/pdfs/Economic_Impact_of_Adult_Autism_2014-2028.pdf.

10. Natalie Henninger and Julie Lounds Taylor, "Outcomes in Adults with Autism Spectrum Disorders: A Historical Perspective," *Autism* 17 (January 2013): 103–16. Online: aut.sagepub.com/content/17/1/103.

11. Julie Lounds Taylor and Marsha Mailick Seltzer, "Changes in the Autism Behavioral Phenotype during the Transition to Adulthood," *Journal of Autism and Developmental Disorders* 40 (December 2010): 1441–46. Online: www.ncbi.nlm.nih.gov/pmc/articles/PMC2910794.

12. According to one projection, the number of Alzheimer cases will increase 65 percent between 2015 and 2050, from 5.1 million to 8.4 million. Liesi E. Hebert et al., "Alzheimer Disease in the United States (2010–2050) Estimated Using the 2010 Census," *Neurology* 80 (May 7, 2013): 1778–83. Online: www.ncbi.nlm.nih.gov/pmc/articles/PMC3719424.

13. "The Economic Impact of Autistic Children."

14. By 2025, nearly 65 million people will be receiving Social Security benefits—59 percent more than the number in 2007. Meanwhile, the baby boomers' retirement will hold down growth in the labor force, and thus the income tax base. U.S. Congressional Budget Office, "The Budget and Economic Outlook, 2015 to 2025," January 2015. Online: www.cbo.gov/sites/default/files/cbofiles/attachments/49892-Outlook2015.pdf.

15. Jeff Howe, "Paying for My Special-Needs Child," *Time*, June 24, 2014. Online: time.com/tag/autism/page/2.

16. Kristy Anderson et al., "Prevalence and Correlates of Postsecondary Residential Status among Young Adults with an Autism Spectrum Disorder," *Autism* 18 (July 2014): 562–70. Online: aut.sagepub.com/content/18/5/562.full.pdf+html.

17. Anita Creamer, "Aging Parents Worry about Adult Children with Disabilities," *Sacramento Bee*, March 3, 2013. Online: www.sacbee.com/news/local/article2576765.html.

18. Jeff Howe, "Paying for My Special-Needs Child," *Time*, June 24, 2014. Online: time. com/tag/autism/page/2.

19. "Judge Glen on Her Groundbreaking Opinion on Special Needs Trusts," Autism Speaks, July 26, 2013. Online: www.autismspeaks.org/news/news-item/judge-glen-her-ground breaking-opinion-special-needs-trusts.

20. Marina Vornovitsky, Alfred Gottschalck, and Adam Smith, "Distribution of Household Wealth in the U.S.: 2000 to 2011," U.S. Census Bureau, August 21, 2014. Online: www. census.gov/people/wealth/files/Wealth%20distribution%202000%20to%202011.pdf.

21. Rakesh Kochhar and Richard Fry, "Wealth Inequality Has Widened along Racial, Ethnic Lines since End of Great Recession," Pew Research Center, December 12, 2014. Online: www. pewresearch.org/fact-tank/2014/12/12/racial-wealth-gaps-great-recession.

22. American Academy of Pediatrics, "Black, Hispanic Children with Autism More Likely to Regress Than Whites," *ScienceDaily*, May 6, 2014. Online: www.sciencedaily.com/releases/ 2014/05/140506074725.htm.

23. Paul Taylor, ed., "The Rising Cost of Not Going to College," Pew Research Center, February 11, 2014. Online: www.pewsocialtrends.org/files/2014/02/SDT-higher-ed-FINAL-02-11-2014.pdf.

24. Paul Shattuck, "Postsecondary Education and Employment among Youth with an Austicm Spectrum Disorder," *Pediatrics* 129 (June 2012): 1042–49.

25. Xin Wei et al., "Science, Technology, Engineering, and Mathematics (STEM) Participation among College Students with an Autism Spectrum Disorder," *Journal of Autism and Developmental Disorders* 43 (July 2013): 1539–46. Online: link.springer.com/content/pdf/10. 1007%2Fs10803-012-1700-z.pdf.

26. Kathleen Wilson, "Programs Help Autistic Students Succeed in College," *Ventura County Star*, September 23, 2012. Online: www.vcstar.com/news/2012/sep/23/programs-help-autistic-students-succeed-in.

27. Nicholas W. Gelbar, Isaac Smith, and Brian Reichow, "Systematic Review of Articles Describing Experience and Supports of Individuals with Autism Enrolled in College and University Programs," *Journal of Autism and Developmental Disorders* 44 (October 2014): 2593–601. Online: link.springer.com/article/10.1007/s10803-014-2135-5.

28. Paige Carlotti, "More Colleges Expanding Programs for Students on Autism Spectrum," *Forbes*, July 31, 2014. Online: www.forbes.com/sites/paigecarlotti/2014/07/31/more-colleges-expanding-programs-for-students-on-autism-spectrum.

29. Paul T. Shattuck et al., "Disability Identification and Self-Efficacy among College Students on the Autism Spectrum," *Autism Research and Treatment* (2014), Article ID 924182. Online: www.hindawi.com/journals/aurt/2014/924182/#B1.

30. See the experiences of European students in Valérie Van Hees, Tinneke Moyson, and Herbert Roeyers, "Higher Education Experiences of Students with Autism Spectrum Disorder: Challenges, Benefits and Support Needs," *Journal of Autism and Developmental Disorders*, December 2, 2014. Online: link.springer.com/article/10.1007%2Fs10803-014-2324-2.

31. Paul T. Shattuck and Anne M. Roux, "Commentary on Employment Supports Research," *Autism* 19 (February 2014): 246–47. Online: aut.sagepub.com/content/19/2/246.full.

32. Christina Wilkie, "Young Adults with Autism Seek Out White-Collar Careers for First Time," *Huffington Post*, September 27, 2012. Online: www.huffingtonpost.com/2012/09/27/ autism-employment-white-collar-jobs_n_1916611.html.

33. Katherine Bouton, "Quandary of Hidden Disabilities: Conceal or Reveal?" *New York Times*, September 21, 2013. Online: www.nytimes.com/2013/09/22/business/quandary-of-hidden-disabilities-conceal-or-reveal.html.

34. U.S. Senate Committee on Health, Education, Labor and Pensions, "Fulfilling the Promise: Overcoming Persistent Barriers to Economic Self-Sufficiency for People with Disabilities," majority committee staff report, September 18, 2014. Online: www.help.senate.gov/imo/media/ doc/HELP%20Committee%20Disability%20and%20Poverty%20Report.pdf.

35. Daniela Caruso, "Autism in the U.S.: Social Movement and Legal Change," *American Journal of Law and Medicine* 36 (2010). Online: papers.ssrn.com/sol3/Delivery.cfm/SSRN_ ID1623215_code355514.pdf?abstractid=1577194&mirid=5.

36. Ibid.

37. Michael Bernick and Richard Holden, *The Autism Job Club* (New York: Skyhorse, 2015).

38. Julie Lounds Taylor, Leann E. Smith, and Marsha R. Mailick, "Engagement in Vocational Activities Promotes Behavioral Development for Adults with Autism Spectrum Disorders," *Journal of Autism and Developmental Disorders* 44 (June 2014): 1447–60. Online: www.waisman.wisc.edu/family/pubs/Autism/2013EngagementVocationalActivitiesPromotes BehavioralDevelopmentAdultsWithASD.pdf.

39. Brigid Schulte and Tim Craig, "Unknown to Va. Tech, Cho Had a Disorder," *Washington Post*, August 27, 2007. Online: www.washingtonpost.com/wp-dyn/content/article/2007/08/26/AR2007082601410_pf.html.

40. Alice Park, "Don't Blame Adam Lanza's Violence on Asperger's," *Time*, March 11, 2014. Online: time.com/19957/adam-lanzas-violence-wasnt-typical-of-aspergers.

41. Jo Ashline, "Special Needs: Autism Didn't Pull the Trigger," *Orange County Register*, December 28, 2012. Online: www.ocregister.com/news/autism-381971-son-people.html.

42. John J. Pitney Jr., "Seven Times?" *Autism Policy and Politics*, August 24, 2014. Online: www.autismpolicyblog.com/2014/08/seven-times.html.

43. Claire King and Glynis H. Murphy, "A Systematic Review of People with Autism Spectrum Disorder and the Criminal Justice System," *Journal of Autism and Developmental Disorders* 44 (November 2014): 2717–33. Online: link.springer.com/article/10.1007/s10803-014-2046-5.

44. Tim Waller, "Arrest of Autistic Man Prompts Call for Police Training," WYFF, January 2, 2015. Online: www.wyff4.com/news/Arrest-of-autistic-man-prompts-call-for-police-training/30491078.

45. David Dennis Jr., "My Son Is Black. With Autism. And I'm Scared of What the Police Will Do to Him," *Medium*, December 4, 2014. Online: medium.com/@DavidDWrites/my-son-is-black-with-autism-and-im-scared-of-what-the-police-will-do-to-him-1af15a203d57.

46. Mary Ann Spoto, "Autism Training for Law Enforcement in NJ Often Leads to Better Outcomes, Expert Says," *Newark Star-Ledger*, March 18, 2014. Online: www.nj.com/union/index.ssf/2014/03/post_26.html.

47. Greg Hambrick, "Recent Special 'Autism' Code on Virginia Driver's Licenses and ID Cards Goes into Law: Helpful or Discriminatory for Individuals on the Autistic Spectrum?" *Ashburn Patch*, July 14, 2014. Online: patch.com/virginia/ashburn/recent-special-autism-code-on-virginia-drivers-licenses-and-id-cards-goes-into-law-helpful-or-discriminatory-for-individuals-on-the-autistic-spectrum.

48. Cara Spoto, "Autistic Child Sign Sought," *Journal Times* (Racine, WI), October 12, 2014. Online: journaltimes.com/news/local/autistic-child-sign-sought/article_bdf73cda-c198-5b7f-aac4-f3593cf87cd2.html.

49. Erika Harrell, "Crime against Persons with Disabilities, 2009–2012—Statistical Tables," U.S. Bureau of Justice Statistics, February 2014. Online: www.bjs.gov/content/pub/pdf/capd0912st.pdf.

50. S. M. Brown-Lavoie, M. A. Viecili, and J. A. Weiss, "Sexual Knowledge and Victimization in Adults with Autism Spectrum Disorders," *Journal of Autism and Developmental Disorders* 44 (September 2014): 2185–96. Online: link.springer.com/article/10.1007/s10803-014-2093-y.

51. Orac, "'Autism Biomed' and the Murder of Alex Spourdalakis," *Respectful Insolence*, June 14, 2013. Online: scienceblogs.com/insolence/2013/06/14/autism-biomed-and-murder-of-alex-spourdalakis.

52. Kelli Stapleton, "When a Power Player Takes You Down," *Status Woe*, September 3, 2013. Online: thestatuswoe.wordpress.com/2013/09/03/when-a-power-player-takes-you-down/.

53. "Exclusive: Kelli Stapleton: A Mother's Worst Nightmare," *Dr. Phil*, September 16, 2014. Online: drphil.com/shows/show/2257.

54. "ASAN Statement on Dr. Phil Episode Featuring K. Stapleton," Autistic Self Advocacy Network, September 19, 2014. Online: autisticadvocacy.org/2014/09/asan-statement-on-dr-phil-episode-featuring-k-stapleton.

55. Leslie Kane, "Medscape Ethics Report 2014, Part 1: Life, Death, and Pain," Medscape, December 16, 2014. Online: www.medscape.com/features/slideshow/public/ethics2014-part1#2.

56. Dennis Thompson, "Most Americans Agree with Right-to-Die Movement," *Health Day*, December 5, 2014. Online: consumer.healthday.com/general-health-information-16/suicide-health-news-646/most-americans-embrace-right-to-die-movement-694268.html.

57. Elizabeth Picciuto, "Why Disability Advocates Say No to Doctor-Assisted Death," *Daily Beast*, February 20, 2015. Online: www.thedailybeast.com/articles/2015/02/20/why-disability-advocates-say-no-to-doctor-assisted-death.html.

58. "ASAN and Not Dead Yet Testify against Physician Assisted Suicide in Massachusetts," Autistic Self Advocacy Network, December 19, 2013. Online: autisticadvocacy.org/2013/12/asan-and-not-dead-yet-testify-against-physician-assisted-suicide-in-massachusetts.

59. Monica Friedman, "Ten Questions for Tom Angleberger." Online: eurekasolutions.net/monica/tom-angleberger.php3.

60. David Dale, "From Rain Man to the Bridge—The Art of Aspergacting," *The Age*, July 27, 2013. Online: www.theage.com.au/entertainment/blogs/the-tribal-mind/from-rain-man-to-the-bridge--the-art-of-aspergacting-20130724-2qi45.html.

61. Youth Transitions Collaborative, "Power in Numbers: A Profile of American Voters with Disabilities," July 12, 2013. Online: heath.gwu.edu/files/downloads/power innumbersexecutivesummary_508.pdf.

62. Michelle Diament, "Congress to 'Combat' Autism No More," *Disability Scoop*, June 12, 2014. Online: www.disabilityscoop.com/2014/06/12/congress-combat-autism-no/19436.

63. "On Easter Seals," *Yes, That, Too*, June 16, 2013. Online: yesthattoo.blogspot.com/2013/06/on-easter-seals.html.

64. Michael Hiltzik, "Chili's Autism Misstep and the Downside of Sloppy Philanthropy," *Los Angeles Times*, April 7, 2014. Online: www.latimes.com/business/hiltzik/la-fi-mh-chilis-autism-20140407-story.html.

65. John Elder Robison, "What's MSSNG In #Autism?" *Wrong Planet*, December 11, 2014. Online: jerobison.blogspot.com/2014/12/whats-mssng-in-autism.html.

66. John Elder Robison, "Fixing Autism Research," *Technology Review*, December 18, 2014. Online: www.technologyreview.com/view/533366/fixing-autism-research.

67. Erika Hayasaki, "The Debate over an Autism Cure Turns Hostile," *Newsweek*, February 18, 2015. Online: www.newsweek.com/2015/02/27/one-activists-search-cure-his-autism-drawing-violent-backlash-306998.html.

68. Jody Allard, "My Daughter Is a Gift, But Her Autism Is Not," *Huffington Post*, March 3, 2015. Online: www.huffingtonpost.com/ravishly/my-daughter-is-a-gift-but-her-autism-is-not_b_6763052.html.

69. Simon Cushing, "Autism: The Very Idea," in *The Philosophy of Autism*, ed. Jami L. Anderson and Simon Cushing (Lanham, MD: Rowman and Littlefield, 2013), 17–45.

70. Will Boggs, "'Autisms' a More Appropriate Term Than 'Autism,' Geneticists Say," Reuters, January 26, 2015. Online: www.reuters.com/article/2015/01/26/us-autism-genetics-siblings-idUSKBN0KZ1WH20150126.

71. Therese K. Grønborg, Diana E. Schendel, and Erik T. Parner, "Recurrence of Autism Spectrum Disorders in Full- and Half-Siblings and Trends over Time: A Population-Based Cohort Study," *JAMA Pediatrics* 167 (October 2013): 947–53. Online: archpedi.jamanetwork.com/article.aspx?articleid=1728998.

72. Thomas J. Hoffmann et al., "Evidence of Reproductive Stoppage in Families with Autism Spectrum Disorder: A Large, Population-Based Cohort Study," *JAMA Psychiatry* 71 (August 2014): 943–51. Online: archpsyc.jamanetwork.com/article.aspx?articleid=1878923.

73. Emily Willingham, "Embryo Sex Selection to Select against Autism?" *Forbes*, October 21, 2013. Online: www.forbes.com/sites/emilywillingham/2013/10/21/embryo-sex-selection-to-select-against-autism.

74. "Autism as Reason for Sex Selection," Gender Selection Authority, November 18, 2013. Online: www.genderselectionauthority.com/autism-reason-sex-selection-0.

75. Andrew Whitehouse, "Prenatal Screening and Autism," *The Conversation*, November 17, 2013. Online: theconversation.com/prenatal-screening-and-autism-20395.

76. Wesley Smith, "Eugenic Pre-Natal Cleansing Spreads to Autism," *National Review Online*, November 23, 2013. Online: www.nationalreview.com/human-exceptionalism/364704/eugenic-pre-natal-cleansing-spreads-autism-wesley-j-smith.

77. David Cox, "Are We Ready for a Prenatal Screening Test for Autism?" *The Guardian*, May 1, 2014. Online: www.theguardian.com/science/blog/2014/may/01/prenatal-screening-test-autism-ethical-implications.

78. Jaime L. Natoli et al., "Prenatal Diagnosis of Down Syndrome: A Systematic Review of Termination Rates (1995–2011)," *Prenatal Diagnosis* 32 (February 2012): 142–53. Online: onlinelibrary.wiley.com.ccl.idm.oclc.org/doi/10.1002/pd.2910/pdf.

79. Shixi Zhao et al., "Prenatal Genetic Testing for Autism: Abortion Decision-Making among Taiwanese Parents of Children with Autism Spectrum Disorders," paper presented at the annual meeting of the American Public Health Association, November 17, 2014. Online: apha.confex.com/apha/142am/webprogram/Paper308530.html.

80. Joseph M. Shapiro, *No Pity: People with Disabilities Forging a New Civil Rights Movement* (New York: Three Rivers Press, 1994), 279.

81. Avital Hahamy, Marlene Behrmann, and Rafael Malach, "The Idiosyncratic Brain: Distortion of Spontaneous Connectivity Patterns in Autism Spectrum Disorder," *Nature Neuroscience* 18 (February 2015): 302–9. Online: www.nature.com/neuro/journal/v18/n2/full/nn.3919.html.

82. Jami L. Anderson, "A Dash of Autism," in *The Philosophy of Autism*, ed. Jami L. Anderson and Simon Cushing (Lanham, MD: Rowman and Littlefield, 2013), 123.

83. R. Eric Barnes and Helen McCabe, "Should We Welcome a Cure for Autism? A Survey of the Arguments," *Medicine, Health Care and Philosophy* 15 (August 2012): 255–69. Online: link.springer.com/article/10.1007%2Fs11019-011-9339-7#page-1.

84. National Center for Special Education Research, "Secondary School Experiences of Students with Autism," April 2007. Online: ies.ed.gov/ncser/pdf/20073005.pdf.

85. Lauren Bishop-Fitzpatrick, Nancy J. Minshew, and Shaun M. Eack, "A Systematic Review of Psychosocial Interventions for Adults with Autism Spectrum Disorders," *Journal of Autism and Developmental Disorders* 43 (March 2013): 687–94. Online: link.springer.com/article/10.1007%2Fs10803-012-1615-8.

86. Shattuck and Roux, "Commentary on Employment Supports Research."

87. Steven K. Kapp et al., "Deficit, Difference, or Both? Autism and Neurodiversity," *Developmental Psychology* 49 (January 2013): 59–71. Online: psycnet.apa.org/journals/dev/49/1/59.

Index

About the Author

John J. Pitney, Jr., is the Roy P. Crocker Professor of American Politics at Claremont McKenna College in Claremont, California. He received his B.A. in political science from Union College, where he was co-valedictorian. He earned his Ph.D. in political science at Yale, where he was a National Science Foundation Fellow. From 1978 to 1980, he worked in the New York State Senate. From 1983 to 1984, as a Congressional Fellow of the American Political Science Association, he worked for Senator Alfonse D'Amato of New York and the House Republican Policy Committee. From 1984 to 1986, he was senior domestic policy analyst for the House Republican Research Committee. He joined the Claremont McKenna College faculty in 1986. From 1989 to 1991, during a leave of absence, he worked at the Research Department of the Republican National Committee, first as deputy director, then as acting director. He has won several teaching awards, and in 2012, *The Princeton Review* named him as one of America's top 300 college professors. He is the author of *The Art of Political Warfare* and the coauthor of several books, including *American Government: Deliberation, Democracy, and Citizenship*, *Epic Journey: The 2008 Elections and American Politics* and *After Hope and Change: The 2012 Elections and American Politics*. He has written articles for many publications, such as *The Washington Post*, *The Wall Street Journal*, *The Christian Science Monitor*, and *Politico*. He is a frequent commentator on politics and public policy for National Public Radio and American Public Radio. He maintains several blogs, including *Epic Journey* and *Autism Policy and Politics*.